America Between the Wars
1919–1941

Uncovering the Past: Documentary Readers in American History
Series Editors: Steven Lawson and Nancy Hewitt

The books in this series introduce students in American history courses to two important dimensions of historical analysis. They enable students to engage actively in historical interpretation, and they further students' understanding of the interplay between social and political forces in historical developments.

Consisting of primary sources and an introductory essay, these readers are aimed at the major courses in the American history curriculum, as outlined further below. Each book in the series will be approximately 225–50 pages, including a 25–30 page introduction addressing key issues and questions about the subject under consideration, a discussion of sources and methodology, and a bibliography of suggested secondary readings.

Published

Paul G. E. Clemens
The Colonial Era: A Documentary Reader

Sean Patrick Adams
The Early American Republic: A Documentary Reader

Stanley Harrold
The Civil War and Reconstruction: A Documentary Reader

Steven Mintz
African American Voices: A Documentary Reader, 1619–1877

Robert P. Ingalls and David K. Johnson
The United States Since 1945: A Documentary Reader

Camilla Townsend
American Indian History: A Documentary Reader

Steven Mintz
Mexican American Voices: A Documentary Reader

Brian Ward
The 1960s: A Documentary Reader

Nancy Rosenbloom
Women in American History Since 1880: A Documentary Reader

Jeremi Suri
American Foreign Relations Since 1898: A Documentary Reader

Carol Faulkner
Women in American History to 1880: A Documentary Reader

David Welky
America Between the Wars, 1919–1941: A Documentary Reader

America Between the Wars 1919–1941

A Documentary Reader

Edited by David Welky

WILEY-BLACKWELL

A John Wiley & Sons, Ltd., Publication

This edition first published 2012
Editorial material and organization © 2012 John Wiley & Sons, Inc.

Wiley-Blackwell is an imprint of John Wiley & Sons, formed by the merger of Wiley's global
Scientific, Technical and Medical business with Blackwell Publishing.

Registered Office
John Wiley & Sons Ltd, The Atrium, Southern Gate, Chichester, West Sussex, PO19 8SQ,
United Kingdom

Editorial Offices
350 Main Street, Malden, MA 02148-5020, USA
9600 Garsington Road, Oxford, OX4 2DQ, UK
The Atrium, Southern Gate, Chichester, West Sussex, PO19 8SQ, UK

For details of our global editorial offices, for customer services, and for information about
how to apply for permission to reuse the copyright material in this book please see our website at
www.wiley.com/wiley-blackwell.

The right of David Welky to be identified as the author of the editorial material in this work has
been asserted in accordance with the UK Copyright, Designs and Patents Act 1988.

Wiley also publishes its books in a variety of electronic formats. Some content that appears in print
may not be available in electronic books.

Designations used by companies to distinguish their products are often claimed as trademarks.
All brand names and product names used in this book are trade names, service marks, trademarks
or registered trademarks of their respective owners. The publisher is not associated with any
product or vendor mentioned in this book. This publication is designed to provide accurate and
authoritative information in regard to the subject matter covered. It is sold on the understanding
that the publisher is not engaged in rendering professional services. If professional advice or other
expert assistance is required, the services of a competent professional should be sought.

Library of Congress Cataloging-in-Publication Data

America between the wars, 1919–1941 : a documentary reader / edited by David Welky.
   p.   cm. – (Uncovering the past : documentary readers in American history ; 7)
   Includes bibliographical references and index.
   ISBN 978-1-4443-3896-6 (hardback) – ISBN 978-1-4443-3897-3 (paperback)
1. United States–History–1919–1933–Sources.   2. United States–History–1933–1945–
Sources.   3. United States–Social conditions–1918–1932–Sources.   4. United States–Social
conditions–1933–1945–Sources.   I. Welky, David.
   E784.A66 2011
   973.91–dc23

                                                                    2011023519

A catalogue record for this book is available from the British Library.

Set in 10/12.5pt Sabon by SPi Publisher Services, Pondicherry, India
Printed and bound in Malaysia by Vivar Printing Sdn Bhd

1   2012

Contents

List of Illustrations

Series Editors' Preface

Primary sources have become an essential component in the teaching of history to undergraduates. They engage students in the process of historical interpretation and analysis and help them understand that facts do not speak for themselves. Rather, students see how historians construct narratives that recreate the past. Most students assume that the pursuit of knowledge is a solitary endeavor; yet historians constantly interact with their peers, building upon previous research and arguing among themselves over the interpretation of documents and their larger meaning. The documentary readers in this series highlight the value of this collaborative creative process and encourage students to participate in it.

Each book in the series introduces students in American history courses to two important dimensions of historical analysis. They enable students to engage actively in historical interpretation, and they further students' understanding of the interplay among social, cultural, economic, and political forces in historical developments. In pursuit of these goals, the documents in each text embrace a broad range of sources, including such items as illustrations of material artifacts, letters and diaries, sermons, maps, photographs, song lyrics, selections from fiction and memoirs, legal statutes, court decisions, presidential orders, speeches, and political cartoons.

Each volume in the series is edited by a specialist in the field who is concerned with undergraduate teaching. The goal is not to offer a comprehensive selection of material but to provide items that reflect major themes and debates; that illustrate significant social, cultural, political, and economic dimensions of an era or subject; and that inform, intrigue, and inspire undergraduate students. The editor of each volume has written an introduction that discusses the central questions that have occupied historians in this field and the ways historians have used primary sources to answer them. In addition, each introductory essay contains an explanation of the kinds of materials available to investigate a particular subject, the methods by which scholars analyze them, and the considerations that go into interpreting them. Each source selection is introduced by a short head note that gives students the necessary information and context for understanding the document. Also, each section of the volume includes questions to guide student reading and stimulate classroom discussion.

David Welky's *America Between the Wars, 1919–1941* offers a superb array of documents dealing with political, social, economic, and cultural developments from the end of World War I to the beginning of World War II. This period featured the growth of uneven prosperity during the 1920s accompanied by a transformation of social and cultural mores. These changes exposed fault lines along ideological, religious, racial, ethnic, and sexual terrains and occasioned clashes between different groups of Americans seeking to shape the direction of the country. The economy of the so-called "Roaring Twenties" brimmed with a wide assortment of consumer goods from automobiles to radios and household appliances. Within this unparalleled decade of mass production and consumption, individual heroes such as the aviator Charles A. Lindbergh thrilled Americans by showing that human beings remained the masters of technology. However, the optimism occasioned by the return of peace and prosperity crashed with the onset of the Great Depression of the 1930s. The business and financial excesses and government indifference of the 1920s should resonate with those Americans coping with the economic collapse in the first decade of the twenty-first century. Readers of these documents will surely take an interest in comparing the ways in which the nation responded to the ravages of the Great Depression through President Franklin D. Roosevelt's New Deal programs with government efforts in the early twenty-first century to tackle the Great Recession. Still, for all of Roosevelt's attempts to restore prosperity, it took World War II to end the Great Depression. Although dealing mainly with domestic matters, Welky devotes careful attention to the foreign policy debates that ultimately led the United States to enter the second great war of the twentieth century.

David Welky furnishes an assortment of rich documents with head notes and questions in each chapter that will encourage students to create history and show that facts do not speak for themselves. Students can analyze the views of politicians, diplomats, journalists, novelists, poets, advertisers, and ordinary people – farmers and workers, women and men, black, white, Native, Asian, and Hispanic Americans – as they grappled with the opportunities and challenges of prosperity, depression, and war.

Steven F. Lawson and Nancy A. Hewitt,
Series Editors

Source Acknowledgments

2.1 Grand Dragon Hiram Evans on the Klan and Americanism, 1926: Hiram Wesley Evans, "The Klan's Fight for Americanism" *North American Review* 223 (March 1926): 38–9, 41–3, 44, 45, 46, 49, 52, 53–54, 57, 60. Reprinted with permission of the *North American Review*.

2.2 "The Menace of Fundamentalism," 1925: *The Independent* 114 (May 30, 1925): 602.

2.4 "Why Boston Wishes to Hang Sacco and Vanzetti," 1927: *New Republic* 51 (May 25, 1927): 4–5, 6. Reprinted with permission of *New Republic*.

3.1 Floyd J. Calvin, Criticizing Southern Lynching, 1923: From "Eight Weeks in Dixie" by Floyd J. Calvin, *The Messenger*, January 1923: 576–7. Reprinted with permission.

3.2 Marcus Garvey Addresses UNIA Supporters in Philadelphia, 1919: Cary D. Wintz, ed., *African American Political Thought, 1890–1930: Washington, DuBois, Garvey, and Randolph* (London: Armonk, 1996), pp. 199, 200–2, 204, 205, 207; first appeared in *Negro World*, November 1, 1919.

3.3 Alain Locke, "Harlem," 1925: *The Survey* 53 (March 1925): 629, 630.

3.4 Pace Phonograph Corporation, Supporting Black Businesses, 1921: *The Crisis* 22 (June 1921): 41

3.5 Zora Neale Hurston, "How It Feels to Be Colored Me," 1928: *The World Tomorrow* 11 (May 1928): 215–16. Used with the permission of the Zora Neale Hurston Trust.

3.6   Douglas, Aaron. *Aspects of Negro Life: From Slavery through Reconstruction*, 1934: Art & Artifacts Division, Schomburg Center for Research in Black Culture, The New York Public Library, Astor, Lenox and Tilden Foundations.
Aaron Douglas, *Into Bondage*, 1936. Oil on canvas, 60³/₈ × 60¹/₂ inches. Corcoran Gallery of Art, Washington, DC. Museum Purchase and partial gift from Thurlow Evans Tibbs, Jr., The Evans-Tibbs Collection 1996.9.

4.2   Sinclair Lewis, Main Street, 1920: "Main Street," in *Lewis at Zenith: A Three-Novel Omnibus* (New York: Harcourt, Brace & World, 1961), pp. 37, 38–41.

4.3   Countee Cullen, "Heritage", 1925: Copyrights held by the Amistad Research Center, Tulane University, and administered by Thompson and Thompson, Brooklyn, NY. Reprinted with permission.

5.2   Letters from Mothers to the Children's Bureau, 1920–7: Original letters in National Archives, RG 102, Records of the Children's Bureau, Central Files, 1914–1940. from Molly Ladd-Taylor, *Raising a Baby the Government Way: Mothers' Letters to the Children's Bureau 1915–1932* (New Brunswick, NJ: Rutgers University Press, 1986). Reprinted with permission of the author.

5.3   Crystal Eastman, Radical Feminism, 1920: Original appeared in *The Liberator* (December 1920): 23–4.

5.4   Margaret Sanger Defends Birth Control, 1923: *The Margaret Sanger Papers* [Microfilm] reel 69 frames 389–401, and in the Sophia Smith Collection, Smith College, Northampton MA. Reprinted with kind permission of Alexander Sanger.

6.1   Bruce Bliven, How Radio is Reaching the World, 1924: "Radio's Promise and Pitfalls," *Century Magazine* 108 (June 1924): 149–50, 151, 152, 153, 154.

6.3   Motion Pictures in Middletown, 1929: Robert S. Lynd and Helen Merrell Lynd, *Middletown: A Study in American Culture* (New York: Harcourt, Brace & Company, 1929), pp. 263–5, 266, 267–9. Copyright © 1937 by Harcourt Inc., 1965 by Robert S. Lynd and Helen M. Lynd. Reprinted with kind permission of Houghton Mifflin Harcourt Publishing Company and Staughton M. Lynd.

6.4   John R. Tunis on College Football, 1928: *Harper's Magazine* 157 (November 1928): 742, 743–4, 745, 746.

6.5   Paul Gallico Discusses the Relevance of Babe Ruth, 1932: *Vanity Fair* 38 (May 1932): 38, 73. Reprinted with permission of Conde Nast Publications.

7.1   Paul Abbott on the National Economy, 1929: *Outlook and Independent* 151 (January 23, 1929): 142–3, 155.

7.2   *New York Times*, First Day of the Crash, 1929: From "Stocks Collapse in 16,410,030-Share Day," *New York Times* (October 30, 1929). Reprinted with permission.

7.4   Calvin Coolidge, A Bright Economic Future If We Stay the Course, 1932: *American Magazine* 113 (February 1932): 11–12, 13, 108, 110.

8.1   Walter Lippmann, Candidate Franklin Roosevelt, 1932: Reprinted with the permission of Scribner, a Division of Simon & Schuster, Inc, from Walter Lippmann, *Interpretations, 1931–1932*. Copyright © 1932 by Walter Lippmann, copyright renewed 1960 by Allan Nevins. All rights reserved.

8.3   Franklin Roosevelt, "Fireside Chat on Banking," 1933. F. B. Graham responds: Lawrence W. Levine and Cornelia R. Levine, eds., *The People and the President: America's Conversation with FDR* (Boston: Beacon Press, 2002), p. 36. Copyright © 2002 by Lawrence W. Levine and Cornelia R. Levine. Reprinted by permission of the author, the Sandra Dijkstra Literary Agency and Beacon Press, Boston.

9.1   Clarence Lee, Riding the Rails during the Great Depression, 1999: Errol Lincoln Uys, *Riding the Rails: Teenagers on the Move During the Great Depression* (Routledge, 2003), pp. 132–2, 133–6. Reprinted with permission of Routledge Publishing Inc.

9.2   Ann Marie Low, Farming in the Dust Bowl, 1930–2: Ann Marie Low, *Dust Bowl Diary* (Lincoln: University of Nebraska Press, 1984), pp. 49–52, 59–60, 67, 95–6. Copyright © 1984 by the University of Nebraska Press. Reprinted with permission.

9.3   John L. Spivak, Migrant Farm Workers, 1934: "A Letter from America to President Roosevelt," *New Masses* 10 (March 20, 1934): 9–10, 11.

9.4   Howard Kester, The Southern Tenant Farmers Union's "Ceremony of the Land," 1937: *Papers of the Southern Tenant Farmers Union*, reel 4.

10.1   James P. Cannon, In Support of Unionization: "What the Union Means," *Organizer Daily Strike Bulletin*, 1934, in James P. Cannon, *Notebook of an Agitator* (Pathfinder Press, 1993). Copyright © 1958, 1973, 1993, by Pathfinder Press. Reprinted with permission.

10.3 Raymond E. Click to Franklin Roosevelt, The New Deal Means Socialism, 1935: Lawrence W. Levine and Cornelia R. Levine, eds., *The People and the President: America's Conversation with FDR* (Boston: Beacon Press, 2002), p. 137. Copyright © 2002 by Lawrence W. Levine and Cornelia R. Levine. Reprinted by permission of the author, the Sandra Dijkstra Literary Agency and Beacon Press, Boston.

10.4 The *Saturday Evening Post* Attacks Intrusive Government, 1935: "Bullheaded Government," *Saturday Evening Post* 207 (May 18, 1935): 26. Reprinted with permission.

10.5 Image 10.1: Editorial cartoon published Feb. 10, 1937, in the Columbus (Ohio) Dispatch. Reprinted with permission.

11.1 Herman J. D. Carter, An Injustice at Scottsboro, 1933: Herman J. D. Carter, *The Scottsboro Blues* (Nashville: Mahlon Publishing, 1933), pp. 10–11. From Claude Barnett Collection, Chicago History Museum.

11.2 James R. Reid, Joe Louis: African-American Hero, 1938: "Reid Cites Qualities of Louis Which Have Inspired Race Youth," *Chicago Defender*, June 25, 1938. Reprinted with permission of the *Chicago Defender*.

11.4 Eva Lowe (Chen Junqi) Describes Chinese American Life during the Depression, 1982: From Judy Yung, ed., *Unbound Voices: A Documentary History of Chinese Women in San Francisco* (Berkeley: University of California Press, 1999), pp. 368–70, 371–3. Reprinted with permission of University of California Press.

11.5 Luisa Moreno, Latinos and American Identity, 1940: From an address delivered at the Panel of Deportation and Right of Asylum of the Fourth Annual Conference of the American Committee for Protection of the Foreign Born. (Washington, DC March 3, 1940, Box 1, Folder 1, Carey McWilliams Collection, University Research Library, Department of Special Collections, University of California, Los Angeles.)

12.1 Babe Didrikson: Viking Girl, 1932: " The World-Beating Girl Viking of Texas," *Literary Digest* 114 (27 August 1932): 26–7, 28.

12.2 Meridel Le Sueur, "I Was Marching," 1934: Copyright © 1948, 1956, 1966 Reprinted with permission of International Publishers Co. Inc.

12.3 Bruce Gould and Beatrice Blackmar Gould, A Modern Marriage, 1937: Originally published as "The Dance of Life" in *Ladies' Home Journal* 54 (October 1934): 4. All rights reserved.

12.4 Eleanor Roosevelt "My Day," 1937, 1939:, Rochelle Chadakoff, ed., *Eleanor Roosevelt's My Day: Her Acclaimed Columns, 1936–1945*, pp. 43–4, 66–7, 69–70, 126–7.

12.5   Letters from African-American Women to the Federal Government, 1935–1941: Gerda Lerner, ed., *Black Women in White America: A Documentary History* (New York: Pantheon, 1972), pp. 399–404, 405. Originals appear in WPA Box, Howard University, Washington, DC.

13.2   Harry Elmer Barnes, World War I Was a Mistake, 1926: From *The Genesis of the World War* by Harry Elmer Barnes. Copyright © 1926, 1927 by Alfred A. Knopf Inc and renewed 1954, 1955 by Harry Elmer Barnes. Used by permission of Alfred A. Knopf, a division of Random House, Inc.

13.4   The Sinking of the *Panay*: Copyright© 1937 by the *Christian Century*, 'The Sinking of the Panay' by the editors is reprinted by permission from the December 22, 1937 issue of the *Christian Century*.

14.1   Franklin Roosevelt, *America Will Be Neutral*, 1939. Taylor's response: Frederick R. Taylor to Franklin Roosevelt, "Supporting FDR's Neutrality Message," 1939. Lawrence W. Levine and Cornelia R. Levine, *The People and the President: America's Conversation with FDR* (Boston: Beacon Press, 2002), p. 276. Copyright © 2002 by Lawrence W. Levine and Cornelia R. Levine. Reprinted by permission of the author, the Sandra Dijkstra Literary Agency and Beacon Press, Boston.

14.3   Franklin Roosevelt, "An Arsenal of Democracy," 1940. Wessel's response: Lisette M. Wessel to Franklin Roosevelt, You Are Leading Us Into War, 1940. Lawrence W. Levine and Cornelia R. Levine, *The People and the President: America's Conversation with FDR* (Boston: Beacon Press, 2002), p. 331. Copyright © 2002 by Lawrence W. Levine and Cornelia R. Levine. Reprinted by permission of the author, the Sandra Dijkstra Literary Agency and Beacon Press, Boston.

14.4   A. Philip Randolph Calls for a March on Washington, 1941: *Pittsburgh Courier*, January 25, 1941. Reprinted with permission.

15.1   Will Hays, *The Motion Picture in a Changing World*, 1940: Will H. Hays, *The Motion Picture in a Changing World: Annual Report to the Motion Picture Producers and Distributors of America, Inc.* (March 25, 1940): 3–5, 6–7. Found in Franklin Roosevelt Presidential Library, John Boettiger Papers, box 20, file Hays, Will H. 1938–1946.

15.2   Henry Luce, America and the War, 1940: Henry Luce, "America and Armageddon," *Life* 8 (June 3, 1940): 40, 100. Reprinted with permission of *Life*.

15.3   Edward R. Murrow, *This is London*, 1940: Elmer Davis, ed., *This is London* (New York: Simon & Schuster, 1941), pp. 150, 151–3, 162–64, 221–4. Reprinted with permission of Casey Murrow.

Introduction

A wise man once explained to me the difference between a history student and a professional historian. Studying history, he said, was like eating. College undergraduates consume material provided by a professor. Introductory history classes require them to digest a buffet's worth of information in a single semester. Students may not relish the food set before them – political history might be too bland, or cultural history too heavy, or gender history too spicy – but they are all capable of eating if they are in the right mood. Everyone enjoys eating *something*, and every history student can find something palatable if they sign up for the right courses.

Being a historian is a different proposition. Historians certainly consume history, whether in the form of books, documentaries, historical sites, or scholarly journal articles. But they also produce history. They *write* books and articles. They assist in the production of documentaries. They create the base of knowledge needed to understand the significance of historical sites. Historians therefore resemble chefs, cooking what one hopes are tasty dishes for others to devour. While eating is an instinctive activity, not everyone knows how to cook, or is interested in learning how to cook. Chefs work behind the scenes and rarely see customers enjoying the fruits of their labor. Although an occasional compliment or complaint gets relayed to the kitchen, the chef – like the historian – generally labors in anonymity, as if the food – or history – prepared itself.

America Between the Wars, 1919–1941: A Documentary Reader, First Edition.
Edited by David Welky. Editorial material and organization © 2012 John Wiley & Sons, Inc.
Published 2012 by John Wiley & Sons, Inc.

This book aims to help you shift from thinking like a student of history to thinking like a historian. Think of it as your first semester at chef's school. It aspires to push you beyond being told what happened in the past – consuming – to begin devising your own conclusions regarding what happened in the past – producing. It does this by presenting an array of primary sources, organized thematically, created between 1919 and 1941. A primary source is a piece of evidence created during whatever period one is examining. In a legal sense, it is an eyewitness account, as opposed to hearsay testimony. Primary sources are the historian's ingredients. If properly handled and combined, they can produce amazing dishes, in the form of exciting new scholarship. Without them the historian-chef can only reheat dishes others have already cooked for them.

Our list of available ingredients has lengthened over the past few decades. Early-twentieth-century historians perceived the past through a narrow lens. To conclude our metaphor, their work ignored most cuisines. For them "history" meant the study of great men. These scholars believed that presidents, generals, brilliant orators, statesmen, and business leaders drove human events. For the most part they limited their use of primary sources to political speeches, letters between prominent thinkers, and the diaries of powerful people. No one argues that the subjects these historians selected were not worth studying. Presidents, generals, and statesmen are important, and their actions can profoundly affect humanity's future direction. The focus upon great men, however, deprived the vast majority of people from having any place in the past. Historians wrote about George Washington, not those who elected him, and turned out books about General Robert E. Lee, not those who fought under him.

Beginning in the 1960s, new directions in history expanded the definition of a legitimate primary source. College enrollments exploded as the baby boomer generation came of age. For the first time, large numbers of Hispanics, African Americans, and Asian Americans pursued higher education. More working- and middle-class students entered college than ever before. These people resolved to fill the knowledge gaps that traditional historians had left. They wanted to paint themselves into America's past. Since the late 1960s historians have tended to write history from the bottom up, focusing more on the masses than on "great men." Older surveys of the 1930s, for example, focused upon Franklin Roosevelt, his inner circle, and the political phenomenon known as the New Deal. More recent contributions flesh out the era by discussing how workers, migrant laborers, the unemployed, women, and minorities survived the Depression and influenced the New Deal. These studies assume that these once-voiceless Americans are not only appropriate historical subjects, but also that they played major roles in determining the character of the age.

This more expansive conception of history liberated scholars once limited to writing about wars, politics, and diplomacy. Now historians can explore social movements, ethnic groups, gender, sexuality, religious minorities, race, movies, sports, and music. Even those who study politics and war approach their material from fresh angles. Rather than provide a blow-by-blow account of a battle from a general's perspective, a military historian might approach a conflict from a private's point of view. Historians might also examine how popular culture depicted a war, how public opinion influenced political decision making, or how fighting overseas impacted the home front. The result is a broader, more nuanced, more inclusive depiction of the past than traditional accounts provided.

But how do historians give voices to people who left few paper trails? It is the rare nineteenth-century steelworker who left a voluminous diary. Humble immigrants did not write daily newspaper columns. African American slaves could not keep up an extensive correspondence. Historians have had to creatively apply the available scraps of information to recapture these lost worlds. Lyrics from black spirituals speak to a culture of resistance against the gloom of slavery. Foreign-language newspapers, minutes of union meetings, and corporate timesheets offer insight into factory workers' lives. Depending upon what questions a historian asks of them, seemingly mundane sources such as household inventories, census data, and recipe books can yield valuable insights. To give just one example, imagine that a historian working in a county courthouse finds a list of items recorded in a probate inquiry conducted after the death of, say, an Alabama farmer in 1934. That document would be of little interest to someone interested in America's diplomatic relations with Europe but would be of great interest to someone researching the material lives of ordinary citizens during the Depression.

This reconsideration of historical sources has affected studies of the era between World War I and World War II. Historians have, for example, used Hollywood movies to explore the national debate over America's role in the Second World War. Long-forgotten files from the Civilian Conservation Corps, a job-creation program from the 1930s, provided a wealth of information about the young men who worked on reclamation, erosion, park improvement, and flood-control projects. Tax records, local newspapers, and even maps offer material about impoverished sharecroppers in the Mississippi Delta.

Two points bear mentioning. First, except for oral history interviews, no new primary sources concerning the years covered in this book have been created since Japan's 1941 attack on Pearl Harbor closed the interwar era. These sources have been sitting around since the 1920s and 1930s, often ignored by generations of researchers. New collections sometimes emerge from dusty attics or are unsealed after being classified or locked in private collections. For the most part, however, changes in our understanding of the time have not resulted from the discovery of new sources so much as from historians asking different questions of existing sources. New questions revealed the inadequacy of the traditional base of sources, compelling historians to search elsewhere for answers.

Second, most of the writers of these "new" sources never intended them to become historical documents. "Great men" composed their letters and diaries with one eye on posterity. They knew later generations would comb their works for insights into their age. But plantation managers never imagined future researchers compiling statistics on how much they fed their slaves. Social Security administrators could not have fathomed historians scouring their records for evidence of the New Deal's gender biases. The lack of self-consciousness within these materials, the very fact that they were not written with history in mind, provides a refreshing dose of candor to those accustomed to reading self-aware writers. At the same time, it is often difficult to pry relevant evidence from these sources precisely *because* they were not created with history in mind. People from the past rarely say exactly what historians need them to say in order to help make a point or prove an argument. Researchers have to read between the lines, use additional materials to fill gaps, make inferences and assumptions, and apply a series of other intellectual devices to make sense of the past.

Dealing with primary sources is an art, not a science. Arithmetic offers the simplicity of "it's right" versus "it's wrong" – 2+2 will always equal 4. History has no such assurances. Certainly there are indisputable facts. No matter how hard one tries to prove otherwise, World War I did, does, and always will precede World War II. That's a fact. On the other hand, showing how World War I helped to cause World War II, or explaining how World War I influenced military tactics used during World War II, takes us beyond the realm of unarguable facts.

History is much more than a collection of names and dates. History is an effort to impose organization, cohesion, and structure on past events. I live near the William J. (you may know him as Bill) Clinton Presidential Library and Museum, a facility with the slogan: "History doesn't change, but our exhibits do." Intended to inform potential visitors that the museum constantly rotates its featured attractions, this catchphrase irks me every time I see it (historians get outraged by things normal people view as trivial). I expect more from a building dedicated to a man with a deep love for history. History *does* change. It changes all the time. If history didn't change we could all entrust a single historian with the task of churning out an annual volume containing *the* history of the previous year. That would certainly shorten your reading list, and mine too.

Back in the bad old days of communism, the Soviets had a joke that went something like this: "The future is certain, it is only the past that is unpredictable." Besides showing a misguided confidence in the longevity of totalitarian governments, this line also demonstrates an awareness that history is contested ground. History is an interpretation of the past that reflects a particular way of viewing the world. Different generations and interest groups shape and reshape history to serve their own needs and purposes. For example, present-day advocates of smaller, less powerful government portray the New Deal's vast expansion of the federal government as a disaster. Those who believe government can help solve problems too large for individuals to tackle present the New Deal in a more positive light.

There are multiple explanations for why history is a fluid creature. Varying interpretations of the past result in some cases from sheer ignorance or a willful desire to impose one's ideology upon earlier events no matter what the facts. More often variations occur because of history's subjective nature. Two plus two will always equal four, but none of your classmates will read the following documents in exactly the same way you do. They will draw different conclusions, perceive different motivations, and construct different impressions of what the authors hoped to accomplish. From these diverse interpretations will emerge opportunities to debate what "really" happened, to build a more solid, if always imperfect, understanding of the interwar era. Just because there is no absolute truth does not mean that some explanations are more convincing than others. A good argument is grounded in verifiable fact and demonstrates a firm grasp of all available primary sources. Like a detective building a case around the clues at hand or a scientist basing a theory upon mathematical equations or observable realities, the historian organizes evidence from primary sources into its most plausible form.

This book is intended to develop your ability to analyze primary sources and to shape them into larger narratives. You probably already have some experience with primary sources but may never have thought about how to approach them in a systematic way. To my mind, there are six things to consider when reading any primary source: context, author, intention, audience, content, and personal biases.

Primary sources appeared within a particular *context*, and they make little sense unless read within that context. Just as we are products of our time, historical actors lived, thought, and wrote at a specific moment. They understood the world in a way that made sense to them, even if it does not make sense to us. Someone writing in 1930, for example, might quite confidently predict that the economic downturn would soon end.

We, having the benefit of hindsight, know that they are in for another decade of hard times. White supremacists, anti-immigration activists, and radical feminists might offer perspectives that strike you as ridiculous, far-fetched, or offensive. Recall that they existed at a different time and in a different intellectual universe from our own. Our task is to understand their positions, not to criticize them for failing to echo our own beliefs. The headnote preceding each document will help you place entries within their appropriate context.

Next, note the *author*. Is it a man? Woman? White? Black? Powerful? Oppressed? Consider how their identity might color their opinions. What is their *intention*? Why did they write this article, or draw this cartoon, or compose this poem? What did they hope to accomplish? Are they trying to persuade other people to follow them? To win assistance from an authority figure? To make people laugh, cry, or feel outrage? What is the *audience* for this document? We change our literary voice depending upon whom we are talking to. A union activist might make their case one way to a stuffy business journal and adopt quite another style when speaking to a radical newspaper. As readers we must also bear in mind that different audiences will respond to the same argument in diverse ways.

People create documents for reasons. Think about the traces you leave of your own existence, whether they be phone calls, diary entries, e-mails, text messages, or comments on websites. Each of these serves a purpose in your life. They have an author, an intention, and an audience. You need something, you're bored, you're arranging a gathering, you have an opinion – all of these motivations say something about who you are and, by extension, the world you live in. If you're feeling particularly puckish you could even use this book as a primary source for studying me! Why did I undertake this project? Why did I select these documents instead of others? What does this introduction say about my personality and beliefs? Apply this same thought process to the strangers from the interwar era you encounter in the following pages.

With all these things to consider, there hardly seems time for the most basic element of reading primary sources: *content*. It is important to understand what the document is trying to say. What points does it try to make? What perspective does it offer? How does it support its contentions? Remember also that an assertion does not become truthful simply by appearing on a page. Read these documents with a skeptical eye. Examine them with context, author, intention, and audience in mind. Separate fact from opinion.

Finally, in reading primary sources we need to be aware of our *personal biases*. Just as these 1920s and 1930s authors approached their topics from a particular perspective, we encounter these documents with our own set of opinions, principles, and values. Our attitudes inevitably influence how we receive voices from the past. Resist the urge to dismiss a document that conflicts with your world view. Also resist the urge to embrace arguments that jibe with your own. To do otherwise is to construct a history that merely projects into the past what you already believe to be true. This is lazy history, scholarship without thought. Always be prepared to see alien worlds – and the past is most assuredly an alien world – through alien eyes. Celebrate the fact that history, when studied well, challenges our preconceptions. It forces us to detach from our perception of what the world is today, to accept immersion in a foreign environment. You come to this book with assumptions of what the 1920s and 1930s were like. If you close your eyes and think about the era you may see flappers, gangsters, and breadlines. Don't shut your eyes to documents that expand, challenge, and contradict those stereotypes. Doing so would not only deny the rich diversity of this period, but also cheat your own intellectual development.

This book does not present a comprehensive treatment of the period between the world wars. It instead illuminates several themes that ran through this turbulent time. First, it is crucial to understand that World War I's impact loomed over these decades. The war left Americans embittered, confused, and paranoid. Most failed to grasp why the United States had entered the conflict or what it had gained. Fueled by wartime propaganda that smeared dissidents, ethnics, unionists, civil rights activists, and radicals as less than "100 per cent American," the country's suspicions of perceived outsiders marked the peacetime years.

The 1920s witnessed several battles to define postwar America. African Americans, who served with distinction during the war, demanded equality with whites. This New Negro movement gained strength through sheer numbers. Hundreds of thousands of black southerners abandoned the fields for greener pastures in the North. Many of them settled in New York, Chicago, and other cities, where they discovered greater freedom of movement and more opportunities than the rural South offered. A New Woman also emerged as feminists savoring victory in the decades-long battle for suffrage rights charted bold paths towards gender equity. Some women exchanged Victorian notions of chastity and purity for more liberated lifestyles. Stereotyped as flappers, these rebels smoked, drank, wore makeup and revealing clothes, traveled unchaperoned in automobiles, talked openly about sex, and generally thumbed their noses at convention.

These developments inspired counterattacks. Conservatives resented threats to the social fabric. A postwar onslaught of strikes, riots, and economic problems also troubled them, as did the resumption of immigration from eastern and southern Europe. Evidence of the desire to preserve older and presumably safer ways abound. Passed in 1920, Prohibition was in part a slap at the immigrant culture of saloons and communal drinking. The Ku Klux Klan experienced massive growth on the strength of its anti-black, anti-immigrant platform. Nativists scored a victory when the 1924 National Origins Act closed the American gates to all but a handful of potential immigrants. Conservative social movements battled with liberal trends throughout the interwar period.

The 1920s also marked the rise of a mass, national culture that stood alongside, and sometimes supplanted, local byways. Several factors were at work here. Improved broadcasting, reception, and amplification technology made the radio a standard piece of American domestic life. Without leaving their homes, families could share a musical performance, a sporting event, or an on-air sitcom with millions of other people. Hollywood's introduction of talking pictures in the late 1920s transformed a popular medium into an entertainment colossus. Economic prosperity played a role in the widespread acceptance of mass culture, at least during the 1920s. Higher per-capita incomes meant that more Americans had extra dollars to spend on luxuries. Adopting a leisure-based culture also necessitated a shift away from the Victorian conviction that culture should teach solid morals and improve one's character toward a new definition of "culture" as a way to have a good time.

Good times ended with the fiscal disaster known as the Great Depression. The catastrophe, which started in 1929 and endured until massive defense spending revived the economy around 1940, challenged Americans' basic assumptions about their economic, social, and political systems. Beginning under Herbert Hoover's administration and accelerating under Franklin Roosevelt (FDR), the size and power of the federal government swelled as Washington officials tried to devise mechanisms to counter the Depression. Under Roosevelt's New Deal, Washington put the unemployed to work, regulated financial markets, and created a social safety net. The federal government, although miniscule compared to today, assumed a role modern Americans would recognize. Washington had been a practical nonentity between 1921 and 1929, when conservative Republicans Warren Harding and Calvin Coolidge held the presidency. Coolidge's assertion that "four-fifths of all our troubles would disappear if we would only sit down and keep still" crystallized the prevailing *laissez-faire* attitude. The New Deal shattered this hands-off ideology. Not even conservative presidents such as Ronald Reagan and George W. Bush did much to steer Washington away from Roosevelt's central governing assumption: that the state bore some responsibility for the well-being of all members of society.

As if guiding the country through its worst-ever economic crisis was not enough of a burden, Roosevelt faced the additional responsibility of leading the nation through World War II. FDR saw Hitler as a grave threat to American power. He understood that the Nazis had global ambitions. If these were realized, Germany and its Axis allies Italy and Japan would isolate the United States diplomatically, economically, and militarily, leaving it friendless in a hostile world. Roosevelt hoped to slow the Axis surge without directly involving the United States in the fight. He initiated a defense buildup and boosted aid to Great Britain, Hitler's only surviving opponent following the 1940 fall of France. These halting steps ignited enormous controversy. Americans defined their global interests narrowly after World War I. They were willing to commit troops to ensure the United States' continued dominance of the western hemisphere. The prospect of deploying them to Europe and Asia, however, struck many as lunacy. They remained convinced that crafty European propagandists had tricked the nation into joining the last war and were determined to avoid making the same mistake again. Not until Pearl Harbor did most Americans come to see the conflict as their fight. After two decades of cultural change, social upheaval, and economic chaos, they entered a war that sparked additional socioeconomic transformations, consolidated the country's superpower status, and thrust it into the role of global champion of democracy.

Chapter 1   Challenges to Postwar Readjustment

1 W. E. B. DuBois, "Returning Soldiers," 1919

The armistice of November 11, 1918 ended the World War without stopping wartime-era introspection, unrest, and paranoia in the United States. Citizen spy groups and federal agencies continued surveillance of anyone who struck them as less than 100 per cent American. A communist revolution in Russia and radical uprisings in postwar Europe sparked fears that the red tide might swamp the western hemisphere. Labor strikes, racial unrest, and a struggling postwar economy fueled impressions that America stood on the brink of disaster.

Black intellectuals such as W. E. B. DuBois saw opportunity in this unsettled environment. DuBois, a founding member of the National Association for the Advancement of Colored People (NAACP) and editor of the organization's magazine, the Crisis, *traveled to Paris after the war to press President Wilson and other delegates at the peace conference to end European colonization of Africa and white domination of the United States. His pleas fell upon deaf ears. DuBois vented his frustrations in a* Crisis *editorial written upon his return to New York City. "Returning Soldiers" highlighted the gap between America's egalitarian principles and its bigoted reality. In arguing that the 200,000 African Americans in uniform had fought for victory at home as well as abroad, DuBois helped set the stage for the New Negro movement that revolutionized black thought during the 1920s. His intemperate words also caused the postal*

America Between the Wars, 1919–1941: A Documentary Reader, First Edition.
Edited by David Welky. Editorial material and organization © 2012 John Wiley & Sons, Inc.
Published 2012 by John Wiley & Sons, Inc.

service to briefly block delivery of the Crisis *on the grounds that it threatened national security.*

    How valid are DuBois's complaints? How do you think white Americans would have responded to them? How well does DuBois link his appeal to traditional conceptions of American patriotism?

We are returning from war! The Crisis and tens of thousands of black men were drafted into a great struggle. For bleeding France and what she means and has meant and will mean to us and humanity and against the threat of German race arrogance, we fought gladly and to the last drop of blood; for America and her highest ideals, we fought in far-off hope; for the dominant southern oligarchy entrenched in Washington, we fought in bitter resignation. For the America that represents and gloats in lynching, disfranchisement, caste, brutality and devilish insult – for this, in the hateful upturning and mixing of things, we were forced by vindictive fate to fight, also.

But today we return! We return from the slavery of uniform which the world's madness demanded us to don to the freedom of civil garb. We stand again to look America squarely in the face and call a spade a spade. We sing: This country of ours, despite all its better souls have done and dreamed, is yet a shameful land.

It *lynches*.

And lynching is barbarism of a degree of contemptible nastiness unparalleled in human history. Yet for fifty years we have lynched two Negroes a week, and we have kept this up right through the war.

It *disfranchises* its own citizens.

Disfranchisement is the deliberate theft and robbery of the only protection of poor against rich and black against white. The land that disfranchises its citizens and calls itself a democracy lies and knows it lies.

It encourages *ignorance*.

It has never really tried to educate the Negro. A dominant minority does not want Negroes educated. It wants servants, dogs, whores and monkeys. And when this land allows a reactionary group by its stolen political power to force as many black folk into these categories as it possibly can, it cries in contemptible hypocrisy: "They threaten us with degeneracy; they cannot be educated."

It *steals* from us.

It organizes industry to cheat us. It cheats us out of our land; it cheats us out of our labor. It confiscates our savings. It reduces our wages. It raises our rent. It steals our profit. It taxes us without representation. It keeps us consistently and universally poor, and then feeds us on charity and derides our poverty.

It *insults* us.

It has organized a nation-wide and latterly a world-wide propaganda of deliberate and continuous insult and defamation of black blood wherever found. It decrees that it shall not be possible in travel nor residence, work nor play, education nor instruction for a black man to exist without tacit or open acknowledgment of his inferiority to the dirtiest white dog. And it looks upon any attempt to question or even discuss this dogma as arrogance, unwarranted assumption and treason.

This is the country to which we Soldiers of Democracy return. This is the fatherland for which we fought! But it is *our* fatherland. It was right for us to fight. The faults of *our* country are *our* faults. Under similar circumstances, we would fight again. But by the God of Heaven, we are cowards and jackasses if now that that war is over, we do not marshal every ounce of our brain and brawn to fight a sterner, longer, more unbending battle against the forces of hell in our own land.

We *return*.

We *return from fighting*.

We *return fighting*.

Make way for Democracy! We saved it in France, and by the Great Jehovah, we will save it in the United States of America, or know the reason why.

Source: W. E. B. DuBois, "Returning Soldiers," *Crisis* 18 (May 1919): 13–14.

2 Jack Gaveel, Workers Need to Radicalize, 1919

Postwar Europe was a powder keg. Lenin's Bolsheviks were consolidating communist rule over the former Russia, known as the Soviet Union, and leftist forces marched in defeated Germany and elsewhere. Enthused by developments in Europe and eager to provoke social revolution at home, American radicals stepped up efforts to mobilize the working class behind Marxist ideas, or at least to foster a sense of class identification that strengthened the unionist movement. Labor militancy was indeed rising. Workers who had endured stagnant wages even as the cost of living skyrocketed during the war now agitated for raises, shorter working days, better conditions, and more job security. Jack Gaveel's broadside in the radical Chicago newspaper Golos Truzenika (Voice of the Laborer) *paired these demands with a cynical, disillusioned take on the recent war. A general strike rocked Seattle a few weeks after Gaveel's article appeared. Tens of thousands of protesters brought the city to a standstill. Their actions whipped fears of an imminent communist takeover to hysterical levels. Conservative Americans who saw the strike as further evidence of a Bolshevik conspiracy demanded a patriotic backlash against supposedly un-American elements often tarred as "foreign agitators." The Red Scare had begun.*

How does Gaveel present World War I? Why would this interpretation appeal to his readers? According to Gaveel, what should American workers do to promote a better future? What would that future look like?

The war of the capitalists is concluded. The capitalist ambition is satisfied with the enormous fortune the war has brought; new markets which will facilitate further accumulation of wealth; as to profits, more expansion of trade is in view. The merciless fetters of the capitalists wait for new and foreign people to tie them to the machines of profit. But whatever will happen in consequence of the bloody and merciless war which now is in its last hour, the word revolution sounds in our ear, shaking like thunder.

It is a fact, that the war between the money-magnates (Kings) is ended, but class-struggle has only now started on its way. The red terror of revolution breaks its way throughout the entire world and looks into the eyes of the capitalist class with a grinning defiance. In Europe thrones are being crushed, tumbling into the dust; they hold trials over czars; Emperors hurry (flee) away dragging their dirty hide (body) to some hiding place where they are safe. The shameful flags of slavery are torn down and the flag of revolution which was hoisted in its place, waves lively in the fresh air of love of mankind. That was the first year in [the] history of the world, when it was interesting to celebrate Christmas according to the doctrines of Christ. The capitalist doctrines are overthrown with an astounding rapidity all over Europe in order to make place for the new doctrine: "peace on earth and good will towards men." Just for that reason Christian capitalism, with a grimace of contempt, draws its lips together, its heart filled with hatred against the Bolsheviki because they announce that "there will be no peace and brotherhood on earth as long as the army of the workers will be under the yoke of capitalism."

Workers of America, the world has changed! The social system of a ramshackle State lies on its death-bed and the industrial democracy of a new world [is] knocking at our door. They await the birth of democracy and we can not be quiet about the birth of our democracy. We must no longer be indifferent towards the trend of events but, whether we want or not, we have to face them under all circumstances. Every one will be forced to this by the industrial and financial crisis in this country, too, within a very short time.

Capitalism is driven out of certain parts of Europe and looks in America for a shelter.

While you American workers have shed your blood and sacrificed your lives over there for freedom and democracy your brothers who remained here were deprived of all that in the meanest manner. The yoke of slavery was wearing harder upon the necks of those who remained at home, than at any other time in history. The jails and prisons are filled with untold numbers of your fellow-workers; in these hell-holes they have to die a slow, merciless death and they were put there by the judges and executioners appointed through you. The workers of Russia, Finland, Germany, Sweden, Norway, Holland, France and England are fighting now in their own countries for such democracy which will be the democracy for all, men, women and children.

That is the kind of democracy for which you too have to fight against the industrial kaisers of America; that means nothing else than to enlighten your fellow-workers in the factories, mines and shops, to organize them into trade unions, so that the workers may dictate the conditions under which they are willing to work and continue production. You must do that if you do not want that the workers of the world point out towards you with their finger, at the time when the crisis will set in and you, who have sacrificed your lives for democracy, will have to stretch out your hand like a beggar for a miserable "job."

The capitalists of this country hold their hands tightly around the neck of their slaves to what they became entitled through the opportunities of the war and they will not let loose until they are forced to. Every worker in this country faces a dangerous situation; those who fought for democracy are already looking for work in the factories all over the country. And then the good news will come out that new labor-saving machines are employed everywhere.

These events will create the conditions of times when there is no sufficient work, that is low wages, longer working hours, and in its footsteps follow the result, as sickness, crime and prostitution; then the most doubtful eye will see already that they can not find here even a trace of that freedom for which they went to Europe to fight. We only need to look into the capitalist press and we can find that the returned soldiers who are looking for their old job do not get it at all; they also may find often that their job is held by women!

Workers of America! What do you think to do in this question? Do you perhaps have confidence in the wisdom of your masters and their conscience, that they will settle that question? Or will you perhaps curse the workers who are in the same condition as you?

We tell you, every one of you: rally all branches behind *one big organization*.

Why? Because the employer will not reduce your working hours in order that everybody can get work and he will not give you higher wages because in doing so he would act against his own interests. . . .

You can not help the case either if you blame the bad labor conditions upon the cursed immigrants. It would not help any if, out of mere selfishness, you would care only for yourself. . . .

You have to create a connection with the unemployed and the unemployed shall act with those who work who are employed. In such action only will there be any power and that will be the only remedy. That is the way you have to act; the eyes of the world are directed at you; because the capitalist beasts are trying to entrench themselves already that the attacks of the workers shall find them prepared. . . .

You workers, who gave up everything in this war shall have only that right left, to go back to the servant's position in which the war has found you. Or is it your only duty to sacrifice your lives in the interest of the greedy, money-hungry capitalistic class?

The time of action is here. We have to show the working-class of Europe that we are with them just as they are with us in our common struggles, because that struggle is that of the world's workers against the blood-thirsty capitalist class.

Source: Jack Gaveel, "The Duties of the Working Class," *Golos Truzenika* (*Voice of the Laborer*), January 25, 1919.

3 A. Mitchell Palmer on Communism in America, 1920

Attorney General A. Mitchell Palmer seized upon the Red Scare to further his presidential ambitions. A wave of terrorist attacks in summer 1919 startled a nation still coming to grips with the war, strikes, race riots, and a horrific influenza epidemic that killed around 600,000 Americans. Anarchists mailed a few dozen bombs to Palmer and other prominent individuals. Post Office officials intercepted many of them, but some got through. One anarchist died when he tripped on Palmer's front steps while carrying a bomb. The explosion destroyed the front of the attorney general's house (the bomber's scalp landed on the roof of Palmer's across-the-street neighbors, Franklin and Eleanor Roosevelt). Americans blamed communists for these incidents despite clear evidence of anarchist involvement – many failed to grasp the distinctions between the two groups. Palmer launched a series of raids against alleged communists during the winter of 1919–20. His campaign netted thousands of suspects, most of them arrested without warrants and held without charges. The great majority went free within a few weeks. Immigration officials deported the rest as "undesirables." Fear was in the air. In February 1920, the month this article appeared, an Indiana man shot an immigrant who said "to hell with the United States" during an argument about the proposed Treaty of Versailles. A jury deliberated for just two minutes before finding the shooter not guilty by reason of patriotism. Palmer's political aspirations evaporated a few months later when his hysterical predictions of further attacks proved false.

How does Palmer characterize communists? Does his depiction sound reasonable? Considering the circumstances of the times, do you feel it was proper to arrest or deport suspected communists?

. . . Like a prairie-fire, the blaze of revolution was sweeping over every American institution of law and order a year ago. It was eating its way into the homes of the American workman, its sharp tongues of revolutionary heat were licking the altars of the churches, leaping into the belfry of the school bell, crawling into the sacred corners of American homes, seeking to replace marriage vows with libertine laws, burning up the foundations of society.

Robbery, not war, is the ideal of communism. This has been demonstrated in Russia, Germany, and in America. As a foe, the anarchist is fearless of his own life, for his creed is a fanaticism that admits no respect of any other creed. Obviously it is the creed of any criminal mind, which reasons always from motives impossible to clean thought. Crime is the degenerate factor in society.

Upon these two basic certainties, first that the "Reds" were criminal aliens, and secondly that the American Government must prevent crime, it was decided that there could be no nice distinctions drawn between the theoretical ideals of the radicals and their actual violations of our national laws. An assassin may have brilliant intellectuality, he may be able to excuse his murder or robbery with fine oratory, but any theory which excuses crime is not wanted in America. This is no place for the criminal to flourish, nor will he do so, so long as the rights of common citizenship can be exerted to prevent him.

It has always been plain to me that when American citizens unite upon any national issue, they are generally right, but it is sometimes difficult to make the issue clear to them. If the Department of Justice could succeed in attracting the attention of our optimistic citizens to the issue of internal revolution in this country, we felt sure there would be no revolution. The Government was in jeopardy. My private information of what was being done by the organization known as the Communist Party of America, with headquarters in Chicago, of what was being done by the Communist Internationale under their manifesto planned at Moscow last March by Trotzky, Lenine and others, addressed "To the Proletariats of All Countries," of what strides the Communist Labor Party was making, removed all doubt. In this conclusion we did not ignore the definite standards of personal liberty, of free speech, which is the very temperament and heart of the people. The evidence was examined with the utmost care, with a personal leaning toward freedom of thought and word on all questions. . . .

My information showed that communism in this country was an organization of thousands of aliens, who were direct allies of Trotzky. Aliens of the same misshapen caste of mind and indecencies of character, and it showed that they were making the same glittering promises of lawlessness, of criminal autocracy to Americans, that they had made to the Russian peasants. How the Department of Justice discovered upwards of 60,000 of these organized agitators of the Trotzky doctrine in the United States, is the confidential information upon which the Government is now sweeping the nation clean of such alien filth. . . .

One of the chief incentives for the present activity of the Department of Justice against the "Reds" has been the hope that American citizens will, themselves, become voluntary agents for us, in a vast organization for mutual defense against the sinister agitation of men and women aliens, who appear to be either in the pay or under the criminal spell of Trotzky and Lenine. . . .

Behind, and underneath, my own determination to drive from our midst the agents of Bolshevism with increasing vigor and with greater speed, until there are no more of them left among us, so long as I have the responsible duty of that task, I have discovered the hysterical methods of these revolutionary humans with increasing amazement and suspicion. In the confused information that sometimes reaches the people, they are compelled to ask questions which involve the reasons for my acts against the "Reds." I have been asked, for instance, to what extent deportation will check radicalism in this country. Why not ask what will become of the United States Government if these alien radicals are permitted to carry out the principles of the Communist Party as embodied in its so-called laws, aims and regulations?

There wouldn't be any such thing left. In place of the United States Government we should have the horror and terrorism of bolsheviki tyranny such as is destroying Russia now. Every scrap of radical literature demands the overthrow of our existing government. All of it demands obedience to the instincts of criminal minds, that is, to the lower appetites, material and moral. The whole purpose of communism appears to be a mass formation of the criminals of the world to overthrow the decencies of private life, to usurp property that they have not earned, to disrupt the present order of life regardless of health, sex or religious rights. By a literature that promises the wildest dreams of such low aspirations, that can occur to only the criminal minds, communism distorts our social law.

The chief appeal communism makes is to "The Worker." If they can lure the wage-earner to join their own gang of thieves, if they can show him that he will be rich if he steals, so far they have succeeded in betraying him to their own criminal course. . . .

These are the revolutionary tenets of Trotzky and the Communist Internationale. Their manifesto further embraces the various organizations in this country of men and women obsessed with discontent, having disorganized relations to American society. These include the I. W. W.'s, the most radical socialists, the misguided anarchists, the agitators who oppose the limitations of unionism, the moral perverts and the hysterical neurasthenic women who abound in communism. . . .

It has been inferred by the "Reds" that the United States Government, by arresting and deporting them, is returning to the autocracy of Czardom, adopting the system that created the severity of Siberian banishment. My reply to such charges is, that in our determination to maintain our government we are treating our alien enemies with extreme consideration. To deny them the privilege of remaining in a country which they have openly deplored as an unenlightened community, unfit for those who prefer the privileges of Bolshevism, should be no hardship. It strikes me as an odd form of reasoning that these Russian Bolsheviks who extol the Bolshevik rule, should be so unwilling to return to Russia. The nationality of most of the alien "Reds" is Russian and German. There is almost no other nationality represented among them. . . .

It is my belief that while they have stirred discontent in our midst, while they have caused irritating strikes, and while they have infected our social ideas with the disease of their own minds and their unclean morals, we can get rid of them! [A]nd not until we have done so shall we have removed the menace of Bolshevism for good.

Source: A. Mitchell Palmer, "The Case Against the 'Reds,' " *Forum* 63 (February 1920): 174–6, 180, 181–2, 183, 185.

4 Warren Harding, "Readjustment," 1920

"He writes the worst English that I have ever encountered," H. L. Mencken once said of Warren Harding, the conservative Republican senator who won the 1920 presidential election. "It reminds me of a string of wet sponges," Mencken continued, "it reminds me of tattered washing on the line; it reminds me of stale bean soup, of college yells, of dogs barking idiotically through endless nights. It is so bad that a sort of grandeur creeps into it." Harding's oratorical skills indeed paled against those of his predecessor, Woodrow Wilson, but for millions of Americans that difference embodied Harding's appeal. Wilson offered soaring rhetoric and grand notions of

remaking the world, while Harding offered stability, tranquility, and – to use his word – normalcy. There was nothing wrong with America that a little old-fashioned common sense couldn't fix, he told voters. Progress would come if we looked to the past for ideas and inspiration. The isolationist, low-tax, smaller-government platform Harding articulated in the following campaign speech helped him trounce Democratic challenger James Cox by a margin of nearly two to one in 1920, ushering in a dozen years of Republican control of the White House.

How would Warren Harding define "normalcy"? Why did his vision appeal to so many voters? Although he never mentions his Democratic opposition, how does his speech implicitly define them? How does this speech compare to other political speeches you have heard? What do you see as its strengths and weaknesses?

My countrymen, there isn't anything the matter with the world's civilization, except that humanity is viewing it through a vision impaired in a cataclysmal war. Poise has been disturbed, and nerves have been racked, and fever has rendered men irrational. Sometimes there have been draughts upon the dangerous cup of barbarity. Men have wandered far from safe paths, but the human procession still marches in the right direction. Here in the United States, we feel the reflex, rather than the hurting wound itself, but we still think straight; and we mean to act straight; we mean to hold firmly to all that was ours when war involved us and seek the higher attainments which are the only compensations that so supreme a tragedy may give mankind.

America's present need is not heroics, but healing; not nostrums, but normalcy; not revolution, but restoration; not agitation, but adjustment; not surgery, but serenity; not the dramatic, but the dispassionate; not experiment, but equipoise; not submergence in internationality but sustainment in triumphant nationality. It's one thing to battle successfully against the world's domination by a military autocracy because the infinite God never intended such a program; but it's quite another thing to revise human nature and suspend the fundamental laws of life and all of life's requirements.

The world calls for peace. America demands peace, formal as well as actual, and means to have it so we may set our own house in order. We challenge the proposal that an armed autocrat should dominate the world, and we choose for ourselves the claim that the representative democracy which made us what we are. This Republic has its ample task if we put an end to false economics which lure humanity to utter chaos. Ours will be the commanding example of world leadership today. If we can prove a representative popular government under which the citizenship speaks what it may do for the government and country rather than what the country may do for individuals, we shall do more to make democracy safe for the world than all armed conflict ever recorded.

The world needs to be reminded that all human ills are not curable by legislation, and that quantity of statutory enactments and excess of government offer no substitute for quality of citizenship. The problems of maintained civilization are not to be solved by a transfer of responsibility from citizenship to government and no eminent page in history was ever drafted to the standards of mediocrity; nor, no government worthy of the name which is directed by influence on the one hand or moved by intimidation on the other.

My best judgment of America's need is to steady down, to get squarely on our feet, to make sure of the right path.

Let's get out of the fevered delirium of war with the hallucination that all the money in the world is to be made in the madness of war and the wildness of its aftermath.

Let us stop to consider that tranquility at home is more precious than peace abroad; and that both our good fortune and our eminence are dependent on the normal forward stride of all the American people.

We want to go on, secure and unafraid, holding fast to the American inheritance, and confident of the supreme American fulfillment.

Source: http://www.americanrhetoric.com/speeches/warrenghardingreadjustment.htm

5 Charlotte Perkins Gilman, Immigration Hurts America, 1923

In one of the greatest demographic shifts in history, millions of southern and eastern Europeans began arriving on American shores in the late 1800s. They came to join family members, improve their economic outlook, or escape religious persecution. Businessmen loved the vast new supply of cheap labor. Other Americans complained that these immigrants were too different, too unlike "us," to ever assimilate. New arrivals spoke unfamiliar languages such as Italian and Hungarian, worshipped in Catholic cathedrals and Jewish synagogues instead of Protestant churches, and appeared willing to take any job no matter the hours or wage. Anti-immigrant, or nativist, organizations backed measures ranging from intelligence tests for potential entrants to sealing the borders. World War I halted the exodus until 1919. The prospect of further "mongrelization" – as some nativists viewed ethnic diversity – led Congress to pass the 1921 Emergency Immigration Act, which set an annual limit of around 350,000 arrivals. Immigration quotas favored the northern and western European nations which were seen as more desirable than their southern and eastern European counterparts.

Detractors such as writer and sociologist Charlotte Perkins Gilman called
for harsher measures. Their efforts paid off when in 1924 Congress passed
the National Origins Act. The new regulations halved the 1921 law's quota.
These tight restrictions stayed in effect until the 1965 Immigration Act
began the process of reopening America's shores.

How does Gilman define Americanism? Why, in her eyes, do immigrants
not fit that definition? What does Gilman's discussion of race reveal about
the era's perspective on human biology?

There is a question, sneeringly asked by the stranger within our gates: "What is an American?" The American, who knows he is one but has never thought of defining himself, is rather perplexed by the question. A simple answer is here suggested: "Americans are the kind of people who make a nation which every other nationality wants to get into."

The sneering stranger then replies: "By no means. It is not your nation we admire, – far from it! It is your great rich country we want to get into."

But Africa is a great rich country, too; why not go there? They do not wish to go there; the country is "undeveloped;" there are savages in it. True, but this country was undeveloped, when we came here, and there were savages in it.

Our swarming immigrants do not wish for a wilderness, nor for enemies. They like an established nation, with free education, free hospitals, free nursing, and more remunerative employment than they can find at home.

The amazing thing is the cheerful willingness with which the American people are giving up their country to other people, so rapidly that they are already reduced to a scant half of the population. No one is to blame but ourselves. The noble spirit of our founders, and their complete ignorance of sociology began the trouble. They honestly imagined that one kind of man was as good as another if he had the same opportunity, – unless his color was different. Consequently they announced, with more than royal magnificence, that this country was "an asylum for the poor and oppressed of all nations.". . .

We used fondly to take for granted that the incoming millions loved the country as we did, and felt eager to join it. Some of them do. Enormous numbers do not. It is quite true that we ourselves are a mixed race, – as are all races today, – and that we were once immigrants. All Americans have come from somewhere else. But all persons who come from somewhere else are not therefore Americans. The American blend is from a few closely connected races.

The idealism of our forefathers with its unavoidable ignorance, is more than matched today by our own idealism, – though we have knowledge enough to modify it. With glowing enthusiasm we have seized upon one misplaced metaphor, and call our country now a "melting pot" instead of an asylum. Our country is our home. Any man who wants to turn his home either into an asylum or a melting pot is, – well, he is a person of peculiar tastes.

Why did we ever so stupidly accept that metaphor? A melting pot is a crucible. It has to be carefully made of special material and carefully filled with weighed and measured proportions of such ores as will combine to produce known results. If you put into a melting pot promiscuous shovelfuls of anything that comes handy you do not get out of it anything of value, and you may break the pot. . . .

Since genus homo is one species, it is physically possible for all races to interbreed, but not therefore desirable. Some combine well, making a good blend, some do not. We are perfectly familiar in this country with the various blends of black and white, and the wisest of both races prefer the pure stock. . . .

Genus canis, like *genus homo*, can interbreed practically without limit. But if you want a watch-dog you do not mate an Italian greyhound with a hairless pup from Mexico.

If dogs are left to themselves, in some canine "asylum" or "melting-pot," they are cheerfully promiscuous, but do not produce a super-dog. On the contrary they tend to revert to the "yaller dog," the jackal type so far behind them.

The present-day idealists have two main grounds of appeal in their defense of unlimited immigration. One is the advantage to us of the special gifts of the imported stock; the other is the advantage to them of the benefits of democracy. This last may be promptly disposed of. Any people on earth who want a democracy and are able to carry it on, can have one at home. There is no power above them which can prevent it. But if they do not want a democracy, or are unable to carry it on, they are a heavy drawback to us.

We are young in our great effort, we have by no means succeeded yet in developing this high form of government in full efficiency, in unimpeachable honesty and wise economy. Democracy moves on by the spread of ideas; majorities must be convinced, converted; a community of intellect is needed. The more kinds of races we have to reach, with all their differing cultures, ideas, tastes, and prejudices, the slower and harder is the task of developing democracy. . . .

The American people, as representing a group culture, brought with them from England and Holland and Scandinavia the demand for freedom and the capacity to get it. Owing to their vast and sudden advantages in soil and climate, in mineral wealth and geographic isolation, they made rapid growth and were able to add to their inherited tendencies a flexible progressiveness, an inventive ingenuity, a patience and broad kindliness of disposition which form a distinct national character.

It is precisely this American character which is taken advantage of by the "poor and oppressed." The poorer and more oppressed they are the more they need it. Some great and good citizens have come to us, from various stocks, but this is a question of race mixture. There is no claim here made as to racial superiority. Almost any race is superior to others in some particular. Each has not only a right but a duty to develop its own special powers. The intellect of India or China is far more highly developed than ours in some lines, but if these races possessed this country they would only make another India or China. Indeed if our land were reinforced with a vast population of angels from heaven it would not be America!

One of the sharpest irritants arising from the various alien elements in our national body comes from an intensely self-satisfied group of young foreigners who come here to criticise and improve us. These, being more vocal than the poor and oppressed, are loud in disapproval. They are not content with founding universities for themselves, but enter ours and seek to dominate them.

They openly scorn our national culture, proclaiming the high superiority of their own. They are particularly sarcastic about our recent feeble efforts to digest the indigestible and assimilate the unassimilable, looking over this great country, in which already there are a full half of varied Unamericans. We have whole colonies of them with their own languages, schools, and newspapers, their children growing to maturity without even learning English, merely using this country as a convenience for temporary profit or permanent colonizing. Observe them in the war, taking flight in great numbers to fight for their respective home-lands, or staying here to work us in their interests. Even so long established residents as the Irish remain Irish, – they are not Americans. They would willingly sacrifice the interests of this country, or of the world as a whole, for the sake of Ireland.

Nationals of such pure intensity should bestow their talents on the lands they love. Internationalists, of the sort who wish to belong to none, but mix all racial ingredients into a smooth paste, should select an uninhabited island for their experiment.

Source: Charlotte Perkins Gilman, "Is America Too Hospitable?" *The Forum* 70 (October 1923): 1983–4, 1985, 1986, 1988–9.

Discussion questions

1   What impact did involvement in the war have on the United States?
2   What were the main sources of frustration in the postwar era?
3   How does Gaveel and DuBois's image of America differ from Palmer, Harding, and Gilman's?

Chapter 2   Social Battles of the 1920s

1 Grand Dragon Hiram Evans on the Klan and Americanism, 1926

Former Confederate soldiers created the Ku Klux Klan in 1865 as a means for perpetuating white supremacy in the defeated South. Members intimidated, beat, and murdered freed slaves and anyone else who opposed the Klan's racist agenda. Internal divisions and the Grant administration's vigorous anti-Klan counteroffensive shattered the group in the early 1870s. William J. Simmons, a former preacher inspired by filmmaker D. W. Griffith's The Birth of a Nation, *revived the Klan in 1915 with a torchlit ceremony atop Georgia's Stone Mountain, a massive monument to Confederate heroes. The second Klan boasted an anti-black, anti-Catholic, anti-Jewish, and anti-foreigner agenda that called for tight immigration quotas, compulsory Bible study in schools, and the prohibition of liquor sales. Klansmen presented themselves as defenders of noble American traditions under siege from alien values.*

Membership topped the 4 million mark in the mid-1920s, giving the Klan such political clout in parts of the South and Midwest that its endorsement turned elections. Klansmen were typically lower- or middle-class, native-born urbanites who feared that immigrants and African Americans would steal their jobs, undermine what they saw as traditional values, and subvert national security. Hiram Wesley Evans, a former dentist who succeeded

America Between the Wars, 1919–1941: A Documentary Reader, First Edition.
Edited by David Welky. Editorial material and organization © 2012 John Wiley & Sons, Inc.
Published 2012 by John Wiley & Sons, Inc.

*William Simmons as Imperial Wizard in 1922, explained his group's mission
in a 1926 article.*
   *What values did the Klan claim to uphold? What forces threatened those
values, and why? What did Evans want for America? How realistic or
desirable were his wishes? How did he define "Americanism"? Why did the
Klan have so many followers in the 1920s? How do the photographs of a
KKK rally add to our understanding of the Klan?*

... The Klan ... has now come to speak for the great mass of Americans of
the old pioneer stock. . . .

These are, in the first place, a blend of various peoples of the so-called
Nordic race, the race which, with all its faults, has given the world almost
the whole of modern civilization. The Klan does not try to represent any
people but these.

... This remarkable race character, along with the new-won continent and
the new-created nation, made the inheritance of the old-stock Americans the
richest ever given to a generation of men.

In spite of it, however, these Nordic Americans for the last generation have
found themselves increasingly uncomfortable, and finally deeply distressed.
There appeared first confusion in thought and opinion, a groping and hesitancy
about national affairs and private life alike, in sharp contrast to the clear,
straightforward purposes of our earlier years. There was futility in religion,
too, which was in many ways even more distressing. Presently we began to
find that we were dealing with strange ideas; policies that always sounded
well, but somehow always made us still more uncomfortable.

Finally came the moral breakdown that has been going on for two decades.
One by one all our traditional moral standards went by the boards, or were so
disregarded that they ceased to be binding. The sacredness of our Sabbath, of
our homes, of chastity, and finally even of our right to teach our own children in
our own schools fundamental facts and truths were torn away from us.
Those who maintained the old standards did so only in the face of constant
ridicule. . . .

The old-stock Americans are learning, however. They have begun to arm
themselves for this new type of warfare. Most important, they have broken
away from the fetters of the false ideals and philanthropy which put aliens
ahead of their own children and their own race.

To do this they have had to reject completely – and perhaps for the
moment the rejection is a bit too complete – the whole body of "Liberal"
ideas which they had followed with such simple, unquestioning faith. . . .

The plain people now see that Liberalism has come completely under the dominance of weaklings and parasites whose alien "idealism" reaches its logical peak in the Bolshevist platform of "produce as little as you can, beg or steal from those who do produce, and kill the producer for thinking he is better than you." Not that all Liberalism goes so far, but it all seems to be on that road. The average Liberal idea is apparently that those who can produce should carry the unfit, and let the unfit rule them. . . .

The old stock Americans believe in Liberalism, but not in this thing. It has undermined their Constitution and their national customs and institutions, it has corrupted the morals of their children, it has vitiated their thought, it has degenerated and perverted their education, it has tried to destroy their God. They want no more of it. They are trying to get back to decency and common sense. . . .

One more point about the present attitude of the old stock-American: he has revived and increased his long-standing distrust of the Roman Catholic Church. . . .

The real indictment against the Roman Church is that it is, fundamentally and irredeemably, in its leadership, in politics, in thought, and largely in membership, actually and actively alien, un-American and usually anti-American. . . .

The hierarchical government of the Roman Church is equally at odds with Americanism. The Pope and the whole hierarchy have been for centuries almost wholly Italian. It is nonsense to suppose that a man, by entering a church, loses his race or national loyalties. The Roman Church today, therefore, is just what its name says – Roman; and it is impossible for its hierarchy or the policies they dictate to be in real sympathy with Americanism. Worse, the Italians have proven to be one of the least assimilable of people. . . .

We are a movement of the plain people, very weak in the matter of culture, intellectual support, and trained leadership. We are demanding, and we expect to win, a return of power into the hands of the everyday, not highly cultured, not overly intellectualized, but entirely unspoiled and not de-Americanized, average citizen of the old stock. . . .

This is undoubtedly a weakness. It lays us open to the charge of being "hicks" and "rubes" and "drivers of second hand Fords". We admit it. Far worse, it makes it hard for us to state our case and advocate our crusade in the most effective way, for most of us lack skill in language. . . .

First in the Klansman's mind is patriotism – America for Americans. He believes religiously that a betrayal of Americanism or the American race is treason to the most sacred of trusts, a trust from his fathers and a trust from God. He believes, too, that Americanism can only be achieved if the pioneer stock is kept pure. . . .

The second word in the Klansman's trilogy is "white". The white race must be supreme, not only in America but in the world. This is equally undebatable, except on the ground that the races might live together, each with full regard for the rights and interests of others, and that those rights and interests would never conflict. Such an idea, of course, is absurd. . . . The future of progress and civilization depends on the continued supremacy of the white race. The forward movement of the world for centuries has come entirely from it.

The third of the Klan principles is that Protestantism must be supreme; that Rome shall not rule America. The Klansman believes this not merely because he is a Protestant, nor even because the Colonies that are now our nation were settled for the purpose of wresting America from the control of Rome and establishing a land of free conscience. He believes it also because Protestantism is an essential part of Americanism; without it America could never have been created and without it she cannot go forward. Roman rule would kill it.

Protestantism contains more than religion. It is the expression in religion of the same spirit of independence, self-reliance and freedom which are the highest achievements of the Nordic race. . . .

Further, the Klan wishes to restore the Bible to the school, not only because it is part of the world's great heritage in literature and philosophy and has profoundly influenced all white civilization, but because it is the basis on which all Christian religions are built, and to which they must look for their authority. . . .

The Negro, the Klan considers a special duty and problem of the white American. He is among us through no wish of his; we owe it to him and to ourselves to give him full protection and opportunity. But his limitations are evident; we will not permit him to gain sufficient power to control our civilization. Neither will we delude him with promises of social equality which we know can never be realized. The Klan looks forward to the day when the Negro problem will have been solved on some much saner basis than miscegenation, and when every State will enforce laws making any sex relations between a white and a colored person a crime. . . .

The Jew is a more complex problem. His abilities are great, he contributes much to any country where he lives. This is particularly true of the Western Jew, those of the stocks we have known so long. Their separation from us is more religious than racial. When freed from persecution these Jews have shown a tendency to disintegrate and amalgamate. We may hope that shortly, in the free atmosphere of America, Jews of this class will cease to be a problem.

Source: Hiram Wesley Evans, "The Klan's Fight for Americanism," *North American Review* 223 (March 1926): 38–9, 41–3, 44, 45, 46, 49, 52, 53–4, 57, 60.

Figures 2.1–2.2   KKK rally in Washington, DC in 1926.

Source: Library of Congress, Prints & Photographs Division, LC-USZ62-59666.

Source: Library of Congress, Prints & Photographs Division, LC-USZ62-96154.

2 "The Menace of Fundamentalism," 1925

Numerous early-twentieth-century theologians sought to reconcile biblical creation stories with the emerging scientific consensus supporting Charles Darwin's theory of evolution. Efforts to revise Christian thought inspired many, especially in small towns and rural areas, to embrace the rising philosophy of fundamentalism. Fundamentalist sects varied in their principles but generally saw Christ's Second Coming as imminent and shared a conviction that the Bible should be read literally rather than as a series of morality tales. Liberal Baptist minister Harry Emerson Fosdick objected to what he saw as the fundamentalists' narrow-minded rejection of contrary teachings. "Has anybody a right to deny the Christian name to those who differ with him?" he asked in one sermon. Fundamentalism nevertheless gained adherents and political clout through the 1920s, culminating in a series of crusades to convince state legislatures to forbid the teaching of evolution in public schools. Tennessee passed such an act in 1925. The American Civil Liberties Union mounted a counter-assault, backing a Dayton, Tennessee teacher named John T. Scopes who defied the law in order to create a test case for the courts. The resulting Scopes Trial attracted some of the day's top legal talents. Chicago lawyer Clarence Darrow represented Scopes. William Jennings Bryan, a three-time presidential candidate known for his fundamentalist, prohibitionist, and pro-rural views, sat with the prosecution team. Here, The Independent *considers the case, Bryan's legal theories, and the role of fundamentalism in American life. A jury eventually found Scopes guilty and fined him $100, a judgment later overturned on a technicality. Tennessee's anti-evolution law remained on the books until 1967.*

What legal issues and consequences does the article foresee in the Scopes Trial? Why is the article so critical of fundamentalism?

. . . Wholly apart from the question of the validity of the theory of evolution or its conflict with religious orthodoxy, certain very profound and significant currents in American life are revealed by the situation in Tennessee which cannot be ignored or dismissed with a laugh. The whole theory of State education and the deeper question of the rights of an individual or of a minority are involved in what at first seems to be merely the deliberate mediævalism of a few ignorant men.

If we follow the Bryan theory that taxpayers have the right to say what shall be taught in the schools which they support, we are bowing to the great god, Majority, and thus presumably acting in accordance with American traditions. But in actual practice we are delivering to the majority the right to decide by ballot what is truth – which is patently absurd. A majority may decide that the theory of evolution is false, or become convinced that the germ theory of medicine is a wicked delusion, or enthusiastically believe that the earth is flat. Then, armed with their ballots and receipted tax bills, they can proceed to vote a law making it a crime to teach in the public schools the theory that the earth is round. At best, such a condition means that the schools of a community will lag definitely behind in the march of knowledge, waiting always until the majority have become convinced of a truth which has long been evident to the intelligent and informed. . . .

Mr. Bryan's plausible claim that the taxpayers are entitled to the kind of teaching they want may be upheld despite these dangers and the hardships inflicted on the young generations of scholars. But hand in hand with this control of public education by the majority comes from the same group of thinkers the clamor against the private school. "Let us pass a law obliging all children to be taught in the public schools," they say, "and then we can make it a crime to teach in those schools anything which is in conflict with the tenets of the Original Fundamental Hard Shell Ebenezer Flat Earth Brotherhood!" It is a beautiful method for standardizing life and thought. Mr. Bryan has a perfect right to attack evolution or to uphold any religious opinion he likes. He will always find an audience charmed to listen to his honeyed phrases. But neither he nor any group of his cothinkers can justify the infliction by statute of their ideas on the youth of the land.

They are doing more than making themselves ridiculous. They are injuring the cause of true religion; they are reverting to mediævalism and setting up a code of what may be taught and thought, an index with authority and legal sanctions behind it, and in so doing they are turning the hands of the clock backward; they are obscuring and befogging the light of truth; they are the children of darkness of these times. . . .

Some observers see in the tide of Fundamentalism sweeping over the American hinterland a menace to our intellectual liberty. In Oklahoma and Tennessee, in Florida, Mississippi, Georgia, West Virginia, Arkansas, Iowa, Illinois, North Dakota, Minnesota, Oregon, and Arizona, bills have either been passed or are pending making the teaching of "evolution" unlawful. This condition argues a very high imbecility coefficient in the States mentioned, much higher than is actually the case. The amazing thing is that there should be any support for a movement so un-American.

It is amazing, too, that there should be so large a support numerically for the basic contentions of the Fundamentalists. Their perilous premises, their bad logic, the suicidal dilemma of their conclusions should be rejected, one would suppose, by the common horse sense of the American public. Why must one assume the literal truth of every line of the Bible? What constitutes the Bible, anyway? What wisdom has decided whether an ancient Hebrew record is divinely inspired or merely apocryphal? It is so patently absurd to

argue that an incredulity as to the account of geologic time of Genesis necessarily affects one's faith in Jesus Christ, that one wonders that Mr. Bryan
and his followers have the effrontery to go up and down the land stabbing
the water and bowling over straw men of their own invention. The theory
of evolution may be only a theory as yet established by no perfection of
proof. But it is founded on observed facts. It deserves the study of all men
except those who prefer to dwell in darkness. Only the bigoted and the
backward can dare to make its consideration and exploration unlawful.

Source: "The Menace of Fundamentalism," *The Independent* 114 (May 30, 1925): 602.

3   Edwin E. Slosson, "The Futility of Anti-Prohibition," 1920

*Organizations such as the Women's Christian Temperance Union and the
Anti-Saloon League spent decades lobbying to abolish alcohol sales.
Prohibition advocates composed screeds against the evils of the saloon and
songs lamenting the unfortunate wives and children of men who floundered
in demon rum's grip. Virtuous Victorian women gathered at pianos to sing
"with us for your guides you shall win by this sign/The lips that touch liquor
shall never touch mine." Early-twentieth-century Progressives endorsed
prohibition on the grounds that it would Americanize immigrants and
transform unruly industrial workers into sober citizens. World War I
provided an additional push as temperance advocates cited the importance
of beer in German culture, the predominance of German Americans in the
brewery business, and the need to conserve grain. Congress and state
legislatures ratified the Eighteenth Amendment to the Constitution in 1919,
banning the "manufacture, sale, or transportation of intoxicating liquors."
Prohibition took effect the following January. Time exposed Prohibition as
a poorly enforced and increasingly unpopular law that fostered the growth
of organized crime and turned thirsty people into common criminals. Still,
repeal seemed unlikely, for Americans had never overturned a constitutional
amendment. Edwin E. Slosson explained why the United States would
remain dry forever, a prediction proved wrong after the Twenty First
Amendment, ratified in 1933, ended Prohibition.*

*Why does Slosson support Prohibition? Why does he believe it will endure
forever? What is his attitude toward those who disagree?*

The frantic and furious indignation of those who find themselves unwillingly
brought under prohibition is merely amusing to those of us who have
witnessed similar scenes when other states went dry. All their objections

have been raised before. All their schemes for circumventing the law have been tried before. Since there is nothing new in their tactics, there is nothing in them to alarm the prohibitionists. Before the war the United States was going dry anyway by popular vote, city by city, county by county, state by state, and the eighteenth amendment was merely a motion to make it unanimous by extending it at once to the backward sections of the nation. . . .

Perhaps it will do no harm, now that the battle is virtually won, to reveal the secret aim of the prohibitionists. They are fighting – not alcohol, as is commonly assumed – but the saloon as an institution and social drinking as a custom. They are not working to save the drunkard but to save society from the drunkard. They are not so foolish as to suppose that they can prevent any man from making and drinking his own alcohol and, altho they may not admit it, they do not care much if he does. . . . Anybody who can afford to buy a yeast cake and a bag of sugar or a bushel of rotten fruit can brew his own beverage and if he has ingenuity enough to attach a glass, copper or tin tube to a tea kettle he can distill his own whisky. But what if he does? It will never be a popular pastime. Wood alcohol, too, is not dangerous – to the teetotaler. It makes a man not merely "blind drunk" or "dead drunk," but permanently blind and permanently dead. . . .

The saloon in America has been gradually becoming disreputable for many years. Self-respecting saloonkeepers have felt the opprobrium and have been getting out of the business for the sake of their children. The saloons thus fell into less respectable hands and so become increasingly obnoxious to the community. . . .

The reason why men drink, and especially why they drink too much, is not in most cases because they find the taste of alcohol irresistible or are anxious to feel its effects, but because it is the custom and to refuse marks one down as a spoil-sport and a holier-than-thou. It is embarrassing to decline a treat and an insult to decline a toast. The student who does not join in the chorus, "Here's to Alma Mater, drink her down!" is viewed with some aversion by his classmates and he cannot excuse himself by saying that he thinks it disrespectful to imbibe the dear old lady as a beverage. . . .

If a whole people could be kept from alcohol long enough to sober up completely and to forget it, say a generation or two, then it might be safe to abolish prohibitory laws for it would be a long time, if ever, before they would fall into the old drinking habits. But there would then be no demand for the repeal of the law, for people would have come to feel it no more an infringement of their freedom than prohibiting spitting on the street, driving to the left or carrying a gun. Already we find the advantages of prohibition becoming recognized and the popular opposition weakening. Employers like it because it increases speed and reduces mistakes. Labor men like it because it gives them more strength to strike. Formerly strikers spent their idle time and strike funds at the saloon and the disorderly acts of those who took too much liquor brought discredit upon their cause. Now it is found that men on a strike hold out longer and behave better. The restaurants, clubs and hotels, that thought they were ruined when their bar was taken away, are making more money than ever. While the liquor men are fighting in courts, legislatures and Congress, the readjustment is being made and even if in the end they should win all round it would be too late for them to set up the business on the old stand. They would then find that the situation was reversed; they would have got the law on their side but the prohibitionists would have established their custom of not drinking.

Source: Edward E. Slosson, "The Futility of Anti-Prohibition," *The Independent* 102 (April 24, 1920): 126, 128.

4   "Why Boston Wishes to Hang Sacco and Vanzetti," 1927

Perhaps no crime of the 1920s gained as much national and international notoriety as the Sacco–Vanzetti case. Nicola Sacco and Bartolomeo Vanzetti were Italian-born anarchists (the following article mislabels them as communists) accused in 1920 of murdering two men while snatching a shoe factory payroll. Sentenced to the electric chair (not hanging, as the article suggests), their plight garnered worldwide attention. Liberals and radicals saw the former shoemaker and fishmonger as victims of an intolerant postwar justice system bent on purging so-called un-American influences. "Before you see us you already know that we were radicals, that we were underdogs, that we were the enemy of the institutions that you can believe in good faith in their goodness," Vanzetti told Judge Webster Thayer. Much of the evidence against the pair was shaky. Some witnesses either denied seeing the defendants at the crime scene or changed their stories. On the other hand, Sacco and Vanzetti belonged to the anarchist cell that conducted the 1919 bombings discussed in reading 1.3. Fellow anarchists struck additional targets in retaliation for the duo's arrest. Present-day opinion as to their guilt or innocence is divided. The State of Massachusetts executed Sacco and Vanzetti in 1927.

What social splits does the author believe the case exposed? How does this division reflect the other social battles discussed in this chapter? What does the author believe should happen to Sacco and Vanzetti? What evidence and arguments does he wield to support his claims?

Although at this writing Governor Fuller of Massachusetts has not announced what he intends to do about the conviction of Sacco and Vanzetti, we take it for granted that he will appoint a reviewing commission. If he is a man of balanced judgment or respect for the traditions of Anglo-American law, what else can he do? It is wholly incredible that, after the volume and the quality of the doubt which competent lawyers and judges of evidence have published as to the fairness of the trial, he will allow the two men to be killed. It is no less incredible that he would consider a commutation of their sentence to be a possible way out. If they have had a fair trial, he should, under the laws of Massachusetts, allow them to be executed. But if there is a reasonable doubt about their guilt, he should either pardon them or appoint a thoroughly impartial commission to investigate the conduct of the trial and the weight of the evidence. . . .

It is, of course, of the utmost importance to prevent the scheduled execution of Sacco and Vanzetti and to secure for them, if not a new trial, then an impartial review of the old trial. But there is another aspect of the episode which is of almost equal importance. It is created by the attitude which the great majority of the lawyers, business men and good society in Boston have assumed toward the effort to obtain a disinterested review of the legal process which resulted in the conviction of the two Italians. Their attitude has been one of fierce and uncompromising hostility. They have avoided for the most part any attempt to pass on the merits of the demand for a new trial. They have merely treated this demand as the evidence of an effort to weaken the foundations of legal and social order in Massachusetts. Respectable lawyers have stated that it now makes no difference whether the convicted Italians are innocent or guilty. They declare it to be disloyal to the system of criminal justice of their state to question the fairness of the trial. They feel themselves justified in abusing and, so far as possible, in persecuting, the people who insist that in this case justice may have stumbled.

In substance, they are insisting that the process of criminal justice in Massachusetts, as it has operated in this case, should be considered infallible. This is an extraordinary position to assume, considering the notorious defects in the existing machinery in this country for detecting, prosecuting, indicting, trying, punishing and reforming criminals, but what renders it the more extraordinary is one somewhat unusual characteristic of the procedure in this instance. The attribution of infallibility to the process of convicting Sacco and Vanzetti is, in effect, an attribution of infallibility to one man – Judge Webster Thayer, who tried the case. It was his conduct of the trial which resulted in the conviction. It was he who, under the law, passed upon and rejected the applications on various grounds for a new trial. . . . The Commonwealth of Massachusetts, which has always prided itself on its allegiance to the best traditions of Anglo-American law, is, consequently, risking its reputation for doing justice on the superiority to error of one man, who in this particular instance has peculiarly powerful personal reasons for closing his eyes to his own possible mistakes.

It is both astonishing and depressing that educated and intelligent people, who occupy responsible positions in society, should be unconscious of the sinister stupidity of assuming such a position. One of the most ordinary facts in the history of the law in all countries and at all times is that the criminal courts occasionally convict innocent people when the prosecuting or judicial officers have strong personal or social motives for wishing to convict, or for wishing to prevent a conviction from being overthrown. Motives of this kind were demonstrably present in the minds of the judicial officers who prosecuted, tried and convicted Sacco and Vanzetti. . . . There is no good reason why the proudest and most loyal citizen of Massachusetts should fear that in asking for a review of the record in this case he is injuring the reputation of his state. On the contrary, the only way whereby, in existing circumstances, he can justify popular confidence in the administration of justice in the Bay State is to provide, in the Sacco-Vanzetti case, for a review of the evidence outside of the ordinary procedure which that procedure itself does not require.

The blindness of Boston Back Bay to these commonplace considerations is itself something which calls for explanation. Why should a group of people, who in their private lives are kindly and decent, object to having certain reasonable doubts removed as to whether two poor Italians were or were not justly convicted of murder? The obvious answer is that the Italians happen to be communist agitators. This fact, which accounted for their conviction, may be assumed to account for the effort to associate the authority of the whole apparatus of criminal justice in Massachusetts with the refusal to reconsider the verdict. But this answer, while it contains a part of the truth, still leaves something to be explained. If Sacco and Vanzetti had been English or American communists, it is most probable either that they would not have been convicted or that it would have been necessary to arouse public opinion as to the need of a review of the justice of the conviction. It is the combination of their being foreigners and communists which is necessary to account for the resolution of good society in Boston that Sacco and Vanzetti shall die, no matter whether they have had or have not had a fair trial. The agitation for a review of the first trial, after the exhaustion of every expedient which the law provides for a reconsideration of the verdict, touches the Back Bay on its tenderest and most vulnerable spot. It is composed of an ethnic minority which still rules in some measure by virtue of wealth and social prestige. It resents the idea that the processes of this rule should be challenged by representatives of other and, in their opinion, inferior, peoples. . . .

The first article in the creed of the Back Bay is that descendants of the early English settlers are entitled by a species of divine right to rule this country and particularly Massachusetts. Its apologists associate the welfare and security of the commonwealth with the unimpaired exercise of this sacred privilege. At present, however, the descendants of these early settlers, particularly those who live in large cities, are hopelessly outnumbered. They are afraid of being overwhelmed and submerged. They are peculiarly sensitive to any attack upon the part of the social machinery, such as legal administration, which they still partly control. They consider their own prestige and that of their class compromised by the challenge of the Sacco-Vanzetti verdict. Thus their stubborn and impassioned defense of a doubtful conviction is chiefly a matter of pathological class consciousness. . . . The best society of Boston shuts its eyes to the danger of legally executing two possibly innocent Italians because the convicts belong to a class of foreign invaders who do not share American traditions or understand American institutions and who, from its point of view, deserve to feel the full rigor of the law which they ignore or protest.

Source: "Why Boston Wishes to Hang Sacco and Vanzetti," *New Republic* 51 (May 25, 1927): 4–5, 6.

Discussion questions

1 What social divisions did the United States experience in the 1920s?
2 How do the more conservative voices presented here define "America" and "American"?
3 In what ways do the social issues of the 1920s continue to affect the United States?

Chapter 3   The New Negro

1 Floyd J. Calvin, Criticizing Southern Lynching, 1923

Black southerners often had little sense of the battle raging between modernity and tradition during the 1920s. For them, life in postwar America closely resembled life before the war. The sharecropping system bound them to poverty and landlessness while segregation limited their educational opportunities and restricted where they could live. Underpinning these inequalities was the ever-present threat of violence. Lynching remained frighteningly common in the early twentieth century; vigilante mobs hung, shot, or otherwise murdered about fifty people every year. The National Association for the Advancement of Colored People (NAACP) began marking these tragic events in 1920 by hanging a black flag emblazoned with "A Man was Lynched Yesterday" from its New York City headquarters. Floyd J. Calvin, a reporter whose articles appeared in most of the nation's major black newspapers, discussed the causes and consequences of lynching in "The Present South." Here Calvin describes his recent visit to Hope, Arkansas.

What was the status of African Americans in the South? How did white southerners justify this status? Why was John West lynched? What does his murder, and the response to it, say about the nature of southern life?

America Between the Wars, 1919–1941: A Documentary Reader, First Edition.
Edited by David Welky. Editorial material and organization © 2012 John Wiley & Sons, Inc.
Published 2012 by John Wiley & Sons, Inc.

... On July 27th, John West, Negro, was taken from the streets of Hope and lynched.

I didn't see it. I saw its effect.

John West was an elderly man, concrete finisher, from Emporia, Kansas; imported by a paving company then engaged in paving the streets. He was one of the highest paid men on the job and had white men as subordinates. He drank from the same cup the white men used. One white man objected and an argument and fight ensued. West whipped the white man up terribly, then said in public what he thought of the White South in general. Both men paid fines for disturbing the peace – West about three times what the white man paid. Then he (West) bought a ticket for Texarkana and boarded train No. 35, at 12:10 P.M., starting home. The mob knew his moves and had everything planned. Six miles below Hope the train stopped for water. A crowd of white men rushed into the colored coach, overpowered the Negro, took him off and there was the mob which took him into the woods and shot him to death.

The afternoon papers reported the fate that met a "presumptuous nigger" and that was all.

The town moved on quite normally and I went ahead enjoying myself. It was the second Negro lynched in Hope within eighteen months. The first I knew personally, and his wife's voice tremored when she spoke to me. One of his friends explained the tragedy as she pointed out his grave in the colored cemetery where the white people dumped him and called it a burial. Those were *"the good 100 per cent American white people"* the Superintendent referred to when he was imploring Negroes not to join the Catholics. That is why I laughed! *"How can I hear what you say, when what you are is continually ringing in my ears?"*

The tragedy was on Friday. The following Monday a crowd of the younger set left for Detroit, Chicago and Gary, some declaring they never wanted to see the town again.

Politics timidly showed itself too. I say timidly – referring, of course, to its bearing on Negroes. The one party – the Democratic – held its primary during my sojourn, for the entire state as well as for local offices which I could observe at close range. The newspapers were always filled with the regular political activities of the Klan, from paid advertisements espousing the cause of their candidates to front-page news features describing their sensational campaign meetings. In the end the Klan triumphed.

No Negroes voted. They are plainly told they are not wanted in the Democratic party. Many attend the "stump speech" gatherings, and others even do much minor work in behalf of long-standing friends, but that is all. (I heard of rare instances where sentimental servants were taken along and allowed to vote with their employers, but this was both "personal and private.") The City (white) Superintendent of the Hope public schools (including the Negro) however, did say before the colored teachers assembled that he wished the Democrats would change the law and allow Negroes to vote the Democratic ticket, for he felt sure the time would come when the ("100 per centers") would need good, loyal, colored people to help defeat the Catholics. . . .

Out of this mass of observation and experience I have attempted to reach some conclusions, to wit:

On the surface the black people of Dixie seem happy enough: but underneath a peaceful revolution is slowly but surely making headway. *Times are surely growing worse.* There is a reason. Progress means change. When the change among the Negroes is for the better the Southern whites can't stand it. Theoretically they want the Negro to go to school, become educated, acquire property. But with that comes something else. *A man of education and property is a man of standing.* He should be consulted on important questions. He should be respected. He shouldn't have to suffer petty indignities.

But where is the Southerner who won't tell you: "Education is all right, *but a nigger is a nigger just the same."* . . .

There will always be some poor Southern whites. They are the proudest people in the world. *You can't insist that they treat you as a human being.* They do so if they want to – but it is optional with them. The better element may sympathize with you, but you are still helpless. "A chain is no stronger than its weakest link." *Basically the most prosperous Southern Negro is at the mercy of the most ignoble Southern white. There is no law* when it comes to a *showdown* between black and white.

All Negroes know this. Some may live 40 years and never have a single instance of trouble. But the brutal fact stares them in the face – *if it ever comes to a showdown.* And the *least thing* can bring this showdown. "*Would you put a nigger before a white man?*". . . Where is the Southerner who wouldn't quail? They may *all* regret it afterwards – but for the moment: "*White Supremacy*" with capital letters. And those whites who would bravely stand out against it – "*they are 'nigger' lovers – shoot 'em like dogs!*"

This is the actual situation. It is not true in *every* case, but it may be true in *any* case. And every Negro knows that *any* case might be *his own.*

Underneath the revel and merrymaking is a nervous tremor. *Always be careful.* The *mob* is a *possibility* for *any* Negro. Each fine house and each automobile may be in ashes next week this time, or they may be here indefinitely.

Source: "Eight Weeks in Dixie" by Floyd J. Calvin, *The Messenger,* January 1923, 576–7.

2 Marcus Garvey Addresses UNIA Supporters in Philadelphia, 1919

African Americans faced new frustrations in the postwar era. Hundreds of thousands of black veterans discovered that wartime service did not translate into social, political, or economic equality. Many who journeyed from the rural South to the urban North to pursue high-paying wartime jobs found themselves unemployed once white workers returned and the economy contracted. W. E. B. DuBois and other black intellectuals called for a New Negro, one infused with a desire to seize equality rather than wait for the white establishment to grant it. Jamaican-born New Yorker Marcus Garvey was the most radical New Negro to attract a substantial following. As leader of the United Negro Improvement Association (UNIA) and owner of the weekly Negro World, *Garvey promoted black empowerment, black-owned businesses, and a black liberation of Europe's African colonies. Garvey's claim that the UNIA had 4 million members surely exaggerated, but his message nevertheless resonated among lower-class northern urbanites and downtrodden Mississippi River Valley sharecroppers who felt disconnected from erudite, middle-class reformers such as DuBois. Garvey's popularity tumbled after a 1923 arrest for mail fraud in connection with his Black Star steamship line. His conversations with the Ku Klux Klan, another organization interested in racial separation, also antagonized supporters.*

What is Garvey's attitude towards white people? Why does he feel this way? Why do you think Garvey's message appealed to so many people?

[T]he Universal Negro Improvement Association and African Communities League is the greatest movement in the world, because it is the only movement today that is causing the white man to tremble in his shoes. (Cheers.) . . .

We have our foe, our ancient foe, puzzled. He does not know what to do with the New Negro; but the New Negro knows what to do with himself. And the thing that we are going to do is to blast a way to complete independence and to that democracy which they denied us even after we left the battlefields of France and Flanders. We, the New Negroes, say there is no turning back for us now. There is nothing else but a going forward, and if they squeal in America or anywhere else we are going forward. Why, we are not organized as four hundred millions yet, and they are so scared. Now, what will happen in the next five years when the entire four hundred millions will have been organized? All the lynching in the South will be a thing of the past. We are determined in this association to bring the white man to his senses. We are not going to fight and kill anybody because he has more than we have. But if there is anybody taking advantage of the Negro, whether he be white, red or blue, we are going to organize to stop him. . . .

[T]his is the age of action – action on the part of each and every individual of every race. If there is a white man who does not love the white race, to his race he is an outcast; if there is a yellow man that does not love his race, to the yellow race he is an outcast: if there is a Negro who does not love the black race, to his race such a Negro is an outcast and should be trampled to death.

We have lived upon the farce of brotherhood for hundreds of years, and if there is anybody who has suffered from that farce it is the Negro. The white man goes forth with the Bible and tells us that we are all brothers, but it is against the world to believe, against all humanity to believe, that really there is but one brotherhood. And if there are six brothers in any family, at least those six brothers from natural tie ought to be honest in their dealings with each other to the extent of not seeing any of the six starve. If one has not a job, naturally the others would see to it that the one that is out of a job gets something to eat and a place to sleep so as to prevent him from starving and dying. This is brotherhood. Now there is one brother with all the wealth; he has more than he wants, and there is the other brother. What is he doing to the other brother? He is murdering the other brother. He is lynching the other brother, and still they are brothers. Now, if I have any brother in my family who has no better love for me than to starve me, to whip me and to burn me, I say, brother, I do not want your relationship at all. To hell with it. . . .

The Negro peoples of the world should be so determined to reclaim Africa and found a government there, so that if any black man in any part of the world is abused we can call the mighty power of Africa to come to our aid. Men, a Negro government we had once, and a Negro government we must have again. Tell me that I must live everlastingly under the domination of a white man, that I must bequeath to my children white overlordship, then I say, let me die now, Almighty God. If there is no better future in the world for me than to be the slave of a white man, I say, take the life you gave me. I do not want it. You would not be my God if you created me to be a slave to other men; but you are my God and will continue to be my God if you created me an equal of all men. . . .

We have started an agitation all over the world. It is the agitation of self-reliance wherein the Negro must do for himself. I want you to understand that if you do not get behind this agitation and back it up morally and financially you are only flirting with your own downfall, because the world in which we live is today more serious than ever it was. . . . During this selfish, soulless age it falls to the province of the Negro to take the initiative and do for himself; otherwise he is going to die. He is going to d[ie] as I stand on this platform tonight[,] economically in America; he is going to die economically under the yoke of Britain, of France and of Germany. He is going to die in the next one hundred years if he does not start out now to do for himself. . . .

This war brought about new conditions in America and all over the world. America sent hundreds of thousands of colored soldiers to fight the white man's battles, during which time she opened the doors of industry to millions of white American men and women and created a new problem in the industrial market. And now the war is over and those millions who took the places of the soldiers who have returned home say: "We are not going to give up our jobs. We are going to remain in the industrial life of the world.["] This makes it difficult for returned soldiers to get work now. There will be sufficient jobs now for returned soldiers and for white men, because abnormal conditions are still in existence, but in the next two years these abnormal conditions will pass away and the industries will not be opened up for so long. It means that millions are going to starve. Do you think the white industrial captains are going to allow the white men and the white women to starve and give you bread? To the white man blood is thicker than water.

Therefore, in the next two years there is going to be an industrial boomerang in this country, and if the Negroes do not organize now to open up economic and industrial opportunities for themselves there will be starvation among all Negroes. . . .

Men become noble through service. Therefore, if any Negro wants to call himself an aristocrat, a nobleman, before he will get that respect from me he will have to do some service to the Negro race. . . .

Source: Cary D. Wintz, ed., *African American Political Thought, 1890–1930: Washington, DuBois, Garvey, and Randolph* (London: Armonk, 1996), pp. 199, 200–2, 204, 205, 207.

3 Alain Locke, "Harlem," 1925

Harlem was the epicenter of the New Negro movement. Marcus Garvey lived there. Black intellectuals hosted parties in its apartment buildings. Editors assembled magazines intended for black audiences. Novelists walked its streets seeking subject material. Painters toiled behind its windows. Jazz musicians honed their skills in its nightclubs. Harvard University philosophy professor Alain Locke sought to define the borough and the intellectual fervor within it when he edited a special edition of Survey Graphic *magazine devoted to "Harlem: The Mecca of the New Negro." Locke hoped the issue would alert a large audience to the African American community's new assertiveness and inspire black readers to better understand the significance and meaning of race in the United States.*

What, in Locke's eyes, makes Harlem so special? Why does Locke say that "Harlem represents the Negro's latest thrust toward Democracy?"

If we were to offer a symbol of what Harlem has come to mean in the short span of twenty years it would be another statue of liberty on the landward side of New York. It stands for a folk-movement which in human significance can be compared only with the pushing back of the western frontier in the first half of the last century, or the waves of immigration which have swept in from overseas in the last half. Numerically far smaller than either of these movements, the volume of migration is such none the less that Harlem has become the greatest Negro community the world has known – without counterpart in the South or in Africa. But beyond this, Harlem represents the Negro's latest thrust towards Democracy. . . .

Harlem has come into being and grasped its destiny with little heed from New York. And to the herded thousands who shoot beneath it twice a day on the subway, or the comparatively few whose daily travel takes them within sight of its fringes or down its main arteries, it is a black belt and nothing more. The pattern of delicatessen store and cigar shop and restaurant and undertaker's shop which repeats itself a thousand times on each of New York's long avenues is unbroken through Harlem. Its apartments, churches and storefronts antedated the Negroes and, for all New York knows, may outlast them there. For most of New York, Harlem is merely a rough rectangle of commonplace city blocks, lying between and to east and west of Lenox and Seventh Avenues, stretching nearly a mile north and south – and unaccountably full of Negroes.

Another Harlem is savored by the few – a Harlem of racy music and racier dancing, of cabarets famous or notorious according to their kind, of amusement in which abandon and sophistication are cheek by jowl – a Harlem which draws the connoisseur in diversion as well as the undiscriminating sightseer. This Harlem is the fertile source of the "shufflin'" and "rollin'" and "runnin' wild" revues that establish themselves season after season in "downtown" theaters. It is part of the exotic fringe of the metropolis.

Beneath this lies again the Harlem of the newspapers – a Harlem of monster parades and political flummery, a Harlem swept by revolutionary oratory or draped about the mysterious figures of Negro "millionaires," a Harlem pre-occupied with naive adjustments to a white world – a Harlem, in short, grotesque with the distortions of journalism.

Yet in final analysis, Harlem is neither slum, ghetto, resort or colony, though it is in part all of them. It is – or promises at least to be – a race capital. Europe seething in a dozen centers with emergent nationalities, Palestine full of a renascent Judaism – these are no more alive with the spirit of a racial awakening than Harlem; culturally and spiritually it focuses a people. Negro life is not only founding new centers, but finding a new soul. . . . The wash and rush of this human tide on the beach line of the northern city centers is to be explained primarily in terms of a new vision of opportunity, of social and economic freedom, of a spirit to seize, even in the face of an extortionate and heavy toll, a chance for the improvement of conditions. With each successive wave of it, the movement of the Negro migrant becomes more and more like that of the European waves at their crests, a mass movement toward the larger and the more democratic chance – in the Negro's case a deliberate flight not only from countryside to city, but from medieaval America to modern.

The secret lies close to what distinguishes Harlem from the ghettos with which it is sometimes compared. The ghetto picture is that of a slowly dissolving mass, bound by ties of custom and culture and association, in the midst of a freer and more varied society. From the racial standpoint, our Harlems are themselves crucibles. Here in Manhattan is not merely the largest Negro community in the world, but the first concentration in history of so many diverse elements of Negro life. It has attracted the African, the West Indian, the Negro American; has brought together the Negro of the North and the Negro of the South; the man from the city and the man from the town and village; the peasant, the student, the business man, the professional man, artist, poet, musician, adventurer and worker, preacher and criminal, exploiter and social outcast. Each group has come with its own separate motives and for its own special ends, but their greatest experience has been the finding of one another. Proscription and prejudice have thrown these dissimilar elements into a common area of contact and interaction. Within this area, race sympathy and unity have determined a further fusing of sentiment and experience. So what began in terms of segregation becomes more and more, as its elements mix and react, the laboratory of a great race-welding. . . .

A railroad ticket and a suitcase, like a Bagdad carpet, transport the Negro peasant from the cotton-field and farm to the heart of the most complex urban civilization. Here, in the mass, he must and does survive a jump of two generations in social economy and of a century and more in civilization. Meanwhile the Negro poet, student, artist, thinker, by the very move that normally would take him off at a tangent from the masses, finds himself in their midst, in a situation concentrating the racial side of his experience and heightening his race-consciousness. These moving, half-awakened newcomers provide an exceptional seed-bed for the germinating contacts of the enlightened minority. And that is why statistics are out of joint with fact in Harlem, and will be for a generation or so.

Harlem, I grant you, isn't typical – but it is significant, it is prophetic. No sane observer, however sympathetic to the new trend, would contend that the great masses are articulate as yet, but they stir, they move, they are more than physically restless. The challenge of the new intellectuals among them is clear enough – the "race radicals" and realists who have broken with the old epoch of philanthropic guidance, sentimental appeal and protest. But are we after all only reading into the stirrings of a sleeping giant the dreams of an agitator? The answer is in the migrating peasant. It is the "man farthest down" who is most active in getting up. . . .

When the racial leaders of twenty years ago spoke of developing race-pride and stimulating race-consciousness, and of the desirability of race solidarity, they could not in any accurate degree have anticipated the abrupt feeling that has surged up and now pervades the awakened centers. Some of the recognized Negro leaders and a powerful section of white opinion identified with "race work" of the older order have indeed attempted to discount this feeling as a "passing phase," an attack of "race nerves," so to speak, an "aftermath of the war," and the like. It has not abated, however, if we are to gage by the present tone and temper of the Negro press, or by the shift in popular support from the officially recognized and orthodox spokesmen to those of the independent, popular, and often radical type who are unmistakable symptoms of a new order. It is a social disservice to blunt the fact that the Negro of the Northern centers has reached a stage where tutelage, even of the most interested and well-intentioned sort, must give place to new relationships, where positive self-direction must be reckoned with in ever increasing measure.

Source: Alain Locke, "Harlem," *The Survey*, 53 (March 1925): 629, 630.

4 Pace Phonograph Corporation, Supporting Black Businesses, 1921

Most white-owned corporations limited African Americans to janitorial and general labor jobs. The same was true for culture-making industries. Black writers, photographers, and musicians struggled to find rewarding jobs with mainstream newspapers, magazines, movie studios, or recording companies. New Negroes therefore promoted black-owned businesses as avenues to economic success and social respectability. Cultural productions targeted at black audiences had existed before this time, but never on such a grand scale. Weekly papers such as the Chicago Defender *and* Pittsburgh Courier *built national followings. W. E. B. DuBois's* Crisis, *A. Philip Randolph's* Messenger, *and the National Urban League's* Opportunity *appealed to black audiences. Director Oscar Micheaux's so-called "race films" were screened in segregated movie theaters. And, as of 1921, the Pace Phonograph Corporation recorded black musicians for its Harlem-based Black Swan label.*

Based on what you read in the other articles in this chapter, how does this advertisement (next page) reflect the spirit of the New Negro?

Buy New Black Swan Records Every Month and Encourage Negro Singers, Musicians and Composers

Our monthly program will contain music that every home can use, no matter what your tastes may be.

We will record popular songs of the day, dance melodies, blues, high class ballads, sacred songs, Spirituals and operatic selections just as the other phonograph companies do.

We will give opportunities to our own singers such as they can get from no other companies. Every record you buy means encouragement to some Negro singer and some Negro musician to continue their work and to develop their talent.

Every record you buy means employment along new lines to a large number of our talented people, in addition to clerks, stenographers and others.

BLACK SWAN RECORDS are not "colored records" in the sense that they are cheaper or inferior. In appearance, in finish, in tone and in lasting qualities BLACK SWAN RECORDS will stand the test with any records made today.

Ask your dealer to carry all our records in stock. Buy from him regularly. If he does not carry them send direct to us and we will supply you. Or send us the name of a Live young man or young woman agent who will handle our records in your community.

Buy BLACK SWAN RECORDS and you will help preserve the best voices of the race, besides getting music which the race wants but which other companies do not record.

BLACK SWAN RECORDS are the only records using exclusively Negro voices and Negro musicians.

Pace Phonograph Corporation

257 W. 138th Street **New York, N. Y.**

Figure 3.1 Pace Phonograph Corporation, supporting black businesses, 1921.

Source: *The Crisis* 22 (June 1921): 41.

5 Zora Neale Hurston, "How It Feels to Be Colored Me," 1928

*"Being a Negro writer these days is a racket and I'm going to make the most
of it while it lasts," remarked Sweetie May Carr, a fictionalized version of
author Zora Neale Hurston who appeared in Wallace Thurman's novel*
Infants of the Spring *(1932). Hurston was a popular if puzzling figure
within Harlem's literary circles. She happily accepted charity from wealthy
white benefactors and acted out stereotyped roles of a jungle primitive or a
simple "darky" for their amusement. Some of her friends saw such behavior
as a winking disguise intended to dupe whites into financially supporting
her literary endeavors. Others believed that this grinning buffoon was the
"real" Zora. Hurston's 1928 autobiographical essay "How It Feels to Be
Colored Me" reflects this confusion. On the one hand, she plays up her
supposed primitivism and happy-go-lucky willingness to let whites have
their way. The narrative also suggests a deeper, more thoughtful side when
Hurston argues for the essential humanity of all people no matter their
skin color.*

*How does Hurston simultaneously support and subvert traditional white
understandings of African Americans' character? What message does her
final paragraph convey?*

I remember the very day that I became colored. Up to my thirteenth year. I
lived in the little Negro town of Eatonville, Florida. It is exclusively a colored
town. The only white people I knew passed through the town going to or
coming from Orlando. The native whites rode dusty horses, the Northern
tourists chugged down the sandy village road in automobiles. The town
knew the Southerners and never stopped cane chewing when they passed.
But the Northerners were something else again. They were peered at cau-
tiously from behind curtains by the timid. The more venturesome would
come out on the porch to watch them go past and got just as much pleasure
out of the tourists as the tourists got out of the village.

The front porch might seem a daring place for the rest of the town,
but it was a gallery seat to me. My favorite place was atop the gate-post.
Proscenium box for a born first-nighter. Not only did I enjoy the show, but
I didn't mind the actors knowing that I liked it. I usually spoke to them in
passing. I'd wave at them and when they returned my salute, I would say
something like this: "Howdy-do-well-I-thank-you-where-you-goin'?" Usually
automobile or the horse paused at this, and after a queer exchange of
compliments, I would probably "go a piece of the way" with them, as we say
in farthest Florida. If one of my family happened to come to the front in
time to see me, of course negotiations would be rudely broken off. But even

so, it is clear that I was the first "welcome-to-our-state" Floridian, and I hope the Miami Chamber of Commerce will please take notice.

During this period, white people differed from colored to me only in that they rode through town and never lived there. They liked to hear me "speak pieces" and sing and wanted to see me dance the parse-me-la, and gave me generously of their small silver for doing these things, which seemed strange to me for I wanted to do them so much that I needed bribing to stop. Only they didn't know it. The colored people gave no dimes. They deplored any joyful tendencies in me, but I was their Zora nevertheless. I belonged to them, to the nearby hotels, to the county – everybody's Zora.

But changes came in the family when I was thirteen, and I was sent to school in Jacksonville. I left Eatonville, the town of the oleanders, as Zora. When I disembarked from the river-boat at Jacksonville, she was no more. It seemed that I had suffered a sea change. I was not Zora of Orange County any more, I was now a little colored girl. I found it out in certain ways. In my heart as well as in the mirror, I became a fast brown – warranted not to rub nor run.

But I am not tragically colored. There is no great sorrow dammed up in my soul, nor lurking behind my eyes. I do not mind at all. I do not belong to the sobbing school of Negrohood who hold that nature somehow has given them a lowdown dirty deal and whose feelings are all hurt about it. Even in the helter-skelter skirmish that is my life, I have seen that the world is to the strong regardless of a little pigmentation more or less. No, I do not weep at the world – I am too busy sharpening my oyster knife.

Someone is always at my elbow reminding me that I am the grand-daughter of slaves. It fails to register depression with me. Slavery is sixty years in the past. The operation was successful and the patient is doing well, thank you. . . .

The position of my white neighbor is much more difficult. No brown specter pulls up a chair beside me when I sit down to eat. No dark ghost thrusts its leg against mine in bed. The game of keeping what one has is never so exciting as the game of getting.

I do not always feel colored. Even now I often achieve the unconscious Zora of Eatonville before the Hegira. I feel most colored when I am thrown against a sharp white background.

For instance at Barnard. "Beside the waters of the Hudson" I feel my race. Among the thousand white persons, I am a dark rock surged upon, over-swept by a creamy sea. I am surged upon and overswept, but through it all, I remain myself. When covered by the waters, I am; and the ebb but reveals me again.

Sometimes it is the other way around. A white person is set down in our midst, but the contrast is just as sharp for me. For instance, when I sit in the drafty basement that is The New World Cabaret with a white person, my color comes. We enter chatting about any little nothing that we have in common and are seated by the jazz waiters. In the abrupt way that jazz orchestras have, this one plunges into a number. It loses no time in circumlocutions, but gets right down to business. It constricts the thorax and splits the heart with its tempo and narcotic harmonies. This orchestra grows rambunctious, rears on its hind legs and attacks the tonal veil with primitive fury, rending it, clawing it until it breaks through to the jungle beyond. I follow those heathen – follow them exultingly. I dance wildly inside myself; I yell within, I whoop; I shake my assegai above my head, I hurl it true to the mark *yeeeoowwl* I am in the jungle and living in the jungle way. My face is painted red and yellow and my body is painted blue. My pulse is throbbing like a war drum. I want to slaughter something – give pain, give death to what, I do not know. But the piece ends. The men of the orchestra wipe their lips and rest their fingers. I creep back slowly to the veneer we call civilization with the last tone and find the white friend sitting motionless in his seat, smoking calmly.

"Good music they have here," he remarks, drumming the table with his fingertips.

Music! The great blobs of purple and red emotion have not touched him. He has only heard what I felt. He is far away and I see him but dimly across the ocean and the continent that have fallen between us. He is so pale with his whiteness then and I am *so* colored.

At certain times I have no race, I am *me*. . . . The cosmic Zora emerges. I belong to no race nor time. I am the eternal feminine with its string of beads.

I have no separate feeling about being an American citizen and colored. I am merely a fragment of the Great Soul that surges within the boundaries. My country, right or wrong.

Sometimes, I feel discriminated against, but it does not make me angry. It merely astonishes me. How *can* any deny themselves the pleasure of my company! It's beyond me.

But in the main, I feel like a brown bag of miscellany propped against a wall. Against a wall in company with other bags, white, red and yellow. Pour out the contents, and there is discovered a jumble of small things priceless and worthless. A first-water diamond, an empty spool, bits of broken glass, lengths of string, a key to a door long since crumbled away, a rusty knife-blade, old shoes saved for a road that never was and never will be, a nail bent under the weight of things too heavy for any nail, a dried flower or two, still a little fragrant. In your hand is the brown bag. On the ground before you is the jumble it held – so much like the jumble in the bags, could they be emptied, that all might be dumped in a single heap and the bags refilled without altering the content of any greatly. A bit of colored glass more or less would not matter. Perhaps that is how the Great Stuffer of Bags filled them in the first place – who knows?

Source: Zora Neale Hurston, "How It Feels to Be Colored Me," *The World Tomorrow* 11 (May 1928): 215–16.

6 Aaron Douglas, *Aspects of Negro Life*, 1934, and *Into Bondage*, 1936

A number of black artists gave visual form to the New Negro spirit. Sargent Johnson and Richmond Barthé created masks, busts, and full-figure sculptures of powerful black men and women. Often combining African imagery with Western elements, their works conveyed strength, soulfulness, and a uniquely black character. Painters such as Aaron Douglas communicated a similar sensibility. The Kansas-born artist moved to New York in 1925 to develop his distinctive, flat style and his belief that African Americans could connect with their African heritage by studying music, dance, and ritual – cultural artifacts he considered key to understanding the African "soul." Douglas's paintings often imply continuity between the Old and New World, a feeling of one unbroken historical line. They also suggest that black people – whether as Africans or African Americans – have a long history of significant achievements that endures to the present day. Rather than seeking acceptance by merging into the white mainstream, Douglas proudly emphasizes the differences between blacks and whites. He insists that African Americans should celebrate, not hide, even the most regrettable moments from their past.

What "story" do you think Douglas is trying to tell with each painting? How do these works express black pride and accomplishment?

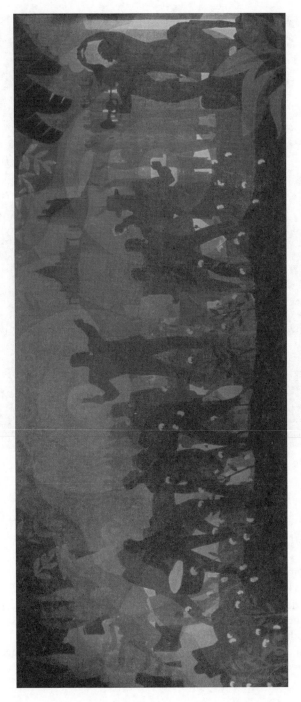

Figure 3.2 Aaron Douglas. "Aspects of Negro Life: From Slavery through Reconstruction," 1934.

Source: Aaron Douglas, *Aspects of Negro Life: From Slavery through Reconstruction*, 1934. Oil on canvas. Art & Artifacts Division, Schomburg Center for Research in Black Culture, The New York Public Library, Astor, Lenox and Tilden Foundations.

Figure 3.3   Aaron Douglas, "Into Bondage," 1936.

Source: Aaron Douglas, *Into Bondage*, 1936. Oil on canvas, 60⅜ × 60½ inches.
Corcoran Gallery of Art, Washington, DC. Museum Purchase and partial gift from
Thurlow Evans Tibbs, Jr., The Evans-Tibbs Collection 1996.9.

Discussion questions

1 How would you define the "New Negro"?
2 What points of agreement and disagreement do you see between Marcus
   Garvey and the other authors in this chapter?
3 What did it mean to be an African American in the 1920s? What challenges
   and opportunities did an African American identity present?

Chapter 4   New Trends in Literature

1 Edna St. Vincent Millay, "Spring," 1920

*American literature entered a new phase as the guns of World War I fell silent
in Europe. The brutal slaughter of millions shocked a generation of writers.
To them, old certainties that man was a rational creature and that civilization
followed an inevitable path toward progress and prosperity seemed ludicrous.
Such aspiring authors as Ernest Hemingway and E. E. Cummings witnessed
the war firsthand. Others, including F. Scott Fitzgerald, William Faulkner, and
Sinclair Lewis, experienced it through reports and newsreels. All, however,
were dismayed by the repressive atmosphere of wartime America and the
postwar paranoia that manifested itself in the Red Scare, nativism, and
the Ku Klux Klan. They responded with poems, short stories, and novels
reflecting their weary cynicism and their disillusionment with Western society.
These works featured emotionally and physically impotent men, helpless
characters adrift in an impersonal mass society, and impetuous firebrands
determined to party through their meaningless existences. Poet Edna
St. Vincent Millay captured this live-free-die-young attitude when she wrote:*

> *My candle burns at both ends;*
> *It will not last the night;*
> *But ah, my foes, and oh, my friends–*
> *It gives a lovely light!*

America Between the Wars, 1919–1941: A Documentary Reader, First Edition.
Edited by David Welky. Editorial material and organization © 2012 John Wiley & Sons, Inc.
Published 2012 by John Wiley & Sons, Inc.

Here she contributes a more reflective verse that encapsulates the bitterness of the "lost generation."

What unexpected tonal shift does the poem contain? What larger events do you think caused that shift? How does her poem contrast with what we typically think of as poems about spring? What is the symbolic importance of the "empty cup" and "uncarpeted stairs"?

To what purpose, April, do you return again?
Beauty is not enough.
You can no longer quiet me with the redness
Of little leaves opening stickily.
I know what I know.
The sun is hot on my neck as I observe
The spikes of the crocus.
The smell of the earth is good.
It is apparent that there is no death.
But what does that signify?
Not only under ground are the brains of men
Eaten by maggots.
Life in itself
Is nothing, –
An empty cup, a flight of uncarpeted stairs.
It is not enough that yearly down this hill
April
Comes like an idiot, babbling and strewing flowers!

Source: Edna St. Vincent Millay, "Spring," *Vanity Fair* 15 (November 1920): 49.

2 Sinclair Lewis, *Main Street*, 1920

Sherwood Anderson, John Dos Passos, William Faulkner, F. Scott Fitzgerald, Ernest Hemingway, and other young writers extended the 1920s-era literary rebellion into the short story and the novel. They rejected the Victorian novel's flowery style and clear-cut morality, instead presenting a cynical, ambiguous world view. Sinclair Lewis's Main Street (1920) was one of the first novels to articulate this postwar bleakness. Lewis, a product of Sauk Centre, Minnesota, grew up as an outsider. Unpopular among his peers, he came to view small-town life as conformist and backward. Main Street reads like an extended venting of his frustrations. It centers on Carol Kennicott, a naïve, idealistic young woman from the big city who hopes to "reform" the village of Gopher Prairie, a fictionalized version of Sauk Centre. Lewis's book, a big seller, contradicted earlier authors who depicted small towns as warm, moral, and comfortable. In this scene, Gopher Prairie native Dr. Will Kennicott introduces his new wife to some of the town's leading lights. Lewis found additional targets in future novels, including businessmen (Babbitt, 1922), evangelicals (Elmer Gantry, 1927), and society folk (Dodsworth, 1929).

What positions do Lewis's characters take on important political, social, and economic issues? Do you think that Lewis fairly depicts these characters, or does his caricaturing ring false?

. . . Juanita Haydock talked a good deal in her rattling voice but it was invariably of personalities: the rumor that Raymie Wutherspoon was going to send for a pair of patent leather shoes with gray buttoned tops; the rheumatism of Champ Perry; the state of Guy Pollock's grippe; and the dementia of Jim Howland in painting his fence salmon-pink.

Sam Clark had been talking to Carol about motor cars, but he felt his duties as host. While he droned, his brows popped up and down. He interrupted himself, "Must stir 'em up." He worried at his wife, "Don't you think I better stir 'em up?" He shouldered into the center of the room, and cried:

"Let's have some stunts, folks."

"Yes, let's!" shrieked Juanita Haydock.

"Say, Dave, give us that stunt about the Norwegian catching a hen."

"You bet; that's a slick stunt; do that, Dave!" cheered Chet Dashaway.

Mr. Dave Dyer obliged.

All the guests moved their lips in anticipation of being called on for their own stunts.

"Ella, came on and recite 'Old Sweetheart of Mine,' for us," demanded Sam.

Miss Ella Stowbody, the spinster daughter of the Ionic bank, scratched her dry palms and blushed. "Oh, you don't want to hear that old thing again."

"Sure we do! You bet!" asserted Sam.

"My voice is in terrible shape tonight."

"Tut! Come on!"

Sam loudly explained to Carol, "Ella is our shark at elocuting. She's had professional training. She studied singing and oratory and dramatic art and shorthand for a year, in Milwaukee."

Miss Stowbody was reciting. As encore to "An Old Sweetheart of Mine," she gave a peculiarly optimistic poem regarding the value of smiles.

There were four other stunts: one Jewish, one Irish, one juvenile, and Nat Hicks's parody of Mark Antony's funeral oration.

During the winter Carol was to hear Dave Dyer's hen-catching impersonation seven times, "An Old Sweetheart of Mine" nine times, the Jewish story and the funeral oration twice; but now she was ardent and, because she did so want to be happy and simple-hearted, she was as disappointed as the others when the stunts were finished, and the party instantly sank back into coma.

They gave up trying to be festive; they began to talk naturally, as they did at their shops and homes.

The men and women divided, as they had been tending to do all evening. Carol was deserted by the men, left to a group of matrons who steadily pattered of children, sickness, and cooks – their own shop-talk. She was piqued. She remembered visions of herself as a smart married woman in a drawing-room, fencing with clever men. . . .

She made her best curtsy to Mrs. Dawson; she twittered, "I won't have my husband leaving me so soon! I'm going over and pull the wretch's ears." . . . She proudly dipped across the room and, to the interest and commendation of all beholders, sat on the arm of Kennicott's chair.

He was gossiping with Sam Clark, Luke Dawson, Jackson Elder of the planing-mill, Chet Dashaway, Dave Dyer, Harry Haydock, and Ezra Stowbody, president of the Ionic bank.

Ezra Stowbody was a troglodyte. He had come to Gopher Prairie in 1865. He was a distinguished bird of prey – swooping thin nose, turtle mouth, thick brows, port-wine cheeks, floss of white hair, contemptuous eyes. He was not happy in the social changes of thirty years. Three decades ago, Dr. Westlake, Julius Flickerbaugh the lawyer, Merriman Peedy the Congregational pastor and himself had been the arbiters. That was as it should be; the fine arts – medicine, law, religion, and finance – recognized as aristocratic; four Yankees democratically chatting with but ruling the Ohioans and Illini and Swedes and Germans who had ventured to follow them. But Westlake was old, almost retired; Julius Flickerbaugh had lost much of his practise to livelier attorneys; Reverend (not The Reverend) Peedy was dead; and nobody was impressed in this rotten age of automobiles by the "spanking grays" which Ezra still drove. The town was as heterogeneous as Chicago. Norwegians and Germans owned stores. The social leaders were common merchants. Selling nails was considered as sacred as banking. These upstarts – the Clarks, the Haydocks – had no dignity. They were sound and conservative in politics, but they talked about motor cars and pump-guns and heaven only knew what new-fangled fads. Mr. Stowbody felt out of place with them. But his brick house with the mansard roof was still the largest residence in town, and he held his position as squire by occasionally appearing among the younger men and reminding them by a wintry eye that without the banker none of them could carry on their vulgar businesses.

As Carol defied decency by sitting down with the men, Mr. Stowbody was piping to Mr. Dawson, "Say, Luke, when was't Biggins first settled in Winnebago Township? Wa'n't it in 1879?"

"Why no 'twa'n't!" Mr. Dawson was indignant. "He come out from Vermont in 1867 – no, wait, in 1868, it must have been – and took a claim on the Rum River, quite a ways above Anoka."

"He did not!" roared Mr. Stowbody. "He settled first in Blue Earth County, him and his father!" . . .

Dave Dyer interrupted to give tidings, "D' tell you that Clara Biggins was in town couple days ago? She bought a hot-water bottle – expensive one, too – two dollars and thirty cents!"

"Yaaaaaah!" snarled Mr. Stowbody. "Course. She's just like her grandad was. Never save a cent. Two dollars and twenty – thirty, was it? – two dollars and thirty cents for a hot-water bottle! Brick wrapped up in a flannel petticoat just as good, anyway!"

"How's Ella's tonsils, Mr. Stowbody?" yawned Chet Dashaway.

While Mr. Stowbody gave a somatic and psychic study of them, Carol reflected, "Are they really so terribly interested in Ella's tonsils, or even in Ella's esophagus? I wonder if I could get them away from personalities? Let's risk damnation and try."

"There hasn't been much labor trouble around here, has there, Mr. Stow body?" she asked innocently.

"No, ma'am, thank God, we've been free from that, except maybe with hired girls and farm-hands. Trouble enough with these foreign farmers; if you don't watch these Swedes they turn socialist or populist or some fool thing on you in a minute. Of course, if they have loans you can make 'em listen to reason. I just have 'em come into the bank for a talk, and tell 'em a few things. I don't mind their being democrats, so much, but I won't stand having socialists around. But thank God, we ain't got the labor trouble they have in these cities. Even Jack Elder here gets along pretty well, in the planing-mill, don't you, Jack?"

"Yep. Sure. Don't need so many skilled workmen in my place, and it's a lot of these cranky, wage-hogging, half-baked skilled mechanics that start trouble – reading a lot of this anarchist literature and union papers and all."

"Do you approve of union labor?" Carol inquired of Mr. Elder.

"Me? I should say not! It's like this: I don't mind dealing with my men if they think they've got any grievances – though Lord knows what's come over workmen, nowadays – don't appreciate a good job. But still, if they come to me honestly, as man to man, I'll talk things over with them. But I'm not going to have any outsider, any of these walking delegates, or whatever fancy names they call themselves now – bunch of rich grafters, living on the ignorant workmen! Not going to have any of those fellows butting in and telling *me* how to run *my* business!"

Mr. Elder was growing more excited, more belligerent and patriotic. "I stand for freedom and constitutional rights. If any man don't like my shop, he can get up and git. Same way, if I don't like him, he gits. And that's all there is to it. I simply can't understand all these complications and hoop-te-doodles and government reports and wage-scales and God knows what all that these fellows are balling up the labor situation with, when it's all perfectly simple. They like what I pay 'em, or they get out. That's all there is to it!"

"What do you think of profit-sharing?" Carol ventured.

Mr. Elder thundered his answer, while the others nodded, solemnly and in tune, like a shop-window of flexible toys, comic mandarins and judges and ducks and clowns, set quivering by a breeze from the open door:

"All this profit-sharing and welfare work and insurance and old-age pension is simply poppycock. Enfeebles a workman's independence – and wastes a lot of honest profit. The half-baked thinker that isn't dry behind the ears yet, and these suffragettes and God knows what all buttinskis there are that are trying to tell a business man how to run his business, and some of these college professors are just about as bad, the whole kit and bilin' of 'em are nothing in God's world but socialism in disguise! And it's my bounden duty as a producer to resist every attack on the integrity of American industry to the last ditch. Yes – SIR!"

Mr. Elder wiped his brow.

Dave Dyer added, "Sure! You bet! What they ought to do is simply to hang every one of these agitators, and that would settle the whole thing right off. Don't you think so, doc?"

"You bet," agreed Kennicott.

The conversation was at last relieved of the plague of Carol's intrusions and they settled down to the question of whether the justice of the peace had sent that hobo drunk to jail for ten days or twelve. It was a matter not readily determined. Then Dave Dyer communicated his carefree adventures on the gipsy trail:

"Yep. I get good time out of the flivver. 'Bout a week ago I motored down to New Wurttemberg. That's forty-three – No, let's see: It's seventeen miles to Belldale, and 'bout six and three-quarters, call it seven, to Torgenquist, and it's a good nineteen miles from there to New Wurttemberg – seventeen and seven and nineteen, that makes uh, let me see: seventeen and seven's twenty-four, plus nineteen, well say plus twenty, that makes forty-four, well anyway, say about forty-three or -four miles from here to New Wurttemberg. We got started about seven-fifteen, prob'ly seven-twenty, because I had to stop and fill the radiator, and we ran along, just keeping up a good steady gait – "

Mr. Dyer did finally, for reasons and purposes admitted and justified, attain to New Wurttemberg.

Once – only once – the presence of the alien Carol was recognized. Chet Dashaway leaned over and said asthmatically, "Say, uh, have you been reading this serial 'Two Out' in *Tingling Tales*? Corking yarn! Gosh, the fellow that wrote it certainly can sling baseball slang!"

The others tried to look literary. Harry Haydock offered, "Juanita is a great hand for reading high-class stuff, like 'Mid the Magnolias' by this Sara Hetwiggin Butts, and 'Riders of Ranch Reckless.' Books. But me," he glanced about importantly, as one convinced that no other hero had ever been in so strange a plight, "I'm so darn busy I don't have much time to read."

"I never read anything I can't check against," said Sam Clark.

Thus ended the literary portion of the conversation, and for seven minutes Jackson Elder outlined reasons for believing that the pike-fishing was better on the west shore of Lake Minniemashie than on the east – though it was indeed quite true that on the east shore Nat Hicks had caught a pike altogether admirable.

The talk went on. It did go on! Their voices were monotonous, thick, emphatic. They were harshly pompous, like men in the smoking-compartments of Pullman cars. They did not bore Carol. They frightened her. She panted, "They will be cordial to me, because my man belongs to their tribe. God help me if I were an outsider!" . . .

Then a rattle, a daring hope in every eye, the swinging of a door, the smell of strong coffee, Dave Dyer's mewing voice in a triumphant, "The eats!" They began to chatter. They had something to do. They could escape from themselves. They fell upon the food – chicken sandwiches, maple cake, drug-store ice cream. Even when the food was gone they remained cheerful. They could go home, any time now, and go to bed!

They went, with a flutter of coats, chiffon scarfs, and good-bys.

Carol and Kennicott walked home.

"Did you like them?" he asked.

"They were terribly sweet to me." . . .

Source: Sinclair Lewis, *Main Street*, in *Lewis at Zenith: A Three-Novel Omnibus* (New York: Harcourt, Brace & World, 1961), pp. 37, 38–41.

3 Countee Cullen, "Heritage," 1925

African American poets, novelists, and playwrights also investigated new thematic realms. An extraordinary group of black writers descended upon New York City in the period surrounding World War I. Most of them ended up in Harlem, a district churning with excitement and bubbling with talk of a New Negro. Black-owned stores, restaurants, and cabarets lined the streets. Flashily dressed sharps crossed paths with longshoremen in overalls and

businessmen in sober suits. Hot jazz blared from crowded clubs. Street-corner
orators competed for listeners. It was the center of the black intellectual
world. Harlem Renaissance authors shared their white counterparts' disgust
for the recent war and its reactionary aftermath. Frustrated with the slow
pace of social change, many of them turned inward, seeking to create a
vibrant, self-consciously African American intellectual life that peered deep
into the recesses of the black experience. Like painter Aaron Douglas, whose
works appeared earlier, poet Countee Cullen sought connections between
Africa and America. His "Heritage" suggests an ambiguous relationship with
his place of origin. While the poem reflects a deep desire to know Africa, it
also indicates his strong attachment to western ways and an inability to truly
understand the continent.

What does Africa mean to Cullen? Does he base his images on stereotypes
or on actual knowledge of African life? What does Cullen mean when he writes
"With my mouth thus, in my heart/Do I play a double part"? What "double
part" is he playing, and what broader meanings does this statement imply?

What is Africa to me:
Copper sun or scarlet sea,
Jungle star or jungle track,
Strong bronzed men, or regal black
Women from whose loins I sprang
When the birds of Eden sang?
One three centuries removed
From the scenes his fathers loved,
Spicy grove, cinnamon tree,
What is Africa to me?

So I lie, who all day long
Want no sound except the song
Sung by wild barbaric birds
Goading massive jungle herds,
Juggernauts of flesh that pass
Trampling tall defiant grass
Where young forest lovers lie,
Plighting troth beneath the sky.
So I lie, who always hear,
Though I cram against my ear
Both my thumbs, and keep them there,
Great drums throbbing through the air.
So I lie, whose fount of pride,
Dear distress, and joy allied,

Is my somber flesh and skin,
With the dark blood dammed within
Like great pulsing tides of wine
That, I fear, must burst the fine
Channels of the chafing net
Where they surge and foam and fret.

Africa? A book one thumbs
Listlessly, till slumber comes.
Unremembered are her bats
Circling through the night, her cats
Crouching in the river reeds,
Stalking gentle flesh that feeds
By the river brink; no more
Does the bugle-throated roar
Cry that monarch claws have leapt
From the scabbards where they slept.
Silver snakes that once a year
Doff the lovely coats you wear,
Seek no covert in your fear
Lest a mortal eye should see;
What's your nakedness to me?
Here no leprous flowers rear
Fierce corollas in the air;
Here no bodies sleek and wet,
Dripping mingled rain and sweat,
Tread the savage measures of
Jungle boys and girls in love.
What is last year's snow to me,
Last year's anything? The tree
Budding yearly must forget
How its past arose or set –
Bough and blossom, flower, fruit,
Even what shy bird with mute
Wonder at her travail there,
Meekly labored in its hair.
One three centuries removed
From the scenes his fathers loved,
Spicy grove, cinnamon tree,
What is Africa to me?

So I lie, who find no peace
Night or day, no slight release

From the unremittant beat
Made by cruel padded feet
Walking through my body's street.
Up and down they go, and back,
Treading out a jungle track.
So I lie, who never quite
Safely sleep from rain at night –
I can never rest at all
When the rain begins to fall;
Like a soul gone mad with pain
I must match its weird refrain;
Ever must I twist and squirm,
Writhing like a baited worm,
While its primal measures drip
Through my body, crying, "Strip!
Doff this new exuberance.
Come and dance the Lover's Dance!"
In an old remembered way
Rain works on me night and day.

Quaint, outlandish heathen gods
Black men fashion out of rods,
Clay, and brittle bits of stone,
In a likeness like their own,
My conversion came high-priced;
I belong to Jesus Christ,
Preacher of humility;
Heathen gods are naught to me.

Father, Son, and Holy Ghost,
So I make an idle boast;
Jesus of the twice-turned cheek,
Lamb of God, although I speak
With my mouth thus, in my heart
Do I play a double part.
Ever at Thy glowing altar
Must my heart grow sick and falter,
Wishing He I served were black,
Thinking then it would not lack
Precedent of pain to guide it,
Let who would or might deride it;
Surely then this flesh would know

Yours had borne a kindred woe.
Lord, I fashion dark gods, too,
Daring even to give You
Dark despairing features where,
Crowned with dark rebellious hair,
Patience wavers just so much as
Mortal grief compels, while touches
Quick and hot, of anger, rise
To smitten cheek and weary eyes.
Lord, forgive me if my need
Sometimes shapes a human creed.

All day long and all night through,
One thing only must I do:
Quench my pride and cool my blood,
Lest I perish in the flood.
Lest a hidden ember set
Timber that I thought was wet
Burning like the dryest flax,
Melting like the merest wax,
Lest the grave restore its dead.
Not yet has my heart or head
In the least way realized
They and I are civilized.

Source: Countee Cullen, *Color* (New York: Harper & Brothers, 1925), 36–41.

4   Nella Larsen, *Quicksand*, 1928

Born in the Virgin Islands of mixed racial heritage, Harlem Renaissance
novelist Nella Larsen used her most famous works, Quicksand *(1928)*
and Passing *(1929), to examine the importance of color and the relevance*
of African American stereotypes. In the semi-autobiographical Quicksand,
Helga Crane, like Larsen the daughter of a Danish mother and a West Indian
father, travels two continents in search of a community that she can find both
acceptable and accepting. Naxos College, an all-black Southern school that
serves as a stand-in for Booker T. Washington's Tuskegee Institute, is too
provincial, while the white population in Copenhagen, Denmark, views her
as an exciting freak, a jungle sensualist. She spends part of her journey in
Harlem. In the following passage she visits a club with her friend Anne,
a staunch advocate of black pride and self-sufficiency. There they see
Dr. Anderson, president of Naxos College.

How does Larsen characterize Harlem? Does this characterization reinforce or destroy stereotypical images of African Americans? What race-based conflicts does Helga face?

It was night. The dinner-party was over, but no one wanted to go home. Half-past eleven was, it seemed, much too early to tumble into bed on a Saturday night. It was a sulky, humid night, a thick furry night, through which the electric torches shone like silver fuzz – an atrocious night for cabareting, Helga insisted, but the others wanted to go, so she went with them, though half unwillingly. After much consultation and chatter they decided upon a place and climbed into two patiently waiting taxis, rattling things which jerked, wiggled, and groaned, and threatened every minute to collide with others of their kind, or with inattentive pedestrians. Soon they pulled up before a tawdry doorway in a narrow crosstown street and stepped out. The night was far from quiet, the streets far from empty. Clanging trolley bells, quarreling cats, cackling phonographs, raucous laughter, complaining motor-horns, low singing, mingled in the familiar medley that is Harlem. Black figures, white figures, little forms, big forms, small groups, large groups, sauntered, or hurried by. It was gay, grotesque, and a little weird. Helga Crane felt singularly apart from it all. Entering the waiting doorway, they descended through a furtive, narrow passage, into a vast subterranean room. Helga smiled, thinking that this was one of those places characterized by the righteous as a hell.

A glare of light struck her eyes, a blare of jazz split her ears. For a moment everything seemed to be spinning round; even she felt that she was circling aimlessly, as she followed with the others the black giant who led them to a small table, where, when they were seated, their knees and elbows touched. Helga wondered that the waiter, indefinitely carved out of ebony, did not smile as he wrote their order – "four bottles of White Rock, four bottles of ginger-ale." Bah! Anne giggled, the others smiled and openly exchanged knowing glances, and under the tables flat glass bottles were extracted from the women's evening scarfs and small silver flasks drawn from the men's hip pockets. In a little moment she grew accustomed to the smoke and din.

They danced, ambling lazily to a crooning melody, or violently twisting their bodies, like whirling leaves, to a sudden streaming rhythm, or shaking themselves ecstatically to a thumping of unseen tomtoms. For a while, Helga was oblivious of the reek of flesh, smoke, and alcohol, oblivious of the oblivion of other gyrating pairs, oblivious of the color, the noise, and the grand distorted childishness of it all. She was drugged, lifted, sustained, by the extraordinary music, blown out, ripped out, beaten out, by the joyous, wild, murky orchestra. The essence of life seemed bodily motion. And when suddenly the music died, she dragged herself back to the present with a conscious effort; and a shameful certainty that not only had she been in the jungle, but that she had enjoyed it, began to taunt her. She hardened her determination to get away. She wasn't, she told herself, a jungle creature. She cloaked herself in a faint disgust as she watched the entertainers throw themselves about to the bursts of syncopated jangle, and when the time came again for the patrons to dance, she declined. Her rejected partner excused himself and sought an acquaintance a few tables removed. Helga sat looking curiously about her as the buzz of conversation ceased, strangled by the savage strains of music, and the crowd became a swirling mass. For the hundredth time she marveled at the gradations within this oppressed race of hers. A dozen shades slid by. There was sooty black, shiny black, taupe, mahogany, bronze, copper, gold, orange, yellow, peach, ivory, pinky white, pastry white. There was yellow hair, brown hair, black hair; straight hair, straightened hair, curly hair, crinkly hair, woolly hair. She saw black eyes in white faces, brown eyes in yellow faces, gray eyes in brown faces, blue eyes in tan faces. Africa, Europe, perhaps with a pinch of Asia, in a fantastic motley of ugliness and beauty, semi-barbaric, sophisticated, exotic, were here. But she was blind to its charm, purposely aloof and a little contemptuous, and soon her interest in the moving mosaic waned.

She had discovered Dr. Anderson sitting at a table on the far side of the room, with a girl in a shivering apricot frock. Seriously he returned her tiny bow. She met his eyes, gravely smiling, then blushed, furiously, and averted her own. But they went back immediately to the girl beside him, who sat indifferently sipping a colorless liquid from a high glass, or puffing a precariously hanging cigarette. Across dozens of tables, littered with corks, with ashes, with shriveled sandwiches, through slits in the swaying mob, Helga Crane studied her.

She was pale, with a peculiar, almost deathlike pallor. The brilliantly red, softly curving mouth was somehow sorrowful. Her pitch-black eyes, a little aslant, were veiled by long, drooping lashes and surmounted by broad brows, which seemed like black smears. The short dark hair was brushed severely back from the wide forehead. The extreme *décolleté* of her simple apricot dress showed a skin of unusual color, a delicate, creamy hue, with golden tones. "Almost like an alabaster," thought Helga.

Bang! Again the music died. The moving mass broke, separated. The others returned. Anne had rage in her eyes. Her voice trembled as she took Helga aside to whisper: "There's your Dr. Anderson over there, with Audrey Denney."

"Yes, I saw him. She's lovely. Who is she?"

"She's Audrey Denney, as I said, and she lives downtown. West Twenty-second Street. Hasn't much use for Harlem any more. It's a wonder she hasn't some white man hanging about. The disgusting creature! I wonder how she inveigled Anderson? But that's Audrey! If there is any desirable man about, trust her to attach him. She ought to be ostracized."

"Why?" asked Helga curiously, noting at the same time that three of the men in their own party had deserted and were now congregated about the offending Miss Denney.

"Because she goes about with white people," came Anne's indignant answer, "and they know she's colored."

"I'm afraid I don't quite see, Anne. Would it be all right if they didn't know she was colored?"

"Now, don't be nasty, Helga. You know very well what I mean." Anne's voice was shaking. Helga didn't see, and she was greatly interested, but she decided to let it go. She didn't want to quarrel with Anne, not now, when she had that guilty feeling about leaving her. But Anne was off on her favorite subject, race. And it seemed, too, that Audrey Denney was to her particularly obnoxious.

"Why, she gives parties for white and colored people together. And she goes to white people's parties. It's worse than disgusting, it's positively obscene."

"Oh, come, Anne, you haven't been to any of the parties, I know, so how can you be so positive about the matter?"

"No, but I've heard about them. I know people who've been."

"Friends of yours, Anne?"

Anne admitted that they were, some of them.

"Well, then, they can't be so bad. I mean, if your friends sometimes go, can they? Just what goes on that's so terrible?"

"Why, they drink, for one thing. Quantities, they say."

"So do we, at the parties here in Harlem," Helga responded. An idiotic impulse seized her to leave the place, Anne's presence, then, forever. But of course she couldn't. It would be foolish, and so ugly.

"And the white men dance with the colored women. Now you know, Helga Crane, that can mean only one thing." Anne's voice was trembling with cold hatred. As she ended, she made a little clicking noise with her tongue, indicating an abhorrence too great for words.

"Don't the colored men dance with the white women, or do they sit about, impolitely, while the other men dance with their women?" inquired Helga very softly, and with a slowness approaching almost to insolence. Anne's insinuations were too revolting. She had a slightly sickish feeling, and a flash of anger touched her. She mastered it and ignored Anne's inadequate answer.

"It's the principle of the thing that I object to. You can't get round the fact that her behaviour is outrageous, treacherous, in fact. That's what's the matter with the Negro race. They won't stick together. She certainly ought to be ostracized. I've nothing but contempt for her, as has every other self-respecting Negro."

The other women and the lone man left to them – Helga's own escort – all seemingly agreed with Anne. At any rate, they didn't protest. Helga gave it up. She felt that it would be useless to tell them that what she felt for the beautiful, calm, cool girl who had the assurance, the courage, so placidly to ignore racial barriers and give her attention to people, was not contempt, but envious admiration. So she remained silent, watching the girl.

At the next first sound of music Dr. Anderson rose. Languidly the girl followed his movement, a faint smile parting her sorrowful lips at some remark he made. Her long, slender body swayed with an eager pulsing motion. She danced with grace and abandon, gravely, yet with obvious pleasure, her legs, her hips, her back, all swaying gently, swung by that wild music from the heart of the jungle. Helga turned her glance to Dr. Anderson. Her disinterested curiosity passed. While she still felt for the girl envious admiration, that feeling was now augmented by another, a more primitive emotion. She forgot the garish crowded room. She forgot her friends. She saw only two figures, closely clinging. She felt her heart throbbing. She felt the room receding. She went out the door. She climbed endless stairs. At last, panting, confused, but thankful to have escaped, she found herself again out in the dark night alone, a small crumpled thing in a fragile, flying black and gold dress. A taxi drifted toward her, stopped. She stepped into it, feeling cold, unhappy, misunderstood, and forlorn.

Source: Nella Larsen, *Quicksand*, in *Quicksand and Passing* (New Brunswick, NJ: Rutgers University Press, 1986), pp. 58–62.

Discussion questions

1   What themes and trends appeared in 1920s fiction?
2   What is the overall tone of these writings?
3   What do you think are the greatest strengths and weaknesses in these pieces?

Chapter 5   Women in the 1920s

1 Viola I. Paradise, Housekeeping and Childcare in Rural Montana, 1919

World War I devastated Europe's industrial nations, freeing the United States to dominate global markets. Americans spent their surplus income on such new technologies as automobiles, radios, and household appliances. Cities grew at a furious pace, college enrollments boomed, and the number of white-collar workers swelled. But modernity's fruits eluded rural America. Farm families faced rough conditions and low standards of living. In many parts of the West the nearest neighbor might be miles away. Farm women faced special challenges. They not only maintained their primitive homes and cared for the children, but also helped their husbands plant, raise, and harvest the crops. The following report from an investigator from the Children's Bureau, a division of the United States Department of Labor, examines the women of rural Montana. The hardscrabble daily existence detailed below changed little until New Deal-era rural electrification projects ushered in a new, more comfortable world.

How did a farm woman spend an average day? What was the hardest part of being a farm wife? What problems did rural women face that rural men did not? Who worked harder, men or women?

America Between the Wars, 1919–1941: A Documentary Reader, First Edition.
Edited by David Welky. Editorial material and organization © 2012 John Wiley & Sons, Inc.
Published 2012 by John Wiley & Sons, Inc.

... In the area studied all the mothers but 2 – of whom 1 was insane and the other a chronic invalid – did housework, and all except 11 reported washing as part of their usual work during pregnancy or after childbirth or both. In addition to their regular housework, more than half the mothers cooked or did other work for hired help. These services were, as a rule, of brief duration, but so arduous while they lasted that they deserve special mention. Nearly all the women – 92 per cent – reported some chores, such as milking, churning, gardening, care of chickens, care of stock, carrying water, etc.; 76 women reported both chores and field work. ...

[E]specially among the older settlers, the "custom of the country" of hospitality to passers-by, whether friends or strangers, is a very considerable tax on a housewife's strength. One mother whose husband is fairly prosperous said that the first Sunday after she moved onto the homestead, before she was settled, 30 persons, all strangers to her, "dropped in for dinner." ...

The houses are small, most of them one or two room cabins or shacks, with a minimum of furniture. When of sod, unless they are plastered inside, they are hard to keep clean, because the sod gets very dry and dust keeps dropping into the room. To minimize the dirt this creates many women line their walls and ceiling with cloth, gunny sacking, or newspapers. One woman said that for a while she had sprinkled the walls with water, but that she was obliged to discontinue this practice because the water had to be hauled a mile in summer and was too scarce and precious to be used in this way. ...

Even the families who are fairly well to do have very few labor-saving devices. One mother who lived on an exceptionally good ranch explained that, though she could afford some of the conveniences themselves, the prohibitive cost of their transpor[t]ation from the railroad placed them beyond her reach. Another family tried to buy a high chair for the baby, but found that the carriage would cost more than the chair itself. ...

Only a few women had sinks, all but 9 out of 463 having to carry their waste water out of the house. This is laborious at any time, but especially so on wash days.

Only one family had a furnace, all the rest depending for their heat upon stoves, which in most instances were used both for cooking and househeating. ...

Lighting, like heating, is still in a crude state. All the families depend entirely upon the kerosene lamp, except 15 who had gasoline lamps. There is no electric or gas lighting in the area. ...

Various methods of keeping food cool were practiced. The dugout, cave, cellar, or "root house" were the most common, 8 out of 10 of the families reporting these. Often they are nothing more than holes in the ground or in the side of a butte, but sometimes they are fairly large. ...

Carrying water is one of the most arduous of farm duties, especially in an area like the one studied where the water supply is often far from the house. However, when the supply is very far away the father usually hauls it by team in barrels, and the mother need carry it only from the barrel, which is usually kept near the house, into the kitchen. When the father happens to be away, however, if water is needed, the mother must attend to the hauling herself. One mother, who at the time of the investigation was in her fifth month of pregnancy, hauled practically all the water used for household purposes and for six horses, her husband being away a great deal of the time. She would hitch up, drive the wagon one-half a mile to the well, pump the water, and fill the barrels by the bucketful. The strain of lifting the heavy buckets to the top of the barrels certainly entails risk to the pregnant mother. The difficulty, whenever water is needed, of getting it from the barrels in the wagon can be imagined. . . .

Heavy lifting was frequently reported by mothers as the cause of a miscarriage or a stillbirth. . . .

The great majority (68 per cent) of the mothers continued up to the very day of confinement all their housework except washing, and over one-half continued even their washing. Practically the same proportion (one-half) continued their chores. . . .

One mother, for instance, who, besides her housework, reported as her usual tasks milking, churning, care of chickens, gardening, and carrying water from a well over 300 feet from the house, continued all her work up to the day before confinement; and did a large washing on that day. Later in the day she walked 2 miles to a neighbor's, where labor suddenly began – all this in spite of the fact that she had not been well during pregnancy and that the membranes had ruptured five days before parturition. The father was away, "freighting," at the time of confinement, and consequently he could not relieve the mother of her work; moreover, she had the added responsibility of things which must be done on a farm whether or not a man is there to do them. The mother remained at the neighbor's for confinement and for six days following. The day she reached home her husband, who had returned, did her work for her; but beginning the next day – that is, a week after confinement – she resumed her chores, housework, and washing, in addition to the added care of the new baby, who was not very strong. When the baby was 4 months old the mother had to cook for three harvesters for one week, and a month later for six thrashers for one day. . . .

[S]mall and crowded houses are the rule rather than the exception in the area studied; and this despite the fact that the majority of the people have high standards in regard to housing and sanitation. The scarcity of lumber and the difficulty of getting building materials, the dearth of masons and carpenters, the great distances from railroads and markets, the high cost of transportation, the lack of ready money, and the pioneer attitude that to "do without" things is a part of the homesteader's lot – these factors combine to explain the small house and the inevitable crowding.

Seven out of 10 of the homes consisted of one or two rooms, 148 having only one room, and 178 having two rooms. . . .

The following few examples of overcrowded homes will doubtless give the reader a better idea of the house congestion than the figures convey. . . .

A family of nine persons lived in two rooms. The main dwelling was a one-room frame house covered with sod. Three of the children slept in a dugout about 25 yards away.

Another family of seven persons lived in a one-room frame shack 12 by 14 feet. The two beds, a cookstove, and two chairs practically filled the room. The mother said that it was very hard to keep the house clean because it was so small.

In another family seven persons lived in a tiny frame house. A bed, a small table, a stove, and a few chairs entirely filled the main room, in which the whole family slept. . . .

Many families, either because of financial necessity or because of the difficulty of getting furniture from the railroad, were using various makeshifts and substitutes for regular furniture. The most common instances were boxes used for chairs. One family had no bed but used springs set on boxes. In another instance, where a family of seven lived in a one-room house, the mother and two children used a narrow bed and the rest of the family slept in a flax bin which occupied one side of the room. . . .

Some houses, immaculately clean and well screened, were infested with flies. In the homes which were not screened the flies during the hot summer were a great and constant nuisance. The infrequency of sinks aggravates the fly problem, for many of the women throw the waste water out of their doors. Unscreened privies were doubtless prolific breeding places for flies. The unscreened homes have other intruders to contend with besides the flies. In warm weather, when windows and doors must be kept open, the chickens and pigs avail themselves of the housewife's unwilling hospitality and in spite of much shooing and chasing make themselves quite at home, especially on the sod floors. . . .

One hundred and eight families, or nearly one-fourth, had no toilet of any kind. . . .

Source: Viola I. Paradise, *Maternity Care and the Welfare of Young Children in a Homesteading County in Montana* (Washington, DC: Government Printing Office, 1919), pp. 53–4, 55, 56, 57, 58, 59, 61, 62, 65, 67.

2 Letters from Mothers to the Children's Bureau, 1920–7

Americans in the 1920s generally thought of women as wives, homemakers, and, perhaps most importantly, mothers. Yet a society that exalted mothers as symbols of purity and righteousness did little to educate women on the rigors of motherhood or the basics of childcare. Desperate for reliable information, women from around the country wrote to the Children's Bureau, the agency whose study of conditions in rural Montana appeared as document 5.1. Their missives reveal a staggering lack of knowledge about pregnancy and birth control. They also suggest that many women felt overwhelmed by their everyday activities. Their decision to share their fears, questions, and woes with the government rather than friends or family indicates feelings of isolation. It seemed Americans did a better job of promoting the idea of motherhood than they did of helping those who had actually become mothers.

Do you think these correspondents are educated or ignorant, middle class or poor? Why? Why did these women write to the Children's Bureau? How are pregnancy and motherhood similar or different today as compared to the 1920s?

Mrs. W.M. (February 10, 1925)

Dear Friend:–

I am pregnant a little over 6 months. I had a longing for strawberries for breakfast one day; I thought about them before I got up, and while in the bathroom com[b]ing my hair, I wiped out the corners of my eyes with my fingers. I thought, well, it doesn't matter even if I haven't eaten any strawberries yet. I asked a neighbor about it, & she told me I sure must of marked the baby. Is this possible? She told me if you have an appetite for anything & dont eat it, & you put your hand on your face, or scratch your face, that it will mark the baby sure. I'm just worried sick. Its on my mind all the time. I wake up nights & think of things to eat; it seems I just cant get that off my mind & what can you do when you long for watermelon or mush melon, or anything out of season? I cant get these things now. Can that mark or harm the baby in any way? Oh please tell me what to do. All these thoughts about marking the baby when you dont eat what you think of, or long for, just drive me frantic. I think of one thing, & then I think of something else, but I try to overcome these thoughts, & then I worry every time I wash or put my hand to my face that I'm marking the baby because I couldn't get or didn't eat what I longed for last. Does this come from worry? I never worried about these things the first few mo[n]ths, but her[e] of late I'm just sick from worry. I couldn't tell this to anyone else but you, as I have no mother, & no one else cares. I have kept it to myself, but I just had to go to some one. & I'm sure you will help me.

Mrs. N.W., Seattle, Washington (March 4, 1920)

Dear Mrs. Lathrop,

Would I be intruding too much upon your valuable time if I bring you my personal problems and ask your assistance? I would be greatly indebted to you if you would advise me or send me helpful literature.

I am a *busy* mother of three dear babies – aged 3 years, 20 months and 3 months. I am obliged to do all my work and we have not the conveniences and modern utilities that I wish we could afford. I am up-to-date in the care of my babies, reading and following the best literature on the care of babies. The help I need is in planning my work – a work schedule or something to aid me in the daily routine. I do the very best I can. I am busy all day and all evening but my work is never done – I am tired enough to drop when night comes and in the morning look with dread upon the day ahead of me. I want to play with my babies, I want to have time to love them and laugh with them. I have wanted babies for years and now, when Im so tired and with unfinished work every where I turn, I could scream at their constant prattle. I love them until it hurts and know that, when they are out of their babyhood, I can never forgive myself for not making more of these precious years.

Is there not some way that I can do all these scientific and hygienic duties for babies, keep our house up in proper fashion and still have time to rock and play with my babies? What of all my housework and baby-care could best be left undone? I do not ask time for myself but it would be nice to have a short period during the evening in which to read as I feel that I am growing narrow with no thoughts other than my household.

Mrs. M.L., Louisiana (August 27, 1927)

I am coming to you by letter for advice. I am pregnant and need your help. I have been pregnant three months and have been sick most of the time. I have sick stomache, head aches, and feel tired and without any Courage at all. I do all my own housework and besides have four little children to care for; the oldest one is only seven years old. I would appreciate you telling me how to control child birth. I have tried several ways but to no good. I dont have any hard labor at birth. Very seldom sick over an hour or two, but I have children so fast it is wrecking my life. I am nervous at times.

. . . Will be glad to receive any information that you can furnish on these subjects.

Source: Molly Ladd-Taylor, ed., *Raising a Baby the Government Way: Mothers' Letters to the Children's Bureau, 1915–1932* (New Brunswick, NJ: Rutgers University Press, 1986), pp. 57–8, 129–30, 181–2.

3 Crystal Eastman, Radical Feminism, 1920

War's end brought few immediate changes to farm women's demanding and exhausting lives. Urbanites such as Crystal Eastman, however, saw the peace as the harbinger of a new era for women. The brutal, senseless conflict convinced Eastman and other "New Women" that Victorian images of helpless, submissive females were relics of a failed society that had imploded on the battlefields of France. Once the 1920 passage of the Nineteenth Amendment granted women the right to vote in federal elections, activists could move beyond the decades-long struggle for suffrage rights to address other feminist priorities. Eastman used her status as a essayist, public speaker, and editor of The Liberator *to publicize promising female artists and writers and to champion an equal rights amendment to the Constitution. The following piece announces her ambitious feminist agenda for the New Era.*

What is Eastman's vision of the ideal family? Is she anti-family in general or does she oppose only the family in its current form? In what ways does Eastman connect economic and social goals? What ideas does Eastman share with Jack Gaveel, author of "The Duties of the Working Class" (document 1.2, Workers Need to Radicalize, *in this Reader)?*

Now We Can Begin

Most women will agree that August 23, the day when the Tennessee legislature finally enacted the Federal suffrage amendment, is a day to begin with, not a day to end with. Men are saying perhaps "Thank God, this everlasting woman's fight is over!" But women, if I know them, are saying, "Now at last we can begin." In fighting for the right to vote most women have tried to be either non-committal or thoroughly respectable on every other subject. Now they can say what they are really after; and what they are after, in common with all the rest of the struggling world, is *freedom*.

Freedom is a large word.

. . . [T]he true feminist . . . knows, of course, that the vast majority of women as well as men are without property, and are of necessity bread and butter slaves under a system of society which allows the very sources of life to be privately owned by a few, and she counts herself a loyal soldier in the working-class army that is marching to overthrow that system. But as a feminist she also knows that the whole of woman's slavery is not summed up in the profit system, nor her complete emancipation assured by the downfall of capitalism.

Woman's freedom, in the feminist sense, can be fought for and conceivably won before the gates open into industrial democracy. On the other hand, woman's freedom, in the feminist sense, is not inherent in the communist ideal. All feminists are familiar with the revolutionary leader who "can't see" the woman's movement. "What's the matter with the women? My wife's all right," he says. And his wife, one usually finds, is raising his children in a Bronx flat or a dreary suburb, to which he returns occasionally for food and sleep when all possible excitement and stimulus have been wrung from the fight. If we should graduate into communism tomorrow this man's attitude to his wife would not be changed. The proletarian dictatorship may or may not free women. We must begin now to enlighten the future dictators.

What, then, is "the matter with women"? What is the problem of women's freedom? It seems to me to be this: how to arrange the world so that women can be human beings, with a chance to exercise their infinitely varied gifts in infinitely varied ways, instead of being destined by the accident of their sex to one field of activity – housework and child-raising. And second, if and when they choose housework and child-raising to have that occupation recognized by the world as work, requiring a definite economic reward and not merely entitling the performer to be dependent on some man.

This is not the whole of feminism, of course, but it is enough to begin with. . . . And I can agree that women will never be great until they achieve a certain emotional freedom, a strong healthy egotism, and some un-personal sources of joy – that in this inner sense we cannot make woman free by changing her economic status. What we can do, however, is to create conditions of outward freedom in which a free woman's soul can be born and grow. It is these outward conditions with which an organized feminist movement must concern itself.

Freedom of choice in occupation and individual economic independence for women: How shall we approach this next feminist objective? First, by breaking down all remaining barriers, actual as well as legal, which make it difficult for women to enter or succeed in the various professions, to go into and get on in business, to learn trades and practice them, to join trades unions. Chief among these remaining barriers is inequality in pay. Here the ground is already broken. This is the easiest part of our program.

Second, we must institute a revolution in the early training and education of both boys and girls. It must be womanly as well as manly to earn your own living, to stand on your own feet. And it must be manly as well as womanly to know how to cook and sew and clean and take care of yourself in the ordinary exigencies of life. I need not add that the second part of this revolution will be more passionately resisted than the first. Men will not give up their privilege of helplessness without a struggle. . . .

A growing number of men admire the woman who has a job, and, especially since the cost of living doubled, rather like the idea of their own wives contributing to the family income by outside work. And of course for generations there have been whole towns full of wives who are forced by the bitterest necessity to spend the same hours at the factory that their husbands spend. But these bread-winning wives have not yet developed home-making husbands. When the two come home from the factory the man sits down while his wife gets supper, and he does so with exactly the same sense of fore-ordained right as if he were "supporting her." . . .

Cooperative schemes and electrical devices will simplify the business of home-making, but they will not get rid of it entirely. As far as we can see ahead people will always want homes, and a happy home cannot be had without a certain amount of rather monotonous work and responsibility. How can we change the nature of man so that he will honorably share that work and responsibility and thus make the home-making enterprise a song instead of a burden? Most assuredly not by laws or revolutionary decrees. Perhaps we must cultivate or simulate a little of that highly prized helplessness ourselves. But fundamentally it is a problem of education, of early training – we must bring up feminist sons.

Sons? Daughters? They are born of women – how can women be free to choose their occupation, at all times cherishing their economic independence, unless they stop having children? This is a further question for feminism. If the feminist program goes to pieces on the arrival of the first baby, it is false and useless. . . .

The immediate feminist program must include voluntary motherhood. Freedom of any kind for women is hardly worth considering unless it is assumed that they will know how to control the size of their families. "Birth control" is just as elementary an essential in our propaganda as "equal pay." Women are to have children when they want them, that's the first thing. That ensures some freedom of occupational choice; those who do not wish to be mothers will not have an undesired occupation thrust upon them by accident, and those who do wish to be mothers may choose in a general way how many years of their lives they will devote to the occupation of childraising.

But is there any way of insuring a woman's economic independence while child-raising is her chosen occupation? Or must she sink into the dependent state from which, as we all know, it is so hard to rise again? That brings us to the fourth feature of our program – motherhood endowment. It seems that the only way we can keep mothers free, at least in a capitalist society, is by the establishment of a principle that the occupation of raising children is peculiarly and directly a service to society, and that the mother upon whom the necessity and privilege of performing this service naturally falls is entitled to an adequate economic reward from the political government. It is idle to talk of real economic independence for women unless this principle is accepted. But with a generous endowment of motherhood provided by legislation, with all laws against voluntary motherhood and education in its methods repealed, with the feminist ideal of education accepted in home and school, and with all special barriers removed in every field of human activity, there is no reason why woman should not become almost a human thing.

It will be time enough then to consider whether she has a soul.

Source: Original appeared in *The Liberator* (December 1920): 23–4.

4   Margaret Sanger Defends Birth Control, 1923

Like Crystal Eastman, birth-control advocate Margaret Sanger antagonized traditionalist Americans. Sanger was one of eleven children – seven of her mother's 18 pregnancies ended prematurely – and was herself the mother of two sons and of a daughter who died at the age of 5. Sanger's family history and work with New York City slum families convinced her that women could never achieve social and economic equality unless they could dictate the timing and frequency of their pregnancies. Her determination to publicize birth-control methods put her on the wrong side of the authorities. The 1873 Comstock Law, named for purity activist Anthony Comstock, classified literature on contraception as pornographic material subject to confiscation. Sanger tested the limits of the law when she formed the American Birth Control League in 1921. Capitalizing on legal loopholes that allowed doctors to provide birth control for medical reasons, she opened the country's first birth-control clinic two years later. The following document contains a portion of Sanger's testimony before a New York State Assembly committee's hearings on a bill that would have enabled physicians to distribute birth control to married women.

According to Sanger, what special problems do women face? In Sanger's mind, how would broader access to birth control improve America? What prejudices does Sanger display?

MRS. MARGARET SANGER: Ladies and Gentlemen: I want to just say that section 1145 that is probably before you is one in which it claims that a person cannot have information to prevent conception, only for the cure of disease. We are trying to amend that law so that a woman will not have to be diseased to child bearing in order to be spared for her children and for her family.

Some time ago we took a young woman, already a mother of several children, who was suffering from tuberculosis, tuberculosis of the glands, the bones of her hands had been removed – we took this woman with two witnesses to 31 hospitals in New York City. Every one of the 31 hospitals refused to give that woman any information how to prevent having more children and how to prevent conception. They did, however, tell her in some cases that if she became pregnant, and under the laws of this State a woman who becomes pregnant, and suffers from certain diseases, such as tuberculosis, heart disease, kidney disease, may be aborted, and it was possible for that woman after conception had taken place that if her pregnancy was jeopardizing her health or life, under those conditions she could be aborted, if you please, but to give her simply, scientific information how to prevent becoming pregnant was against the law, and they said, it is not our job to change the laws, you people who see this, go and get the laws changed. . . .

[W]e think that it is absolutely unfair that such women are practically conscripted to motherhood under the laws of this State. I say it because it is true, that a woman unless she gives her body to her husband, that the laws of this State do not make that man support her. Then, that really means conscripted motherhood, because there is no way that she can prevent herself from being a mother when she does not want to be. . . .

We believe not in controlling the population after life, after individuals are born, but in controlling the birth rate before life begins. That, it seems to us is more scientific, is far more human. Does a woman who has eight or nine children, does she have to wait for death to take one or two of those children out of the family so as to make a husband's income do for them all? And that is what it means today, it means an infant mortality, maternal mortality, disease, famine, hunger – these are the things that are controlling our population and weeding them out and cutting them down. . . .

It is easy enough for these gentlemen who are not even married to stand up before you and talk about the laws of God. Why I would like to ask them a few things about the laws of the State of New York – I doubt that he knows them so well. The laws of God and the laws of nature are not cornered by any human being. We all have our ideas about the laws of God and we believe in a fine and very much higher regard of the laws of God, that it is better to use our intelligence than it is to be a master of the laws of nature, as some people are today.

Man after all has freed himself by controlling the laws of nature, and so must woman free herself from incessant child bearing, from the slavery of maternity, because that is what it is. Women who have eight, nine, ten, eleven children, they write me by the thousands and thousands. I brought here with me today ten thousand letters from mothers, and these have come to me within the last six weeks. . . . What do they ask? They ask for an opportunity to sleep one whole night before they die, just one night through without being disturbed by children, the crying of babies. They ask for a chance to know their husbands a little better. They say they are keeping them away from them because they are afraid, the man goes out of the home and they write me and say how can we get him back again. They write so they may have an opportunity to know their children, develop their mother love, because they do not do that.

Talk about the sanctity of mother love, in many of these women it has not been developed, it has not a chance of being developed, and these women are asking just for a chance, as they say, to have a breathing spell so they are not overworked. They are overworked far more than the cattle of the State, because after all there are laws in the State which will not allow breeders of animals to breed their cattle when they are diseased, but women of this State, women suffering from insanity, women whose husbands are insane, suffering from epilepsy, kidney disease, who to bear a child means practically death, yet they are compelled to bear children.

THE CHAIRMAN: I do not like to interrupt, you, Mrs. Sanger, but those particular people that you speak about, the women who are epileptic, you might say, are women of low mental standards and so on, they are the people that you want to prevent having children. . . .

MRS. SANGER: . . . There are three kinds of birth control, three kinds. They are classed: continence is certainly a very good method of birth control; sterilization by both exray and surgical means is another means of birth control, and then there are the chemical and the mechanical means of birth control. Now, either one of those three are really means to control birth or prevent conception.

We are not discussing, nor do we want the responsibility of giving methods, that is why we ask for this law. We ask that this be given to the medical profession, that the medical man may, in his judgment, use his judgment according to the individual, and if she is feeble-minded, if her husband is insane and she is not insane, and she is willing to be sterilized, certainly that belongs to her and is her right, if the physician thinks that is the thing to do, and so we say that this belongs to the medical profession.

The Jewish people and Italian families, who are filling the insane asylums, who are filling the hospitals and filling our feeble-minded institutions, these are the ones the tax payers have to pay for the upkeep of, and they are increasing the budget of the State, the enormous expense of the State is increasing because of the multiplication of the unfit in this country and in the State.

ASSEMBLYMAN ESMOND: Isn't it true that sometimes out of the most unpromising stock there comes a genius that by his brilliancy revolutionizes the whole country for good.

MRS. SANGER: Yes, sir, there are, but there is also the fact that if they did not have to support so many feeble-minded and unfit they would have more money to spend on geniuses that are already here. (Applause)

Gentlemen, I believe that this bill is only just, is only right for the women. Women are the sufferers; they are the ones. . . .

And so I say that the women, there are thousands of them in this state, there are hundreds of thousands of them who are bent, bound, broken on the wheel of maternity, and they ask you to do justice, and we ask you to do justice by those women to have this law passed. (Applause)

Source: *The Margaret Sanger Papers* [Microfilm] reel 69 frames 389–401, and in the Sophia Smith Collection, Smith College, Northampton MA.

5 Advertisement for Lysol Disinfectant: Tradition Meets the New Woman, 1928

The rise of mass production techniques such as the assembly line spurred corporations to encourage mass consumption. After all, there was no point in turning out huge quantities of standardized, industrialized goods that no one wanted to buy. Postwar improvements in advertising techniques represented an effort to satisfy this new "need." Businessmen hired marketing firms (many of them staffed by the same people whose efforts had convinced a skeptical public to support the World War), to create ads linking their product with a particular image or a desired lifestyle. Magazines and newspapers used the influx of advertisement revenue to slash subscription rates and broaden readership. Corporations paid some or all of the cost of producing radio programs in exchange for on-air descriptions of the wonders of their products. Advertisers often targeted women, the family's primary consumers. As the advertisement below suggests, companies reached women through several methods, including fear-mongering, associating a product with status or luxury, appealing to tradition, and suggesting the thrill of modernity.

What messages does this advertisement employ? How are these messages similar to or different from those in today's commercials? How does this advertisement balance "old" and "new" conceptions of femininity? What purpose would this mix of messages serve?

Figure 5.1 Advertisement for Lysol Disinfectant: Tradition meets the New Woman, 1928.

Source: *Ladies' Home Journal* 45 (May 1928): 77.

Discussion questions

1   What would a woman from rural Montana think about the demands of "new women" such as Eastman and Sanger?
2   How do these documents portray motherhood?
3   How have feminist issues changed since the 1920s? How have they remained constant?

Chapter 6   Mass Culture

1 Bruce Bliven, Radio's Promise and Pitfalls, 1924

*Popular memories of the interwar era tend to revolve around its mass
entertainment. We may have seen some of the period's great movies – Gone
With the Wind (1939), King Kong (1933), The Wizard of Oz (1939). Some
of its comic strips survive in one form or another – Blondie, Gasoline Alley,
Little Orphan Annie. Most of us can conjure up in our minds newsreel
images of the Hindenburg explosion. Radio stars such as Buck Rogers, Flash
Gordon, the Lone Ranger, and Tarzan endured for decades. Mass culture,
defined simply as culture that reaches a broad, cross-class audience, emerged
in the mass-market magazines and urban newspapers of the late nineteenth
century. It came of age in the 1920s and 1930s, particularly through the
maturation of the motion picture and the popularization of the radio, an
invention that had existed in primitive form since the turn of the century
but became a household staple in the 1920s. It is difficult today to grasp the
revolution embodied within radio's ability to deliver instant entertainment,
news, politics, and sports into the home. It connected isolated communities
into a national whole, furthering the process of creating a unified American
nation. Here, journalist Bruce Bliven ponders the changes radio has wrought
and its possibilities for the future.*

*In Bliven's eyes, what benefits does the radio bring? What promises
will it fail to reach? How accurate are his predictions? How does Bliven's
perspective on the radio compare with today's discussions about the Internet
and other new communication technologies?*

America Between the Wars, 1919–1941: A Documentary Reader, First Edition.
Edited by David Welky. Editorial material and organization © 2012 John Wiley & Sons, Inc.
Published 2012 by John Wiley & Sons, Inc.

... Radio will not change human nature, at least not in any hurry. At present it is a fad, and if you care to note the folly of rash predictions in such a case, go back and read what was promised in the early days of the bicycle or the phonograph.

Having made this point, let me rush into the pit I have digged with six observations of my own about the future of radio, based on a study of what it is already accomplishing.

First, radio is not likely, on the basis of any inventions now perfected or in sight, to become an important factor in the education of the young.

Second, radio will probably have a serious influence on our national political life, and, on the whole, this will be for the better.

Third, radio will not take the place of newspapers and magazines. Its immediate effect will be to hurt the periodicals somewhat, but ultimately it will prove beneficial to serious and intelligent papers which deal with the important questions of the day.

Fourth, the use of the radio for advertising is wholly undesirable and should be prohibited by legislation if necessary, but incidental advertising or publicity which has been the motive behind a great deal of radio broadcasting, if unwanted by the listening public, will probably die of itself in a short time.

Fifth, any monopolistic control of broadcasting is so strongly opposed to national policy that even in the absence of prohibitive legislation it is likely to be held in check by public protest. At least, radio broadcasting should be declared a public utility under strict regulation by the Federal authorities; and it may be necessary to have the Government condemn and buy the whole industry, operating it either nationally or locally on the analogy of the post-office and the public-school system.

Sixth, radio will do much to create a sense of national solidarity in all parts of the country, and particularly in remote settlements and on the farm. It may even be the final factor needed to make rural life attractive to young people, and stop that herding into the cities which is now going on at the rate of 1,200,000 a year, and is causing students of American social conditions much alarm.

Such cold sober prognostications as these would break the heart of any radio engineer, as I have discovered after talking to several of them. They are as delirious as gold-miners about the possibilities of their mushrooming industry. Despite their supposedly conservative engineering turn of mind, they talk to you in terms which leave H. G. Wells's earlier manner simply nowhere. They speak, for instance, of things like these:

World-wide broadcasting from a single station, the greatest artists and lecturers of the five continents being assembled there, or their voices picked up at any other point by special low-power transmitters, and re-broadcast from the central spot.

Great universities, or perhaps only one such institution, giving radio courses in every conceivable subject, and granting degrees on the basis of subsequent written examinations.

One universal language (English or Esperanto) made inevitable by world-wide broadcasting.

World peace facilitated, and perhaps insured, by the close international relationships created through the new art.

Transmitter-receivers which can be carried in the waistcoat pocket like one's watch, so that every human being may have instantaneous communication with every other, no matter where they are. The engineers seem to *like* this prospect, which fills me with nothing but horror.

Wireless transmission of power, from great central stations operated at the taxpayers' expense, the power being free to any one who cares to use it.

Radio transmission not only of pictures, but of motion-pictures, so that the listener in his home will be able both to see and hear the participants in the distant base-ball game or the speaker on his platform. . . .

The question remains, What of radio's social usefulness? . . .

Every one of course thinks of education when this question is asked. It is true that much information of value is already being broadcast, together with an appalling mass of solemn bunk and some really vicious propaganda. Columbia University has conducted a course in Browning's poetry in this way, a syllabus being sent by mail to every one willing to pay a small fee. A large number of letters were received showing a good grasp of the lectures' content, and of adverse criticism there was virtually none. The university, in fact, regards the experiment as an unqualified success, and is planning to repeat it on a wider scale with other subjects. More than fifty schools and colleges now have broadcasting apparatus of their own, and many others use the near-by commercial stations from time to time. . . .

I have already said that I believe radio will have little importance as an aid to formal education for the young. Modern ideas of education have swung completely away from the notion that children ought to be filled with facts by sheer force. Our conception of a good mind is that it must be built, not stuffed; schools are primarily places in which to grow up, and the most useful thing about them, educators are some what mournfully agreed, is the extended opportunity for contact with others of your own age. Radio, of course, faces squarely against this whole tide.

There remains, then, only adult education, as to which the question is, do a sufficient number of grown-ups want this to make its administration by radio possible?

Perhaps I am a pessimist, but I believe the answer is no. I see no signs that more than a highly insignificant minority of adults want to acquire a comprehensive knowledge of anything whatever. They don't mind getting some facts, certainly, if the process is easy enough. . . . Perhaps the convenience of radio listening will induce them to hear such lectures more frequently than at present; but except as to people on farms, I cannot believe that the results will be of much social importance. . . .

In the long run, anybody who wouldn't sit through an hour's discussion of national or local issues in a lecture-hall will probably be equally impatient when tuning in on the oratory. Yet against this must be placed the fact that a President of the United States, for instance, may be heard simultaneously in every part of the country by a number of listeners already supposed to equal one fifth of the population. Persons of sufficient importance – Presidential candidates, certainly, and perhaps those running for senatorial and gubernatorial positions – will be sure of reaching, every time they speak, an audience much greater than the total they could address during a campaign in pre-radio days. . . .

A problem for the politicians is the fact that a radio audience has a psychology utterly different from that of a crowd assembled in one place. The mob spirit, with its factitious enthusiasm, is of course entirely lacking. There is no applause to let the speaker know what is his most popular "line." His ideas will therefore have a better chance of being weighed for what they are really worth. . . .

The present effect of radio upon periodical literature other than newspapers has been to injure the circulations of most of the general magazines. When several million persons suddenly take up a new occupation which keeps them busy virtually all the evening six or seven nights a week, their previous recreations, of which reading was, of course, an important one, must go by the boards. The chief large gains in circulation recently, with a few exceptions, have been among magazines which are themselves devoted to radio.

But such complete devotion to the new toy is unlikely to last forever. Incredible as it may now seem to the devotee, the day is coming when he will tune in only when there is something on the air he wants to hear. This means he will go back to reading for at least a part of the time. . . .

The real danger for radio is not that it will destroy other means of communication, but that its users will fail to live up to the magnificent opportunity it creates. Here is the most wonderful medium for communicating ideas the world has ever been able to dream of, yet at present the magic toy is used in the main to convey outrageous rubbish, verbal and musical, to people who seem quite content to hear it. . . .

Source: Bruce Bliven, "How Radio is Remaking Our World," *Century Magazine* 108 (June 1924): 149–50, 151, 152, 153, 154.

2 Cartoons Celebrating Charles Lindbergh's Transatlantic Flight, 1927

The 1920s and 1930s marked celebrity journalism's coming of age. Fueled by an intensely competitive urban newspaper market, the rise of the radio, and Americans' desire to see individuals transcend the anonymity of modern life, the genre inflated trivial incidents into national phenomena. The unfortunate Floyd Collins became famous when a falling rock trapped him in a cave. Child prodigies Nathan Leopold and Richard Loeb dominated headlines after murdering 14-year-old Bobby Franks. Canada's Dionne Quintuplets were well known in the United States simply because they were born.

None of these celebrities equaled the fame of Charles Lindbergh, a shy, 25-year-old airmail pilot from Minnesota who in May 1927 became the first person to fly solo over the Atlantic Ocean. He was not the first to traverse the ocean, merely the first to do it alone. His accomplishment had no inherent meaning – an airplane took off in New York and landed in Paris – yet millions of people found important messages in his 33-hour journey. "He has shown us that we are not rotten at the core, but morally sound and sweet and good!" one supporter enthused. Lindbergh limited his public comments to praising the aircraft and his financial backers and saw little "meaning" in his flight. Americans interpreted his unwillingness to exploit his notoriety for monetary gain as further evidence that a giant was walking amongst them. Lindbergh remained a reluctant public figure for the rest of his life. His celebrity turned tragic in 1932, when Richard Bruno Hauptmann kidnapped and murdered his son, Charles, Jr.

What arguments do these cartoons make about Lindbergh and his broader social importance?

Source: *Literary Digest* 93 (June 25, 1927): 15.

Figure 6.1   Cartoon celebrating Charles Lindbergh's transatlantic flight, 1927.

Source: *Literary Digest* 93 (June 25,1927): 11.

Figure 6.2   Cartoon celebrating Charles Lindbergh's transatlantic flight, 1927.

Source: *Literary Digest* 93 (June 11, 1927): 6.

HARD-BOILED NEW YORK
—Thomas in the Detroit *News*.

Figure 6.3   Cartoon celebrating Charles Lindbergh's transatlantic flight, 1927.

3 Motion Pictures in *Middletown*, 1929

Social scientists Robert and Helen Merrell Lynd visited Muncie, Indiana,
population 38,000, in the mid 1920s to study how the changes of the
past few decades had affected a typical American city. The resulting book,
Middletown, *examined class structure, family life, work, political thought,*
religion, and leisure. Of particular interest here are the Lynds' conclusions
regarding motion pictures. Movies swept the nation as the art of silent films
matured in the 1920s and as talking films took over at the end of the decade.
Movie stars became national celebrities and Hollywood became a city of
dreams.

*   How did the rise of the motion picture change Middletown? Why did*
Middletown audiences go to the movies?

. . . Like the automobile, the motion picture is more to Middletown than
simply a new way of doing an old thing; it has added new dimensions to the

city's leisure. To be sure, the spectacle-watching habit was strong upon Middletown in the nineties. Whenever they had a chance people turned out to a "show," but chances were relatively fewer. Fourteen times during January, 1890, for instance, the Opera House was opened for performances ranging from *Uncle Tom's Cabin* to *The Black Crook*, before the paper announced that "there will not be any more attractions at the Opera House for nearly two weeks." In July there were no "attractions"; a half dozen were scattered through August and September; there were twelve in October.

Today nine motion picture theaters operate from 1 to 11 P.M. seven days a week summer and winter; four of the nine give three different programs a week, the other five having two a week; thus twenty-two different programs with a total of over 300 performances are available to Middletown every week in the year. In addition, during January, 1923, there were three plays in Middletown and four motion pictures in other places than the regular theaters, in July three plays and one additional movie, in October two plays and one movie.

About two and three-fourths times the city's entire population attended the nine motion picture theaters during the month of July, 1923, the "valley" month of the year, and four and one-half times the total population in the "peak" month of December. . . .

[T]he frequency of movie attendance of high school boys and girls is about equal, business class families tend to go more often than do working class families, and children of both groups attend more often without their parents than do all the individuals or other combinations of family members put together. The decentralizing tendency of the movies upon the family, suggested by this last, is further indicated by the fact that only 21 per cent. of 337 boys and 33 per cent. of 423 girls in the three upper years of the high school go to the movies more often with their parents than without them. On the other hand, the comment is frequently heard in Middletown that movies have cut into lodge attendance, and it is probable that time formerly spent in lodges, saloons, and unions is now being spent in part at the movies, at least occasionally with other members of the family. Like the automobile and radio, the movies, by breaking up leisure time into an individual, family, or small group affair, represent a counter movement to the trend toward organization so marked in clubs and other leisure-time pursuits.

How is life being quickened by the movies for the youngsters who bulk so large in the audiences, for the punch press operator at the end of his working day, for the wife who goes to a "picture" every week or so "while he stays home with the children," for those business class families who habitually attend? . . .

As in the case of the books it reads, comedy, heart interest, and adventure compose the great bulk of what Middletown enjoys in the movies. . . . "Middletown is amusement hungry," says the opening sentence in a local editorial; at the comedies Middletown lives for an hour in a happy sophisticated make-believe world that leaves it, according to the advertisement of one film, "happily convinced that Life is very well worth living."

Next largest are the crowds which come to see the sensational society films. The kind of vicarious living brought to Middletown by these films may be inferred from such titles as: "*Alimony* – brilliant men, beautiful jazz babies, champagne baths, midnight revels, petting parties in the purple dawn, all ending in one terrific smashing climax that makes you gasp"; "*Married Flirts – Husbands:* Do you flirt? Does your wife always know where you are? Are you faithful to your vows? *Wives:* What's your hubby doing? Do you know? Do you worry? Watch out for *Married Flirts.*" . . . While Western "action" films and a million-dollar spectacle like *The Covered Wagon* or *The Hunchback of Notre Dame* draw heavy houses, and while managers lament that there are too few of the popular comedy films, it is the film with burning "heart interest," that packs Middletown's motion picture houses week after week. Young Middletown enters eagerly into the vivid experience of *Flaming Youth:* "neckers, petters, white kisses, red kisses, pleasure-mad daughters, sensation-craving mothers, by an author who didn't dare sign his name; the truth bold, naked, sensational" – so ran the press advertisement – under the spell of the powerful conditioning medium of pictures presented with music and all possible heightening of the emotional content, and the added factor of sharing this experience with a "date" in a darkened room. Meanwhile, *Down to the Sea in Ships*, a costly spectacle of whaling adventure, failed at the leading theater "because," the exhibitor explained, "the whale is really the hero in the film and there wasn't enough 'heart interest' for the women." . . .

Actual changes of habits resulting from the week-after-week witnessing of these films can only be inferred. Young Middletown is finding discussion of problems of mating in this new agency that boasts in large illustrated advertisements, "Girls! You will learn how to handle 'em!" and "Is it true that marriage kills love? If you want to know what love really means, its exquisite torture, its overwhelming raptures, see – ."

"Sheiks and their 'shebas,'" according to the press account of the Sunday opening of one film, ". . . sat without a movement or a whisper through the presentation. . . . It was a real exhibition of love-making and the youths and maidens of [Middletown] who thought that they knew something about the art found that they still had a great deal to learn."

Some high school teachers are convinced that the movies are a powerful factor in bringing about the "early sophistication" of the young and the relaxing of social taboos. One working class mother frankly welcomes the movies as an aid in child rearing, saying, "I send my daughter because a girl has to learn the ways of the world somehow and the movies are a good safe way." The judge of the juvenile court lists the movies as one of the "big four" causes of local juvenile delinquency, believing that the disregard of group mores by the young is definitely related to the witnessing week after week of fictitious behavior sequences that habitually link the taking of long chances and the happy ending. While the community attempts to safeguard its schools from commercially intent private hands, this powerful new educational instrument, which has taken Middletown unawares, remains in the hands of a group of men – an ex-peanut-stand proprietor, an ex-bicycle racer and race promoter, and so on – whose primary concern is making money.

Middletown in 1890 was not hesitant in criticizing poor shows at the Opera House.... The newspapers of today keep their hands off the movies, save for running free publicity stories and cuts furnished by the exhibitors who advertise. Save for some efforts among certain of the women's clubs to "clean up the movies" and the opposition of the Ministerial Association to "Sunday movies," Middletown appears content in the main to take the movies at their face value – "a darned good show" – and largely disregard their educational or habit-forming aspects.

Source: Robert S. Lynd and Helen Merrell Lynd, *Middletown: A Study in American Culture* (New York: Harcourt, Brace & Company, 1929), pp. 263–5, 266, 267–9.

4 John R. Tunis on College Football, 1928

Some doubters questioned the social benefits of mass culture. Detractors accused it of destroying family oriented entertainment, standardizing public tastes, and making mindless entertainment rather than self-improvement the focus of leisure. Working in this vein, children's author John R. Tunis contributed the following attack on college football in 1928. Football had become a mass spectacle during the 1920s as fans across the nation followed University of Illinois running back Harold "Red" Grange, Notre Dame head coach Knute Rockne, and other prominent sportsmen. Schools built vast stadiums to accommodate crowds hungry for a Saturday's worth of entertainment.

According to Tunis, why is college football so popular? Why does he object to college football? What place does he see for it in American life?

"Returning lettermen are Nagurski, Kabela, Hovde, Lekeseles, Brookmeier, Westphal, Pulbrabek, and Teeter. Emlein and Ukkelberg will supplant Apman and Angevik; and Norgaard and Burquist will provide promising material to guard the flanks."

No, this is not, as you might imagine, a list of future citizens of these United States who have passed or are about to pass the rigid requirements of the Quota; but simply a sample of up-to-date football publicity sent out last summer by one of our large Middle Western state universities.

For at present every college worthy of the name of an educational institution maintains a press bureau whose function is to keep the name of the university before the public gaze . . . chiefly by bombarding the press of the land with minute and detailed references to the athletic activities of the university in question, and particularly to its football eleven. Moreover, no longer do these press bureaus wait until the opening of the doors of learning to begin grinding out material for publication. Heavens, no! The advance notices from college press agents start pouring in upon the helpless sporting editors of the nation's newspapers as early as mid-August. By Labor Day the campaign is on in earnest, and the sports pages are full of "Intensive Training to Start To-day," and "Preliminary Practice Begins at Notre Dame," or "University of Pennsylvania Squad Takes to Seashore for Early Conditioning." . . .

[F]ootball is more to the sports follower of this country than merely a game. It is at present a religion – sometimes it seems to be almost our national religion. With fervor and reverence the college man and the non-college man, the athlete and observer approach its shrines; dutifully and faithfully they make their annual pilgrimage to the football Mecca, be it Atlanta or Urbana, Cambridge or Los Angeles, Princeton or Ann Arbor. From far and near they come, the low and the high, the humble in their sports coupés from the neighboring city, the elect in their special cars from all parts of this football-mad nation. . . .

This new religion has its dogma: the doctrine that only through so-called "college spirit" can a man be saved. According to this doctrine in its purest form, anything done for the purpose of bringing victory to the team is justifiable; any news – learned no matter how – about another eleven, any bit of information garnered publicly or privately must be put to use; any amount of time spent in following and cheering and "supporting" the team counts toward the salvation of the faithful. No less than the undergraduate, the graduate is a traitor to his creed does he fail to turn up in the stadium on the day of days, the Homecoming Day, the Big Game Day, the Day when the college demands his all. . . .

The religion of football has its high priests and acolytes, its saints and sanctuaries, as do other religions. The saints are those mighty ones of the game who have gone on, whose names are mentioned with hushed breath by sports writers and football fans alike. The high priests are the saints of the present day; sometime in the future they, too, will have passed away, sometime they, too, will have Memorial Gates and Drives and Locker Buildings constructed in their names and their memory. . . .

The acolytes of the religion are of course the players themselves. They serve and wait upon the Great God Football in his sanctuaries – the grid irons of school and college. These humble flagellants are, need it be said, seldom admitted to the inner holy of holies. The hierarchies that rule the game are composed of the Athletic Directors, Graduate Managers, Graduate Treasurers, Chairmen of Football Committees, and the rest who, with the Head Coaches, are merely names for the lowly graduate and undergraduate to bow down before and worship. The hierarchies and the Head Coaches look with benign approval upon the solemn hocus-pocus of the new religion, for after all, High Priests like everyone else must eat three times daily. . . .

This ritual has pervaded the game little by little, a bit here and a bit there, without anyone being fully aware of what was going on; it has become a part of college life without anyone permanently attached to the colleges realizing what has happened, until to-day it is fixed and standardized from Maine to California. Everyone who has attended an American university large or small is familiar with its manifestations. By way of preparation for the annual football festival there are mass meetings at which the High Priests and Acolytes of the religion speak briefly but passionately and fervently, preaching devotion to the Divine Being. They usually manage to work their audience up to such a pitch that a snake dance follows; headed by the student band playing football songs (which after all are the hymns of the cult), a thousand bare-headed undergraduates swarm across the campus in the dark, swing up Main Street, blocking traffic and pulling the trolleys off the wires, hooting and jeering at the house of Professor Jackson of the Greek Department, who once dared question the sacredness of the gods they worship; and then crowd on to the field back of the gymnasium, where a huge bonfire is lighted and more cheers and songs are heard until everyone is too hoarse and too tired to continue. . . .

But football was not always quite so involved. In fact it is fair to say that football stole up and caught the colleges unaware; almost before they knew it the vast machine which is modern intercollegiate football had been erected and firmly installed in collegiate life. Thirty years ago it was a game. To-day the colleges are waking up to realize that what they have on their hands is a first-class octopus which is strangling many of the legitimate pursuits of the educational institution. As the late President Wilson said before the War:

> "The side shows are so numerous, so diverting, so important if you will – that they have swallowed up the circus, and those who perform in the main tent must often whistle for their audience, discouraged and humiliated."

This, perhaps, represents the opinion of the average educator. I say the average educator, because some college presidents are as completely hypnotized by the effects of football as the most fervent undergraduates. But the majority undoubtedly feel it to be harmful; harmful because it gives both to the students and to a public that knows nothing of colleges an entirely wrong idea of the purpose and functions of a great educational institution. "Yale," said a nine-year-old boy, "is the college that has good football teams." And many boys five times his age share his belief about Yale University.

The purposes of a university and the things a college education accomplish have been defined in many and various ways; but certainly, if four years in a seat of learning has any effect upon its students, it should help them to differentiate between the false and the true, between the sham values of life and the real values. Herein lies the greatest objection of the educators to football. The religion of football, they argue, teaches the most ephemeral of values, brings into prominence in an intellectual institution men who are looked up to solely on account of their ability to catch a thirty-yard pass or turn an opposing end and, instead of assisting the undergraduate to distinguish between what is best and what is worthless in life, tends to befuddle his judgment with its hysterical appeals to his emotion and its irrational standards, and by this setting up of false gods may mislead him for years until he learns for himself, in the world without, to distinguish between the things that are of enduring worth and the things that are not. . . .

Source: John R. Tunis, "The Great God Football," *Harper's Magazine* 157 (November 1928): 742, 743–4, 745, 746.

5 Paul Gallico Discusses the Relevance of Babe Ruth, 1932

To say that Babe Ruth was the most famous baseball player of the interwar era is like saying that Beethoven was a famous composer, or Shakespeare a popular playwright. Just as these artists captured something essential about

their times, Ruth epitomized the mores of a modern, consumerist era.
He lived life to the utmost. His cars were fast, his shirts were silk, and his
appetites were tremendous. A public-relations team ghostwrote newspaper
articles under his byline and arranged endorsements that kept his face before
the public while putting extra money in his pocket. At the same time, he
represented older American values. His rise from a Baltimore orphanage to
worldwide fame offered an updated version of the classic Horatio Alger
"rags to riches" dream. Sportswriter Paul Gallico cast Ruth's multifaceted
appeal into words in this 1932 Vanity Fair *profile.*
   Why did Babe Ruth fascinate Americans? What did his fame say about
American culture?

There is, in all Christendom, no other figure quite like the great, ugly baseball
player, christened George Herman Erhardt, who is now known as Babe
Ruth; and there is no other nation on the face of the globe better fitted to
harbor him, cultivate him, and for that matter, actually bring him into being,
than these goofy United States of America. . . .

The rise, the existence, the *being* of Ruth is purely an American
phenomenon. . . . Ruth's nickname, "Babe", is so much a part of our national
consciousness that the strange message spelled out in letters six inches high
across the top of any afternoon paper, "Babe Conks No. 36" or "Bam Busts
Two", is not, as an English or French cryptologist might imagine, a code for
"Come home, all is forgiven", but a very simple presentation of the news
that Ruth has hit his 36th home run, and that he has made two homers in
one game.

Americans called him Babe because he looks like anything else but and
the sports writers re-nicknamed him the Bambino – also for no good reason,
as there is no Italian in him – and then characteristically they shortened it
to Bam. . . .

Ruth is an American Porthos, a swash buckler built on gigantic and heroic
lines, a great athlete, a Golem-like monster, a huge, vital, vulgar fellow in
whose bosom surge all the well-known elementary emotions and whose tear
ducts lie close to the surface. He lives – ye gods, how he lives! – wholeheartedly,
with complete gusto. He is one of the most completely alive men I have ever
known. He loves to eat, to sleep, to royster and horse play, to drink beer and
play cards with companions, to play hall, to play golf, to swear and shout
and laugh. Everything about him is big – his frame, his enormous head
surmounted by blue-black curly hair, his great blob of a nose spattered
generously over his face, his mouth and his hands – only his ankles are
strangely slim like a woman's. . . .

Ruth is not constituted to do anything unimpressively. When he misses the ball, the force of his swing whirls him around until his legs are twisted like a German pretzel. Sometimes he swings himself clear off his feet. Every miss is its own guarantee of honest effort. . . .

The effect of a home run upon an immediate cross-section of any part of the audience is curious and inexplicable. The ball has fled the park. The Babe trots around the base paths with his arms close to his sides, taking little mincing steps on his small feet and occasionally tipping the peak of his cap to acknowledge the roar of approbation and the patter of applauding hands. Look at your nearest neighbor. You find him acting in a manner that under any other circumstances would call for a spell at Bellevue under close observation. He is grinning from ear to ear, shaking his head from side to side, making strange noises, and thumping the nearest person to him on the back. He is acting like a man who has just been told by the nurse that it's a boy. He looks into his neighbor's face to make sure that there is equal appreciation registered thereon. He lights a fresh cigar and settles back in utter contentment. . . .

The Babe is the only man I have ever known as spectacular in failure as he is in success. His home run is a magnificent thing, a poem of rhythm and timing. The bat meets the ball with a distinctive and peculiar sound all of its own – veterans will say "There she goes," just from the sound, and the ball, a diminishing speck, soars from the inclosures over the top tier of the farthest stands. A strike-out is just as impressive. . . .

There has never been any complaint about Ruth's modesty. The only walls he has ever known have been the parallel columns of the newspapers. Even his sins are public and certainly his expiations have been notably so. In 1925 at Asheville, North Carolina, he fell victim to the gluttony that has beset him for years. . . . Now gluttony with Ruth is not your stuffy napkin -in-collar, bring-me-a-steak-smothered-in-pork-chops kind. The beginning of the tummyache that was felt around the world was engendered by a wayside collation consisting of nine or ten greasy railroad-station frankfurters mounted on papier-mâché rolls, and washed down with some eight bottles of green, red, and yellow soda pop. Anyway, they shipped him up North on a stretcher, and the whole nation trembled with every turn of the wheels that brought him home. He was tucked into a cot in St. Vincent's Hospital, in grave danger of relinquishing his hold upon his great, mortal body, and hung between life and death for many days – on Page One. . . .

Back in 1922 Babe had a bad year. He was untractable, he drank, he fought with Judge Landis, the high priest of baseball, he abused umpires, he committed the gravest sin in baseball, that of chasing a fan up the stands. Also, he played poor baseball. . . .

At the annual dinner of the Baseball Writers Association, Ruth met Senator Jimmy Walker. The Senator was a baseball lover and an admirer of the Babe. He told Ruth that he owed it to the boys of the nation to behave himself. Later when Ruth was called upon to speak, he arose, gulped, and then with tears rolling down his enormous face he solemnly promised the kids of America that he would reform. He swore off drinking (in large quantities). He reformed.

The scene, the speech, the promise, the great reformation rang through the headlines. Here was a great and touching thing, usually seen only in the privacy of the parlor, where the prodigal son breaks down and promises that he will sin no more. Ruth became everybody's son. Everybody forgave him. . . .

The man is a hero out of Horatio Alger or Burt L. Standish. He rose from Rags to Riches, Sink or Swim, Do or Die. He is the prototype of every hackneyed hero of juvenile (and adult) dollar literature come to life. The Alger books used to tell us that a poor boy could eventually triumph over temptation and adversity and acquire wealth and position, but nobody ever knew of anyone who really did.

Ruth came from the slums of Baltimore. He was an orphan. He went to a reform school. At St. Mary's Industrial School in Baltimore, he played baseball. He was a natural athlete. . . .

The Babe has become a member of every family in the country that cares anything about Sport, and a great many that don't. No one goes to see him play ball impersonally. No one can look impersonally upon a public figure about which so much is known. British athletes are presented in the glossy print weeklies wearing blazers and smoking pipes, and that is that. The Frenchman makes a fuss over his athletic hero while he is on the scene, but promptly forgets him between games or matches. The Germans react coldly towards their own world's heavyweight prizefight champion, [Max] Schmeling. A professional athlete relegating political and national news to page two in Europe is simply unthinkable. But snoopiness is a national disease with us. We are a nation of gossips. . . . Snoopiness, our unceasing thirst for information about people in the public eye, and the activity of our press in supplying this information, has built up an orphan boy and a reform school graduate to a high estate where he receives as large a salary as the President of the United States, and far more sustained publicity. It could only occur, we are told, in a democracy, hence we are a democratic nation. It is about the only remaining proof left to us.

Source: Paul Gallico, "The Babe," *Vanity Fair* 38 (May 1932): 38, 73.

Discussion questions

1   Were Americans optimistic or pessimistic about the impact of mass culture?
2   How similar is the interwar era's mass-culture world to today's?
3   What are the strengths and limitations of using mass culture to understand a historical era?

Chapter 7   The Onset of the Great Depression

1 Paul Abbot on the National Economy, 1929

The American economy boomed following a brief but severe postwar recession. A lack of foreign competition due to the war's crushing impact upon Europe, the expansion of the automobile industry and other job-producing businesses, and the perfection of mass-production techniques brought unprecedented prosperity to the urban middle and upper classes. Egged on by the emerging advertising industry, huge numbers of Americans purchased cars, appliances, and new homes. Easy access to credit and the rise of installment buying also fueled consumption. A get-rich-quick spirit spread as speculators made killings in land deals and the stock market. Businessmen such as Henry Ford became heroes in an age that exalted the accumulation of wealth. Enthusiastic investors poured their money into the supercharged market as if the good times would last forever. By 1929, after years of huge profits, a few skeptics were convinced that stocks were dangerously overpriced. President Calvin Coolidge's refusal to dampen the speculative mania was consistent with his small-government, laissez-faire principles. The following writer considers the economic climate and offers his take on what will happen next.

What economic changes does Abbot see coming? How should Americans respond? Is he optimistic or pessimistic about the future?

America Between the Wars, 1919–1941: A Documentary Reader, First Edition.
Edited by David Welky. Editorial material and organization © 2012 John Wiley & Sons, Inc.
Published 2012 by John Wiley & Sons, Inc.

The volume of trading and the rapidly advancing prices on the New York Stock Exchange and to a lesser extent on the other large security exchanges of the country have caused much to be written in the past few months about the speculative fever now sweeping the country. It has been repeatedly stated that the public at large is buying stocks without knowledge of the intrinsic value or the earning power of the particular corporations of which they thus become partial owners, that these purchases are being made only with the idea of reselling at a higher price to others similarly motivated and that necessarily the end men in the line will be left holding the bag when the bubble inevitably bursts. Part of this would appear sound and part unsound.

It has been estimated that, before the War, trading in stocks was limited to some half million people resident in and about New York and the larger cities of the country. In fifteen years conditions have changed so that fifteen million people are now thought to be interested in the market. This is the result of many causes. The Liberty Loan campaign opened the eyes of millions to the fact that there were securities called bonds and that money could be kept in other places besides the savings bank or under the mattress. Later the Allied Governments distributed large volumes of their securities throughout the country.

The last ten years, with the exception of 1921, have been generally prosperous beyond any previous conception and have left the country with a larger surplus for investment than ever before. Many of the larger corporations have sold stock to their employees on a partial payment plan with the idea of allowing them some share in the profits which they help to create and with the hope of thus bringing about a better understanding between capital and labor. At the same time various leading gas and electric light companies have considered it advantageous to place small quantities of their securities with their customers in the hope of improving their mutual relationship.

Since the War hundreds of companies, theretofore owned by a family or at least privately controlled in their own localities, have been publicly financed and the corporations' securities listed on some exchange, or the local company has been absorbed by a larger National unit whose stock is quoted. Now that the New York Stock Exchange ticker quotations are available at reasonable cost throughout the country, the trader in Iowa or Arizona can buy or sell with practically as much facility as the man whose office is on Wall or Broad Street. These and other factors, together with advancing prices, have built up the existing public interest in the security markets.

Basically this transition is sound and the trend may reasonably be expected to continue upward. Trading in corporate securities is economically correct, and the rules and regulations of the leading exchanges of the country are designed to afford security purchasers, large or small, maximum protection.

However, in so rapid a growth there naturally are maladjustments. Many people are frankly speculating and often beyond their means and without adequate information on which to base their judgments. In the smoking rooms of Pullmans, talk largely centers on the stock market. In the subways of New York, office boys and clerks, who, a year or two ago, would have been reading the sporting news, can be seen every night anxiously scanning the day's closing bid and asked quotations, usually with particular interest in the lower priced and more speculative issues. It is undoubtedly true that during the past year many have found it so easy to make money on the New York Stock Exchange that they are neglecting their legitimate businesses for speculation.

It seems likely that as prices rise flurries such as occurred in the market at the end of last November and the first part of December will recur perhaps even more drastically. These market dips will tend to correct this situation as it will teach the amateur trader the folly of purchasing stocks on anything but value, earnings and reasonable prospects and that it is unwise even to purchase the good stocks without sufficient capital to hold them through temporary depressions. . . .

Looking over the range of prices of the better common stocks on the New York Stock Exchange for the year 1928 one sees that many have doubled in value, some have gone up 100 or 200 points and several as much as 300. The obvious conclusion is that the stocks of established companies in relatively stable lines of business cannot be worth two, three or even four times what they sold at a year ago and that such prices cannot represent real values, but must be the result of "speculative fever" and that accordingly a day of drastic reckoning is sure to come.

There have been, however, in the period since the War, certain fundamental changes in our economic system which to a large extent explain and justify the much higher prices at which the common stocks of our *leading* industrial companies are now selling. Most of the companies listed on the New York Stock Exchange are predominant in their respective lines of business and the existing tendency is for all business to concentrate itself into large units.

This is evident in every direction. Banks are combining, railroads are merging, corporations in kindred lines of business are uniting, chain store merchandising is rapidly developing and constantly reaching out into new lines of endeavor. The small grocer is having increasing difficulty, the local druggist is strongly feeling the competition of the chain store. A great merger of department stores has only recently taken place. Mail order houses are opening retail stores in every sizeable community. The number of manufacturers of automobiles is constantly decreasing and it seems likely that the business will eventually be controlled by not more than three or four companies.

Every year thousands of individual shopkeepers, merchants and manufacturers are being driven to the wall by the competition of the big companies. This concentration of power into a few strong hands is rapidly going on and its exponents justify the movement by pointing out that, generally speaking, people at large are able to purchase the product of these larger companies at lower prices than heretofore. The small man finds it increasingly difficult if not impossible to meet their competition, which means in the final analysis that the American people are rapidly becoming a race of employees rather than of independent individualists. Whether in the long run this saving to the consumer will compensate for the change which seems sure to result in the point of view and character of the American people, only time will tell.

What is the outlook for the high priced stocks of these leading industrial companies over the period of the next few years? In attempting to answer this question one must bear in mind that the United States is far and away the largest free trade area in the world with any density of population. Our country is blessed with natural resources of nearly every kind to a greater extent than any similar portion of the earth's surface. We have a homogeneous population which has been educated to the use of the same sort of merchandise, our people are enterprising and audacious and the country's resources are much further from full development than are those of the European countries. Another contributing factor to our prosperity is the fact that we enjoy a stable and liberal form of government and the people as a whole are satisfied with existing conditions politically, socially and economically.

With a background of this sort, it is only natural that industry should prosper, particularly our larger corporations. They can afford to employ the keenest and best equipped executives available, they are able to carry on extensive research and to buy new and better machinery as it is developed. They enjoy better credit, because of this and because of the magnitude of their purchases of materials they are able to secure considerably better prices than their small competitors. Their factories cover the country and accordingly they distribute their goods more cheaply and more rapidly than the individual manufacturer with only one unit. They secure as directors men of experience and proven ability. Their greater sales outlets throughout the country mean that they get more value from a National advertising campaign than a concern in a similar line of business doing a smaller volume, in other words their advertising cost per unit of sales should normally be lower. In addition these large companies enjoy tremendous prestige and public confidence.

Specifically, let us consider the Radio Corporation of America, whose stock was probably more in the public eye during 1928 than that of any other corporation, having sold last year as low as $85.25 a share and as high as $420. . . . What justification can there be for this stock which sold as recently as 1926 at $32 a share rising to over $400?

Radio Corporation of America is the leader in an absolutely new field of activity, the surface of which has in all probability been barely scratched. Among other activities it is developing commercial communication by wireless telegraph, broadcasting, [and] the invention, improvement, exploitation and sale of radio apparatus. It owns exclusive patents to the new low beam wireless which is expected to revolutionize the communication business of the world. Constant progress is being made in the art of transmitting pictures, documents and other facsimile matter by radio and in all probability radio television is not many years away. In fact Mr. Sarnoff, vice president of the company, recently stated that in his estimation radio television broadcasting may be an everyday occurrence within five years. The corporation is working on the synchronization of films with speech. It owns many basic patents and enjoys a considerable income from their lease to manufacturers on a royalty basis. The company's officers and directors include many of the leading electrical and financial minds of the country. . . .

These facts about the position and prospects of the Radio Corporation of America have not been written with the idea of influencing any one to purchase its stock. It has been chosen as it probably represents the most widely known and discussed example of a rapid and violent advance among the common stocks of our leading corporations. Clearly there is considerable justification for its great increase in market value.

Considering the question of whether good common stocks are too high from another angle it is interesting to note that from time to time when lists are published giving the number of shares held by prominent, wealthy and well-informed men in such companies as New York Central, General Electric, United States Steel, etc., these financial leaders have seldom reduced their holdings in such companies and often have increased them.

While securities of the leading corporations have been advancing, the stocks of other companies not so meritorious have in many cases been pushed up to unwarranted levels due to the enthusiasm of public speculation. While business is good, money is dear and gives every indication of remaining so for some time to come. The stock market will from time to time have violent breaks during which the good stocks will go down with the bad. Nevertheless, it is impossible not to feel that over a reasonable period of time the common stocks of our leading and best managed companies in basic lines of industry will continue to advance to higher levels and that there may be more fore-sight than fever in many of the present-day quotations.

Source: *Outlook and Independent* 151 (January 23, 1929): 142–3, 155.

2 *New York Times*, First Day of the Crash, 1929

Americans in the 1920s spoke of a New Era where old economic rules no longer applied. "We in America today are nearer to the final triumph over poverty than ever before in the history of any land," presidential candidate Herbert Hoover declared in 1928. "We shall soon with the help of God be in sight of the day when poverty shall be banished from this earth." That noble dream exploded on October 29, 1929, when the stock market lurched into an unprecedented downturn. Stock prices had flown high for years, partly because of the strong economy and partly because of an unjustified yet widely held conviction that stock prices should be higher. But no longer was it simply enough to believe. Key industries such as automobiles and construction were producing far beyond demand and had to cut back. Unemployment was rising. Agriculture had never recovered from postwar losses. These combined pressures popped the bubble. The stock market, after tripling its value in just four years, lost ninety percent of its value over the next four years. It was not until autumn 1930 that the magnitude of the general downturn – the product not just of events on Wall Street, but also a weak banking system and a slowdown of global trade due to high tariffs – became clear, but the Crash provides a convenient starting date for the Great Depression that haunted Americans for a decade to come.

Why does the author believe the crash happened? On the whole, is the article optimistic or pessimistic?

Stock prices virtually collapsed yesterday, swept downward with gigantic losses in the most disastrous trading day in the stock market's history. Billions of dollars in open market values were wiped out as prices crumbled under the pressure of liquidation of securities which had to be sold at any price.

There was an impressive rally just at the close, which brought many lead-ing stocks back from 4 to 14 points from their lowest points of the day. . . .

From every point of view, in the extent of losses sustained, in total turnover, in the number of speculators wiped out, the day was the most disastrous in Wall Street's history. Hysteria swept the country and stocks went overboard for just what they would bring at forced sale. . . .

There were two cheerful notes, however, which sounded through the pall of gloom which overhung the financial centres of the country. One was the brisk rally of stocks at the close on tremendous buying by those who believe that prices have sunk too low. The other was that the liquidation has been so violent, as well as widespread, that many bankers, brokers and industrial leaders expressed the belief last night that it now has run its course.

A further note of optimism in the soundness of fundamentals was sounded by the directors of the United States Steel Corporation and the American Can Company, each of which declared an extra dividend of $1 a share at their late afternoon meetings. . . .

That there will be a change today seemed likely from statements made last night by financial and business leaders. Organized support will be accorded to the market from the start, it is believed, but those who are staking their all on the country's leading securities are placing a great deal of confidence, too, in the expectation that there will be an over night change in sentiment; that the counsel of cool heads will prevail and that the mob psychology which has been so largely responsible for the market's debacle will be broken.

The fact that the leading stocks were able to rally in the final fifteen minutes of trading yesterday was considered a good omen. . . .

The market has now passed through three days of collapse, and so violent has it been that most authorities believe that the end is not far away. It started last Thursday, when 12,800,000 shares were dealt in on the Exchange, and holders of stocks commenced to learn just what a decline in the market means. This was followed by a moderate rally on Friday and entirely normal conditions on Saturday, with fluctuations on a comparatively narrow scale and with the efforts of the leading bankers to stabilize the market evidently successful. But the storm broke anew on Monday, with prices slaughtered in every direction, to be followed by yesterday's tremendous trading of 16,410,030 shares.

Three factors stood out most prominently last night after the market's close. They were:

Wall Street has been able to weather the storm with but a single Curb failure, small in size, and no member of the New York Stock Exchange has announced himself unable to meet commitments.

The smashing decline has brought stocks down to a level where, in the opinion of leading bankers and industrialists, they are a buy on their merits and prospects, and brokers have so advised their customers.

The very violence of the liquidation, which has cleaned up many hundreds of sore spots which honeycombed the market, and the expected ability of the market to right itself, since millions of shares of stock have passed to strong hands from weak ones.

One of the factors which Wall Street failed to take into consideration throughout the entire debacle was that the banking consortium has no idea of putting stocks up or to save any individuals from loss, but that its sole purpose was to alleviate the wave of financial hysteria sweeping the country and provide bids, at some price, where needed. It was pointed out in many quarters that no broad liquidating movement in the stock market has ever been stopped by so-called good buying. This is helpful, of course, but it never stops an avalanche of liquidation, as was this one.

There is only one factor, it was pointed out, which can and always does stop a down swing – that is, the natual cessation of forced liquidation. It is usually the case, too, that when the last of the forced selling has been completed the stock market always faces a wide-open gap in which there are practically no offerings of securities at all. When that point is reached, buying springs up from everywhere and always accounts for a sharp, almost perpendicular recovery in the best stocks. The opinion was widely expressed in Wall Street last night that that point has been reached, or at least very nearly reached. . . .

Wall Street was a street of vanished hopes, of curiously silent apprehension and of a sort of paralyzed hypnosis yesterday. Men and women crowded the brokerage offices, even those who have been long since wiped out, and followed the figures on the tape. Little groups gathered here and there to discuss the fall in prices in hushed and awed tones. They were participating in the making of financial history.

[It is] the consensus of bankers and brokers alike that no such scenes ever again will be witnessed by this generation. To most of those who have been in the market it is all the more awe-inspiring because their financial history is limited to bull markets.

The machinery of the New York Stock Exchange and the Curb market were unable to handle the tremendous volume of trading which went over them. Early in the day they kept up well, because most of the trading was in big blocks, but as the day progressed the tickers fell further and further behind, and as on the previous big days of this week and last it was only by printing late quotations of stocks on the bond tickers and by the 10-minute flashes on stock prices put out by Dow Jones & Co. and the Wall Street News Bureau that the financial district could get any idea of what was happening in the wild mob of brokers on the Exchange and the Curb.

Source: "Stocks Collapse in 16,410,030-Share Day" *New York Times,* October 30, 1929.

3 Herbert Hoover Speaks to the Press about the Economy, 1929

Herbert Hoover seemed the perfect man for the job of president. His life story seemed cut from the fabric of the American dream. Orphaned at a young age, he rose from the Quaker community of West Branch, Iowa to put himself through Stanford University. He became a prosperous mining engineer and a self-made millionaire in an era that, apart from such skeptics as Sinclair Lewis, deified businessmen. Hoover's wartime work with the Committee for the Relief of Belgium saved countless lives and made him a world-renowned figure. Eight years as commerce secretary under two popular Republican presidents provided crucial insights into how Washington worked. Many who helped elect him president in 1928 saw him as more of a hero than a politician, a "Great Engineer" destined to lead the nation to a glorious future. The Crash and subsequent economic collapse exposed Hoover's weaknesses. A toxic combination of painful shyness and stubborn hardheadedness prevented him from embracing outside perspectives or escaping his ideological box. Hoover could have concealed his poor oratorical skills in an earlier time but had nowhere to hide in this radio-mad age. His nasal voice and stilted syntax failed to inspire a country in desperate need of confidence. "If you put a rose in Hoover's hand it would wilt," remarked one critic. This document captures the president's economic perspective in the days following the Crash, months before anyone recognized the magnitude of the crisis.

Why does Hoover believe the Crash occurred? What should the country do about it? How effectively does Hoover convey his message? What are his strengths and weaknesses as a speaker?

We are dealing here with a psychological situation to a very considerable degree. It is a question of fear. We have had a collapse in the stock market, out of which a good many people have lost money, and a lot of people who could not afford to, and a lot of unfortunate people have been brought in, the effect of which in the American mind creates an undue state of alarm, because our national thinking naturally goes back to previous occasions when events of that character have had a very considerable bearing upon the business situation, and in its final interpretation it is employment.

Now, a great many people lifted their standards of living, and naturally the effect of such a thing tends to decrease consumption particularly for luxury and semiluxury, and those trades are no doubt still affected.

But this occasion so far differs from all others in that the credit situation in the country is entirely isolated from it due to the Federal Reserve and the banks, and there is no credit consideration involved. But the natural recovery of increased interest rates by the withdrawal of capital from speculative securities takes that capital ultimately back into industry and commerce. It is ordinarily the tendency of industrial leaders and everyone else to sit back to see what happens and to be a little more cautious in his business than he might otherwise have been that we have to deal with.

We have also to deal naturally with some unemployment in the seminecessity trades. But the real problem and the interpretation of it is one of maintenance of employment. This is not a question of bolstering stock markets or stock prices or anything of that kind. We are dealing with the vital question of maintaining employment in the United States and consequently the comfort and standard of living of the people and their ability to buy goods and proceed in the normal course of their lives. So that the purpose of this movement is to disabuse the public mind of the notion that there has been any serious or vital interruption in our economic system, and that it is going to proceed in the ordinary, normal manner, and to get that impression over not by preachment and talks but by definite and positive acts on the part of industry and business and the Government and others. As I said before, I do not believe that words ever convince a discouraged person in these situations. The thing that brings him back is courage and the natural sight of other industries and other men going ahead with their programs and business.

So I wanted you to get that background upon it all, because it seriously concerns the press to give the confidence to the public that the business fabric is now organizing itself, taking steps on its own responsibility to carry on; that it is going to go even farther and stretch itself to meet any possible condition of employment is the thing that will give courage to the public rather than to say to them every day that they should not be alarmed. So that I am trying to get this problem across by action in different industries and other groups rather than by too much talking, and, therefore, I don't want to talk about it. . . .

Source: *Public Papers of the Presidents of the United States: Herbert Hoover, March 4 to December 31, 1929* (Washington, DC: Government Printing Office, 1974), pp. 387–8.

4 Calvin Coolidge, A Bright Economic Future If We Stay the Course, 1932

Calvin Coolidge left the White House in 1929 to a chorus of cheers and huzzahs. His low-tax, pro-business administration had apparently set the country on a path to permanent prosperity. The dour, tightlipped Massachusetts Yankee had calmed the nation after Warren Harding died,

promoted conservative fiscal policies, and slashed federal spending to the bare
bones. "If the Federal Government should go out of existence," he argued,
"the common run of people would not detect the difference in the affairs of
their daily life for a considerable length of time." His best-known maxim, "the
chief business of America is business … the man who builds a factory builds
a temple, the man who works there, worships there," summarized his world
view. He suspected the approaching end of good times when he left office but
saw no reason to curb speculation, regulate unhealthy banks, or discourage
industrial overproduction. The market will correct itself, he reasoned, and
government meddling would only make a bad situation worse. Although
ex-President Coolidge generally held his peace – no great challenge for the
man known as "Silent Cal" – he disapproved of Hoover's vigorous measures
to boost the economy. Writing three years after the Crash and one year before
a national bank meltdown set a grim stage for the opening of Franklin
Roosevelt's New Deal, Coolidge shared his thoughts on what most observers
now saw as a severe depression rather than a mere bump on the road to riches.

On what basis does Coolidge conclude that individuals must accept
responsibility for hard times? Is his logic compelling? What advice does
Coolidge offer to those suffering from the Depression? What suggestions
does he have for improving economic conditions?

One of the serious results that come from the experience through which our country has been passing for the past two years is *loss of faith*. Because some have put their trust in things which they have found do not always endure, *they draw the hasty and unwarranted conclusion that it is useless to have faith in anything*. They propose to abandon all standards, seek only the easiest course, and live merely for the present, on the theory that they may as well eat, drink, and be merry, for tomorrow they die.

It cannot be denied that many people have had an experience which at first thought seems to warrant such an attitude. They had profitable employment on which they believed they could rely for a permanent income. That has gone, and they are unable to secure work. They had a house which ultimately they expected would be their own and would make a home for themselves and their family. They have been unable to meet the payments due on it and have seen it taken from them. Others have found that investments on which they relied for provision for their old age have turned out to be of much less value than had been supposed. Some have met with losses through the failure of banks in which they had money deposited.

It is easy, in these circumstances, for the individual to conclude that these disasters have arisen through no fault of his own, that it must be the fault of someone, and he is inclined to blame something he loosely calls society. Sometimes a feeling of injustice results in a threat of defiance against constituted authority.

Among all these people, those who most strongly appeal to our sympathies, those who seem most warranted in their discouragement, are the ones who want work and cannot find it. But even they should take the larger view of their situation. It is no new experience for a wage earner to be without employment. Such a condition has always been temporary. *It will be temporary now. Surely the country will go back to work, back to production and consumption.* The condition of the wage earner in America has long been the despair of all the rest of the world. Some hope should be derived from what has been and some confidence entertained that the same again shall be. . . .

It is true some homes have been lost through default of payments. That risk is always incurred when property is bought on credit. But even in this field, where one home has been lost, an enormous number have been retained. Their owners now find themselves securely and comfortably housed because they saved money and bought when they had an income, instead of spending all their money on rents and expensive living. . . .

When we examine the complaints of those who have lost through investments we find that they fall into three classes: Some lost because they were plainly swindled. We are enacting more and more laws and setting up more and more regulations and safeguards to prevent a recurrence of such abuses. The practice of swindling is very old, and larceny has never been eradicated from any community where property was abundant. But because someone does wrong does not prove that we shall all abandon trying to do right.

Others have used poor judgment in investments. Usually they have been tempted to take large risks by the hope of making large gains. Some did make great profits, while many more suffered heavy losses. *Those who trust to chance must abide by the results of chance. They have no legitimate complaint against anyone but themselves.*

Still others, using all the judgment possible for human beings and guided by the best financial advice obtainable, have seen their investments seriously impaired. But this simply means what everyone should know: that even when surrounded by all the safeguards and all the integrity which it is possible to secure, the ownership of property involves a risk. No law, no regulation, no government supervision, no skill in management, has ever been devised that could protect invested property from temporary fluctuation and occasional loss. These are the hazards of our finite existence. Only omniscience can guard against them.

But that does not excuse us from making the most of what we have and doing the best we can. While no one can tell with certainty what will happen to any particular property or what the market will do at any particular time, the best financial judgment expects that, while further losses may accrue, some time the general level of good standard properties will rise, so that some of the present losses will be reduced. Future prices at which property will sell are always uncertain. There is no one to be blamed for what is unavoidably true. *The great fact of life is uncertainty.* The only thing we can do is to recognize the uncertainty and govern ourselves accordingly.

It is true that a considerable number of people have suffered through bank failures. In a time of declining prices the banks that have not been well managed always have difficulty. Some also that through no fault of their own have met losses have been compelled to close. But that does not mean a total loss to depositors. Sometimes the loss is heavy, but sometimes payment is made in full. In any case, funds are tied up and much inconvenience results.

Our national banking system is as sound as generations of experience have been able to make it. . . . While absolute safety has been impossible to secure, it is probable that the records of money deposited in properly regulated banks in this country would show over a series of years that it has been in the safest place to keep funds. . . .

It might be a great personal comfort if we could lay all the blame for our misfortune upon some source outside ourselves. That is why it is easy to convince some of us that we have not failed, but society has failed. Of course, it would follow that if society were to be blamed for our failures, that same society must be credited with our successes. If we want to look at it that way we shall have to admit that, on the whole, society in this country has done very well by us. Our country, over its span of history, has been considerable of a success.

But while there is a relationship of all of us, which we term society, that differs from each of us, just as a house differs from the individual bricks in it, yet people are not bricks, and moral responsibility cannot be shifted to others. It must rest with the individual. . . .

Under the pressure of events there are some who have become sullen and resentful. They are inclined to refuse to make an effort to pay their taxes and their interest. If they earn anything, they propose to spend it. They have lost faith in the standards by which they have lived.

Such people have made a great mistake. They have been born into the wrong universe for them. They belong in some place where there are no risks to be faced, where a backbone would be considered excess baggage, where courage and perseverance, effort and self-denial, industry and thrift are not virtues in themselves, to be cultivated for their own sakes. The absurdity of this position is revealed by considering what would result if everybody else adopted the same attitude. It may be all right as a rule to die by, but it will not work as a rule to live by.

There is no power that can guarantee us economic security. We think we want relief from toil and worry, forgetful that all our real satisfactions are in our achievements. If we will but make the effort to develop them, if we will apply ourselves faithfully to our tasks, we shall all find we have powers we did not know we possessed.

We shall come nearest to achieving our own economic security by the practice of the old-fashioned, homely virtues of industry and thrift; of buying a few things we can pay for, rather than many which leave us loaded with dangerous debts we can never pay; of small savings securely invested at moderate returns, rather than spectacular financial performances. *The best recipe for financial security is to live within our means. This is our ancient faith. We have found nothing better.*

Source: Calvin Coolidge, "In Times Like These," *American Magazine* 113 (February 1932): 11–12, 13, 108, 110.

Discussion questions

1   How did these observers view the Depression? What were its causes and solutions?
2   Why did these writers so badly underestimate the magnitude of the depression?
3   How should the federal government respond to economic downturns?

Chapter 8   To Fear or Not to Fear

1 Walter Lippmann, Candidate Franklin Roosevelt, 1932

It is easy to assume that voters elected Franklin Delano Roosevelt president in 1932 because they agreed with his vision and goals. So much of what America is today came from FDR's administration – Social Security, the minimum wage, rural electrification, a permanent presence in global affairs – that the president's legacy is presented almost as a given, as the inevitable product of the nation's history to that point. In fact, most people had no idea where then-Governor Roosevelt stood on most issues. Sometimes Roosevelt had no idea where he stood on issues. He came across as a bland if cheerful New York politician eager to please all factions while alienating none. Supreme Court Justice Oliver Wendell Holmes famously dismissed him for possessing "a second-class intellect but a first-class temperament," and nationally syndicated New York Herald-Tribune *columnist Walter Lippmann agreed. Lippmann liked Roosevelt but saw no evidence of greatness in him. FDR was "a kind of amiable Boy Scout," he joked. In the following article the columnist advised readers that the prohibitive favorite for the Democratic Party's nomination had no convictions, political courage, or leadership skills. Among Roosevelt's faults was his troubled relationship with Tammany Hall, New York City's notorious political machine.*

What evidence does Lippmann provide to support his charges? Considering the challenges of running for president in such a diverse country, are there other ways to interpret FDR's actions? How similar or dissimilar does Roosevelt sound compared to other prominent politicians?

America Between the Wars, 1919–1941: A Documentary Reader, First Edition.
Edited by David Welky. Editorial material and organization © 2012 John Wiley & Sons, Inc.
Published 2012 by John Wiley & Sons, Inc.

It is now plain that sooner or later some of Governor Roosevelt's supporters are going to feel badly let down. For it is impossible that he can continue to be such different things to such different men. He is, at the moment, the highly preferred candidate of left-wing progressives like Senator Wheeler of Montana, and of Bryan's former secretary, Representative Howard of Nebraska. He is, at the same time, receiving the enthusiastic support of the New York *Times*.

Senator Wheeler, who would like to cure the depression by debasing the currency, is Mr. Roosevelt's most conspicuous supporter in the West, and Representative Howard has this week hailed the Governor as "the most courageous enemy of the evil influences" emanating from the international bankers. The New York *Times*, on the other hand, assures its readers that "no upsetting plans, no Socialistic proposals, however mild and winning in form," could appeal to the Governor.

The Roosevelt bandwagon would seem to be moving in two opposite directions.

There are two questions raised by this curious situation. The first is why Senator Wheeler and the *Times* should have such contradictory impressions of their common candidate. The second, which is also the more important question, is which has guessed rightly.

The art of carrying water on both shoulders is highly developed in American politics, and Mr. Roosevelt has learned it. His message to the Legislature, or at least that part of it devoted to his Presidential candidacy, is an almost perfect specimen of the balanced antithesis. Thus at one place we learn that the public demands "plans for the reconstruction of a better ordered civilization" and in another place that "the American system of economics and government is everlasting." The first sentence is meant for Senator Wheeler and the second for the New York *Times*.

The message is so constructed that a left-wing progressive can read it and find just enough of his own phrases in it to satisfy himself that Franklin D. Roosevelt's heart is in the right place. He will find an echo of Governor La Follette's recent remarks about the loss of "economic liberty." He will find an echo of Governor La Follette's impressive discussion about the increasing concentration of wealth and how it does not guarantee an intelligent or a fair use of that wealth. He will find references to "plans." On the other hand, there are all necessary assurances to the conservatives. "We should not seek in any way to destroy or to tear down"; our system is "everlasting"; we must insist "on the permanence of our fundamental institutions."

That this is a studied attempt to straddle the whole country I have no doubt whatever. Every newspaper man knows the whole bag of tricks by heart. He knows too that the practical politician supplements these two-faced platitudes by what are called private assurances, in which he tells his different supporters what he knows they would like to hear. Then, when they read the balanced antithesis, each believes the half that he has been reassured about privately and dismisses the rest as not significant. That, ladies and gentlemen, is how the rabbit comes out of the hat, that is how it is possible to persuade Senator Wheeler and the New York *Times* that you are their man.

In the case of Mr. Roosevelt, it is not easy to say with certainty whether his left-wing or his right-wing supporters are the more deceived. The reason is that Franklin D. Roosevelt is a highly impressionable person, without a firm grasp of public affairs and without very strong convictions. He might plump for something which would shock the conservatives. There is no telling. Yet when Representative Howard of Nebraska says that he is "the most dangerous enemy of evil influences," New Yorkers who know the Governor know that Mr. Howard does not know the Governor. For Franklin D. Roosevelt is an amiable man with many philanthropic impulses, but he is not the dangerous enemy of anything. He is too eager to please. The notion, which seems to prevail in the West and South, that Wall Street fears him, is preposterous. Wall Street thinks he is too dry, not that he is too radical. Wall Street does not like some of his supporters. Wall Street does not like his vagueness, and the uncertainty as to what he does think, but if any Western Progressive thinks that the Governor has challenged directly or indirectly the wealth concentrated in New York City, he is mightily mistaken.

Mr. Roosevelt is, as a matter of fact, an excessively cautious politician. He has been Governor for three years, and I doubt whether anyone can point to a single act of his which involved any political risk. . . . I can think of nothing . . . that could be described as evidence of his willingness to attack vested interests, and I can think of one outstanding case in which he has shown the utmost reluctance to attack them. I refer to his relations with Tammany.

It is well known in New York, though apparently not in the West, that Governor Roosevelt had to be forced into assisting the exposure of corruption in New York City. It is well known in New York that, through his patronage, he has supported the present powers in Tammany Hall. It is well known that his policy has been to offend Tammany just as little as he dared in the face of the fact that an investigation of Tammany had finally to be undertaken. It is true that he is not popular in Tammany Hall, but, though they do not like him, they vote for him. For there is a working arrangement between him and Tammany. . . .

I do not say that Mr. Roosevelt might not at some time in the next few months fight Tammany. I do say that on his record these last three years he will fight Tammany only if and when he decides it is safe and profitable to do so. For Franklin D. Roosevelt is no crusader. He is no tribune of the people. He is no enemy of entrenched privilege. He is a pleasant man who, without any important qualifications for the office, would very much like to be President.

It is meaningless for him to talk about "leadership practical, sound, courageous and alert." He has been Governor in the community which has been the financial center of the world during the last year of the boom and the two years of the depression. The Governor of New York is listened to when he speaks. Can anyone point to anything Mr. Roosevelt has said or done in those three years to provide the leadership we should all so much like to have had? I do not think anyone can. He has carefully refrained during these years from exerting any kind of leadership on any national question which was controversial. That was probably shrewd politics. It has helped his candidacy. But as a result of his strategic silence nobody knows where he stands on any of the great questions which require practical, sound, courageous and alert leadership.

Source: Walter Lippmann, "The Candidacy of Franklin D. Roosevelt," *New York Herald-Tribune* (January 8, 1932).

2 Herbert Hoover, The Proposed New Deal Will Ruin Us, 1932

Elected by a landslide in 1928, Herbert Hoover faced long odds in his 1932 re-election bid. Then in its fourth year, the Depression exposed the Great Engineer as a stubborn micromanager with poor communication skills. Hoover at first hoped to simply wait out the downturn. After the spiraling economy proved his optimism misguided he endorsed a series of measures aimed at balancing the federal budget, a goal considered the best answer to a depression. Tax hikes and spending cuts instead sucked money from the flagging economy and sent the country deeper into crisis. He reversed course again, launching ambitious programs designed to inject federal dollars into failing banks, business, and farms. These measures failed to halt the slide even though they provided a foundation for many of the New Deal measures that followed.

Although lightly regarded in many circles, Democratic challenger Franklin Roosevelt seemed poised to topple the incumbent. Roosevelt's cheerful optimism contrasted with Hoover's grim demeanor. The Republican suffered egg-hurling crowds and occasional chants of "Hang Hoover!" as he ground through the campaign. With little to highlight in his own record, he resorted to casting his opponent as the bearer of dangerous, un-American ideologies. His speech at New York City's Madison Square Garden crystallized his argument that the proposed New Deal – a vague phrase Roosevelt employed in his speech accepting the Democratic nomination – meant further disaster for a reeling country.

What kind of America did Hoover envision? How did Franklin Roosevelt threaten this vision? How convincing is Hoover's argument? How effective is he at defending his record and criticizing Roosevelt's? In what ways does Hoover's address remind you of more recent political speeches?

This campaign is more than a contest between two men. It is more than a contest between two parties. It is a contest between two philosophies of government.

We are told by the opposition that we must have a change, that we must have a new deal. It is not the change that comes from normal development of national life to which I object, but the proposal to alter the whole foundations of our national life which have been builded through generations of testing and struggle, and of the principles upon which we have builded the Nation. The expressions our opponents use must refer to important changes in our economic and social system and our system of Government, otherwise they are nothing but vacuous words. And I realize that in this time of distress many of our people are asking whether our social and economic system is incapable of that great primary function of providing security and comfort of life to all of the firesides of our 25,000,000 homes in America, whether our social system provides for the fundamental development and progress of our people, whether our form of government is capable of originating and sustaining that security and progress.

This question is the basis upon which our opponents are appealing to the people in their fears and distress. They are proposing changes and so-called new deals which would destroy the very foundations of our American system. . . .

Our economic system has received abnormal shocks during the past three years, which temporarily dislocated its normal functioning. These shocks have in a large sense come from without our borders, but I say to you that our system of government has enabled us to take such strong action as to prevent the disaster which would otherwise have come to our Nation. It has enabled us further to develop measures and programs which are now demonstrating their ability to bring about restoration and progress. . . .

Our system is the product of our race and of our experience in building a nation to heights unparalleled in the whole history of the world. It is a system peculiar to the American people. It differs essentially from all others in the world. It is an American system.

It is founded on the conception that only through ordered liberty, through freedom to the individual, and equal opportunity to the individual will his initiative and enterprise be summoned to spur the march of progress. . . .

This freedom of the individual creates of itself the necessity and the cheerful willingness of men to act coöperatively in a thousand ways and for every purpose as occasion arises . . .

It is in the further development of this coöperation and a sense of its responsibility that we should find solutions for many of our complex problems, and not by the extension of government into our economic and social life. The greatest function of government is to build up that coöperation, and its most resolute action should be to deny the extension of bureaucracy. . . .

When the political and economic weakness of many nations of Europe, the result of the World War and its aftermath, finally culminated in [the] collapse of their institutions, the delicate adjustment of our economic and social life received a shock unparalleled in our history. . . .

Yet these forces were overcome – perhaps by narrow margins – and this action demonstrates what the courage of a nation can accomplish under the resolute leadership in the Republican Party. . . .

We saved this Nation from a quarter of a century of chaos and degeneration, and we preserved the savings, the insurance policies, gave a fighting chance to men to hold their homes. We saved the integrity of our government and the honesty of the American dollar. And we installed measures which today are bringing back recovery. Employment, agriculture, business – all of these show the steady, if slow, healing of our enormous wound.

I therefore contend that the problem of today is to continue these measures and policies to restore this American system to its normal functioning, to repair the wounds it has received, to correct the weaknesses and evils which would defeat that system. To enter upon a series of deep changes to embark upon this inchoate new deal which has been propounded in this campaign would be to undermine and destroy our American system. . . .

Recently there was circulated through the unemployed in this country a letter from the Democratic candidate in which he stated that he

"would support measures for the inauguration of self-liquidating public works such as the utilization of water resources, flood control, land reclamation, to provide employment for all surplus labor at all times."

I especially emphasize that promise to promote "employment for all surplus labor at all times." At first I could not believe that anyone would be so cruel as to hold out a hope so absolutely impossible of realization to these 10,000,000 who are unemployed. . . . If it were possible to give this employment to 10,000,000 people by the Government, it would cost upwards of $9,000,000,000 a year. . . .

I have said before, and I want to repeat on this occasion that the only method by which we can stop the suffering and unemployment is by returning our people to their normal jobs in their normal homes, carrying on their normal functions of living. This can be done only by sound processes of protecting and stimulating recovery of the existing economic system upon which we have builded our progress thus far – preventing distress and giving such sound employment as we can find in the meantime. . . .

If these measures, these promises, which I have discussed; or these failures to disavow these projects; this attitude of mind, mean anything, they mean the enormous expansion of the Federal Government; they mean the growth of bureaucracy such as we have never seen in our history. . . . It would break down the savings, the wages, the equality of opportunity among our people. These measures would transfer vast responsibilities to the Federal Government from the states, the local governments, and the individuals. But that is not all; they would break down our form of government. . . . At once when these extensions take place by the Federal Government, the authority and responsibility of state governments and institutions are undermined. Every enterprise of private business is at once halted to know what Federal action is going to be. It destroys initiative and courage. . . .

[Y]ou can not extend the mastery of government over the daily life of a people without somewhere making it master of people's souls and thoughts. Expansion of government in business means that the Government in order to protect itself from the political consequences of its errors is driven irresistibly without peace to greater and greater control of the Nation's press and platform. Free speech does not live many hours after free industry and free commerce die. . . .

Source: William Starr Myers, ed., *The State Papers and Other Public Writings of Herbert Hoover* (Garden City, NY: Doubleday, Doran & Company, Inc., 1934), Volume 2, pp. 408–9, 410–11, 412–13, 421–2, 424, 425.

3 Franklin Roosevelt's Fireside Chat on Banking, 1933

Franklin Roosevelt won the 1932 election easily, carrying 42 of 48 states and crushing Herbert Hoover 472–59 in the electoral college. The vote represented a repudiation of Hoover rather than enthusiasm for Roosevelt, who maintained a Sphinx-like silence as to his intentions during the four-month interregnum between election and inauguration. Political watchers predicted everything from a pro-business administration to a socialist revolution. Roosevelt ignored the speculation, preferring to spend

his time absorbing knowledge from advisers of varying ideological stripes.
FDR used his inaugural address to outline general "lines of attack" without
establishing precise goals. Above all else he stressed the need for bold action
and a conviction that brighter days lay ahead.

Roosevelt's first priority was addressing a banking industry standing on
the brink of a collapse that might annihilate the wobbling economy. FDR's
inner circle worked with Hoover's men to craft an Emergency Banking Act
that Roosevelt signed into law just seven hours after Congress introduced it.
With a stroke of the pen the president imposed a broad new set of financial
regulations. More dramatically, FDR temporarily closed the banks to allow
for further tinkering and to give depositors a chance to regain confidence. He
took to the airwaves a few days later to deliver the first of 30 "fireside chats"
he gave during his 12 years in office. In it he displayed an uncanny ability to
connect with unseen listeners. His speech moved the Graham family of
Dubuque, Iowa to write a response, included here.

What does Roosevelt's speech suggest about his audience? How effective is
Roosevelt's speech? How does his speaking style compare to Herbert
Hoover's? How do the Grahams view the president? Do you find their
perspective normal or unusual?

I want to talk for a few minutes with the people of the United States about banking – with the comparatively few who understand the mechanics of banking but more particularly with the overwhelming majority who use banks for the making of deposits and the drawing of checks. I want to tell you what has been done in the last few days, why it was done, and what the next steps are going to be. I recognize that the many proclamations from State capitols and from Washington, the legislation, the Treasury regulations, etc., couched for the most part in banking and legal terms, should be explained for the benefit of the average citizen. I owe this in particular because of the fortitude and good temper with which everybody has accepted the inconvenience and hardships of the banking holiday. I know that when you understand what we in Washington have been about I shall continue to have your cooperation as fully as I have had your sympathy and help during the past week.

First of all, let me state the simple fact that when you deposit money in a bank the bank does not put the money into a safe deposit vault. It invests your money in many different forms of credit – bonds, commercial paper, mortgages and many other kinds of loans. In other words, the bank puts your money to work to keep the wheels of industry and of agriculture turning around. A comparatively small part of the money you put into the bank is kept in currency – an amount which in normal times is wholly sufficient to cover the cash needs of the average citizen. In other words, the total amount of all the currency in the country is only a small fraction of the total deposits in all of the banks.

What, then, happened during the last few days of February and the first few days of March? Because of undermined confidence on the part of the public, there was a general rush by a large portion of our population to turn bank deposits into currency or gold – a rush so great that the soundest banks could not get enough currency to meet the demand. . . .

By the afternoon of March third scarcely a bank in the country was open to do business. Proclamations temporarily closing them in whole or in part had been issued by the Governors in almost all the States.

It was then that I issued the proclamation providing for the nationwide bank holiday, and this was the first step in the Government's reconstruction of our financial and economic fabric.

The second step was the legislation promptly and patriotically passed by the Congress confirming my proclamation and broadening my powers so that it became possible in view of the requirement of time to extend the holiday and lift the ban of that holiday gradually. This law also gave authority to develop a program of rehabilitation of our banking facilities. I want to tell our citizens in every part of the Nation that the national Congress – Republicans and Democrats alike – showed by this action a devotion to public welfare and a realization of the emergency and the necessity for speed that it is difficult to match in our history. . . .

This bank holiday, while resulting in many cases in great inconvenience, is affording us the opportunity to supply the currency necessary to meet the situation. No sound bank is a dollar worse off than it was when it closed its doors last Monday. Neither is any bank which may turn out not to be in a position for immediate opening. . . .

A question you will ask is this: why are all the banks not to be reopened at the same time? The answer is simple. Your Government does not intend that the history of the past few years shall be repeated. We do not want and will not have another epidemic of bank failures.

As a result, we start tomorrow, Monday, with the opening of banks in the twelve Federal Reserve Bank cities – those banks which on first examination by the Treasury have already been found to be all right. This will be followed on Tuesday by the resumption of all their functions by banks already found to be sound in cities where there are recognized clearing houses. That means about two hundred fifty cities of the United States.

On Wednesday and succeeding days banks in smaller places all through the country will resume business, subject, of course, to the Government's physical ability to complete its survey. . . .

Let me make it clear to you that if your bank does not open the first day you are by no means justified in believing that it will not open. A bank that opens on one of the subsequent days is in exactly the same status as the bank that opens tomorrow. . . .

It is possible that when the banks resume a very few people who have not recovered from their fear may again begin withdrawals. Let me make it clear that the banks will take care of all needs – and it is my belief that hoarding during the past week has become an exceedingly unfashionable pastime. . . . I can assure you that it is safer to keep your money in a reopened bank than under the mattress.

The success of our whole great national program depends, of course, upon the cooperation of the public – on its intelligent support and use of a reliable system. . . .

One more point before I close. There will be, of course, some banks unable to reopen without being reorganized. The new law allows the Government to assist in making these reorganizations quickly and effectively and even allows the Government to subscribe to at least a part of new capital which may be required.

I hope you can see from this elemental recital of what your Government is doing that there is nothing complex, or radical, in the process.

We had a bad banking situation. Some of our bankers had shown themselves either incompetent or dishonest in their handling of the people's funds. They had used the money entrusted to them in speculations and unwise loans. This was, of course, not true in the vast majority of our banks, but it was true in enough of them to shock the people for a time into a sense of insecurity and to put them into a frame of mind where they did not differentiate, but seemed to assume that the acts of a comparative few had tainted them all. It was the Government's job to straighten out this situation and do it as quickly as possible. And the job is being performed. . . .

[T]here is an element in the readjustment of our financial system more important than currency, more important than gold, and that is the confidence of the people. Confidence and courage are the essentials of success in carrying out our plan. You people must have faith; you must not be stampeded by rumors or guesses. Let us unite in banishing fear. We have provided the machinery to restore our financial system; it is up to you to support and make it work.

It is your problem no less than it is mine. Together we cannot fail.

Source: B. D. Zevin, ed., *Nothing to Fear: The Selected Addresses of Franklin Delano Roosevelt, 1932–1945* (Freeport, NY: Books for Libraries Press, 1946), pp. 18–20, 21–2.

The President of the greatest Nation on earth honored every home with a personal visit last night. He came into our living-room in a kindly neighborly way and in simple words explained the great things he had done so that all of us unfamiliar with the technicalities might understand. When his voice died away we realized our "friend" had gone home again but left us his courage, his faith and absolute confidence.

As long as you talk to your people there is not one thing you cannot accomplish. From the lips of neighbors, acquaintances and strangers we hear this sentiment. Congress and other law-makers will find themselves puny interference when you have but to turn to the Radio and enter our home a welcome and revered guest. If you could only hear our response – but, I'm sure you sense the great hope and reliance of your people, We believe in you!

Of all precedents you have shattered is the theory that a man must come from the lowly to understand the needs of the common people. We love you for that perception that could only come from a great unselfish heart.

We are just a modest middle-class people having lost what little we had, but, since March 4th, . . . we knew we were not fighting alone. We have a LEADER at last.

If this should ever reach your eyes – don't take anyone's valuable time for acknowledgement when there is so much to be done. I hope that when the major things have been disposed of you will not forget a national old-age bill such as you fostered in New York. It will alleviate so much suffering and humiliation.

Since you addressed us as "friends" we have written our letter in this spirit and to express our faith.

Respectfully,

F. B. Graham
Mrs. F. B. Graham
Dubuque, Iowa

Source: Lawrence W. Levine and Cornelia R. Levine, eds., *The People and the President: America's Conversation with FDR* (Boston: Beacon Press, 2002), p. 36.

4 Cartoon Celebrating the National Recovery Administration, 1933

Roosevelt's first hundred days in office energized a downtrodden nation. Laws enacted during that brief span stabilized the banks, regulated the financial sector, launched an agricultural recovery program, repealed prohibition, and created job programs for the unemployed. FDR sensed that industry also needed assistance. Businessmen, however, disagreed as to how the government could help them. The president intended to let the matter sit until Alabama Senator Hugo Black introduced a bill to establish a 30-hour work week as a way to spread out available jobs. Roosevelt thought the proposal both unconstitutional and bad policy. Merging several competing and sometimes contradictory ideas into a single package, he asked Congress to replace the Black Bill with his own National Industrial Recovery Act (NIRA). Congress complied in June 1933. NIRA guaranteed labor's right to form unions and created a jobs program called the Public Works Administration. It also organized the National Recovery Administration (NRA), a bureaucracy designed to rationalize the economy by bringing together representatives from management, labor, and government to write codes of conduct for hundreds of industries ranging from steel to feather dusters. Each code set minimum wages, safety standards, and prices for an industry. Americans applauded NRA as another tangible assault on the depression, and the agency's blue eagle symbol soon adorned store windows and advertisements for companies looking to connect their products to the president's personal popularity. In New York City, a crowd of 250,000 paraded down Fifth Avenue in a show of support for the measure. This cartoon from the Philadelphia Record *gives a sense of not only the enthusiasm for NRA, but also for Franklin Roosevelt. Despite this early excitement, NRA proved a clear example of well intended but overreaching government intervention. Few lamented its death when the Supreme Court declared it unconstitutional in 1935.*

What "story" does this cartoon tell? What does the cartoon reveal about public images of FDR and the depression?

HIS GREATEST FIGHT LIES AHEAD.

—By Jerry Doyle.

Figure 8.1 Cartoon celebrating the National Recovery Administration, 1933.

Source: *Philadelphia Record*, August 1, 1933.

Discussion questions

1 What did critics believe Franklin Roosevelt would do as president?
2 How does Franklin Roosevelt's speaking style compare with Herbert Hoover's?
3 Judging by these sources, how did the mood of America change between 1929 and 1933?

Chapter 9   Voices from the Great Depression

1 Clarence Lee, Riding the Rails during the Great Depression, 1999

The Great Depression was as much a social phenomenon as an economic disaster. Hard times devastated families. Unemployed and underemployed men bore the shame of being unable to provide for their wives and children. Some became sullen, others combative. Women had to accommodate their damaged spouses while finding ways to stretch the household budget and supplement the family's income. This partial reversal of gender roles often exacerbated household tensions. "Seems like times is changed," observed Pa Joad, one of the protagonists in John Steinbeck's Depression-era masterpiece The Grapes of Wrath. *"Time was when a man said what we would do." Children also felt these pressures as they scuffled to make a few bucks and got used to making do without luxuries. But apprehensions rose as older siblings confronted a barren job market and anxiety-ridden parents bickered about money. One common response was to imagine themselves as a source of household problems. Their desire not to be a burden drove hundreds of thousands of teenagers to adopt the rootless life of a hobo. Little more than children, they floated from town to town begging for scraps and trying to hustle a few days of work. Some disliked life on the road and soon returned to their families. Others disappeared for years, dropping a line now and again to let their parents know that they were still alive. Clarence Lee, the son of a Louisiana sharecropper, left home in 1931 at age 16 and stayed away for 18 months.*

America Between the Wars, 1919–1941: A Documentary Reader, First Edition.
Edited by David Welky. Editorial material and organization © 2012 John Wiley & Sons, Inc.
Published 2012 by John Wiley & Sons, Inc.

How would you describe Lee's childhood? Why did he leave home? What dangers came with the hobo life? How did Lee's adventures affect him?

My childhood ended the day we became sharecroppers. We worked the land of a man who owned a dairy. We had to milk his cows as well as plant crops. I had pain in the ligaments of my knees and couldn't walk. My father woke me in the darkness at 3 A.M., put me on his back, and carried me to the dairy to help with the milking. For three solid months, we worked without pity or mercy.

There was no time to play like other children. I wasn't allowed to go to school. To this day I've no book learning. The kind of cropping we did was with strawberries, sweet peppers, cucumbers, and stuff like that. I was always loaded up with something.

Sharecropping was selling yourself to the devil. . . .

The farmers put a mortgage on our lives. You get deeper and deeper into debt. When you can't stand one landlord any longer, you make a deal with another. He comes and pays what you owe and takes you to his place. One man sold you and another bought you like a slave. This happened over and over again. You were degraded from people down to merchandise. . . .

I could see my parents' sadness. I remember my father saying to me, "Someday we'll see the end of the tunnel," and I replied, "Yes, and we'll have to be careful, there might be a train." My father had to laugh at that, but there was nothing to look forward to.

I'd never seen a dollar. I never knew a dollar had a face on it. . . .

I wanted to stay home and fight the poverty with my family. I didn't have it in my mind to leave until my father told me, "Go fend for yourself. I cannot afford to have you around any longer." Until today it hurts when I think about it but there was nothing I could do. It was eighteen months before I saw my parents again.

We were mostly boys riding the freight trains at harvest time. You'd see some older boys with their little brothers but no fathers. Most of the time it was boys of fifteen or sixteen, teenagers like myself whose parents had put them out to make their own way. Sometimes two or three of us rode together but never a gang of youths. One or two could go and ask for help and a man might let you work in his fields. If he saw a gang of you, he didn't want you around.

It was dangerous riding the freights. You had to be careful not to stumble and fall under the wheels when you climbed on the cars. You had to jump off at the right time too 'cause once the train picked up speed you had a hard time getting off. Sometimes you slept in a boxcar in a rail yard; next morning when you woke up the train would be taking off with you. It was scary and dangerous but you had to do it to survive.

You never knew who was going to be on the train with you. If you hopped on a freight train with white people, you'd sit together in the boxcars. When they hit the ground they went their way and you'd go yours.

What I remember most is the "clunk" sound of the wheels hitting the joints in the track. It was a good sound and a good feeling too. "Clunk, clunk, clunk, clunk. . ." After a while you hear the whistle blow and other noises. "I'm doing OK," I'd say. "I've got a ride, I don't have to walk." You are not wandering without a purpose but going from point A to point B. You felt good 'cause you knew you were gonna get there. You were gonna try to better yourself. . . .

Being on the road was a destructive experience for me. When I was riding the freight trains I didn't feel like an American citizen. I felt like an outcast.

I wasn't treated like a human being. I was nothing but dirt as far as whites were concerned. If you walked into a place to get a soft drink they'd kick you out. If you asked for something to eat, some would give you a piece of bread at the back door and tell you to get off the premises. Some would sic the dogs on you. It was hurtful to be treated like that. I felt very, very down.

When you went to people's houses to ask for food, if the color of your skin was white you fared better. If it was black you didn't fare too well. They might let a white man stay in the house with them, but me, I could sleep in a barn with the mules and hay. . . .

That's what the Depression meant to me: riding freight trains from place to place looking for something to eat. You didn't panhandle and ask for a handout but offered to work. You didn't go around stealing anything.

Once we went to a place where people were selling chickens and they gave us one. There we were, three boys with a chicken like Mr. Hoover said, but no pot! We picked off the feathers, pulled the intestines out, and stuffed it with mud. We dug a hole, put the chicken in the ground and made a fire above it. When the fire burned down, all we had to do was remove the dirt and we had ourselves a chicken dinner.

You wanted to buy a pair of pants or some shoes but you had nothing. I found a shoe and a boot and I wore them so long others nicknamed me "Shoeboot." You could buy second-hand shoes for forty cents, but where are you going to get the money from? You are working twelve hours a day for one dollar just to survive. . . .

I saw too many hungry people to believe that it was just me. Poverty existed all over Louisiana. Nobody had anything much. Practically everybody I met was hungry. I saw little children with bloated stomachs like those you see over in Africa.

I'd see trains coming in and going out of Baton Rouge. People were sticking on the sides or sitting in the boxcar doors with their legs hanging out. People from the country coming to the city, people from the city going to the country to look for work. Passing each other on the tracks and finding nothing when they got to their destination.

I thought the Depression would never end. . . .

I was on a train from Baton Rouge to Denham Springs, Louisiana, going to look for work in the fields. I rode in a boxcar behind the coaches. The train was stopped at a small station along the route. I saw some people climb aboard to talk to the conductor.

After a time they left the coaches and came to the boxcar, where they looked me over real good.

"He'll have to get off," I heard the conductor say.

I asked why they wanted me off the train.

They told me that a white woman had been raped near Denham Springs. They said I fit the description, my color, my height, the way I was dressed. But they figured that I was innocent. I was in the boxcar traveling from Baton Rouge when the woman was raped. I couldn't be going and coming back at the same time.

At Denham Springs they would've ignored this. They would've taken me and lynched me.

I got homesick many nights as I lay in the total darkness of a big empty barn. Sometimes I lay crying, but then I would see myself and say, "I will go on."

I was motivated by poverty. I wanted to overcome it and do better in life. I had no education, no money, no home but I had common sense. I never reached for something that was too high for me nor did I stoop to something that was so low it would drag me down.

That's what kept me going – I wanted to do better so that I could go back and help my parents and my little sister and brother.

Source: Errol Lincoln Uys, *Riding the Rails: Teenagers on the Move During the Great Depression* (London: Routledge, 2003), pp. 131–2, 133–6.

2 Ann Marie Low, Farming in the Dust Bowl, 1930–2

America's rural districts faced economic hardships long before the Great Depression. Farmers purchased additional land and modern farm machinery during World War I to capitalize on high agricultural prices. Their strategy produced huge debts and, at least for a few years, spectacular profits. Declining crop prices in the 1920s left most farmers unable to repay their loans. A bad situation turned worse as teetering banks repossessed failing farms during the Depression. Decades of overgrazing, overplowing, and poor water management rendered soil vulnerable to drought. When the rain stopped falling in 1930, the earth, stripped of the native grasses that bound it together, literally blew away in the breeze. Black clouds of dust rolled eastward across the prairie. Families stuffed wet towels under doors in a vain attempt to keep out the storms. Dust stung the eyes, clogged the nostrils, and invaded the lungs. A lifetime's work could blow away in a few minutes. With nothing to keep them on the land, about 3.5 million former plains farmers joined Clarence Lee and other teenage hobos wandering the country in search of work and a new home. Americans gave them the generic label of "Okies."

Ann Marie Low lived on her father's farm in North Dakota, near the northern edge of the so-called Dust Bowl. Here, she describes life on the land, the family's economic woes, and the family strains that accompanied hard times.

What problems haunted the Lows? Why do you think they stayed on their farm? How did the depression affect the Lows economically and psychologically?

June 30, 1931, Tuesday

It is so hot! Dad's flax just cooked in the ground. It is all gone. Fields and pastures are burned brown.

The heat deaths in the country total 1,231. I mean humans. Lord only knows how many animals have died. Scotts recently lost their dog and a cow to the heat. Cattle are starving all over the state, and there is no market for them. Horses drop dead in the fields from the heat. The milk cows have so little to eat they are going dry. People pasture their grain fields and then plow them up to conserve moisture for next year – if moisture comes. This is our third year of drouth, and in a severe depression.

If good rains don't come soon, the Big Pasture will last only until August. Then the cattle must go to market or starve, and they are not worth shipping.

The turkeys have done fine, but it is so hot the hens I set for baby chicks have just quit setting. There are only 130 baby chicks.

This afternoon, by the time I finished ironing, I had no pep left and lay on the bed in Bud's room watching Dad and Bud cultivate in the heat and dust. It made me cool to think how much hotter they were.

July 25, 1931, Saturday

This was a typical day. Up at 5:00 to go a mile for the cows and milk them. Fed and watered the chickens and turkeys. Separated the milk. Fixed a pancake breakfast for the men and fed the hogs and calves. Washed the dishes and separator, baked and frosted a cake, and put a pudding in the oven. A bull got loose and was attacking the trees in Dad's shelterbelt. Got him back in and scraped the burned edges off the pudding. Rode Piute to the cornfield for Bud to use checking the yearlings. It isn't that Bud doesn't trust me, but he just feels better if he can ride over and check on the yearlings, especially his, himself. I understand. I cultivated corn while he did that and then rode Piute to the Big Pasture. . . .

Nothing has been said – nothing ever is in this family – but I notice my witty, happy-hearted, fun-loving brother doesn't joke much lately. He is mourning about Isabelle.

Five years ago Dad started giving Bud his choice of one of the heifer calves each year, and has laughed that Bud always picks the best. The idea was to give Bud a start on his own herd of breeding stock, plus some steers to sell for college expenses.

Five years ago Bud picked the best calf and asked Dad, "Isn't she a good one?"

"She's a belle."

Bud threw his arms around the calf's neck and said, "Oh, you Isabelle!"

We don't name beef cattle or make pets of them. That one, however, was always called Isabelle and was Bud's pet.

Isabelle produced two good calves. Drouth, heat, and pasture shortages have been hard on the cattle. Whether that was the cause or not, I do not know, but Isabelle did not get with calf in time to calve last spring. She was due in late summer. Because she hadn't calved and seemed weak, we didn't take her to the Big Pasture. As time went on she weakened too much to graze or go to water here on the home place.

Bud and I did our best. We carried water and hay to her and went out with hand sickles to cut grass where we could find it so that she would have something green. When she refused even grain, I ground the grain in Mama's kitchen food grinder, soaked it with water, and made a mash she would nibble on.

Nothing worked. The day came when Isabelle could not eat or rise to her feet.

"Dad, is there anything you can do?"

"I'm sorry, Son."

There were no words or tears. Bud just went into the house and got his gun. Somehow, to me, the look on his face when he shot Isabelle stood for this whole tragedy of a land laid waste, a way of life destroyed, and a boy's long struggle ending in despair.

November 1, 1931, Sunday

Winter is coming. As I brought the cows in last night the sunset was a gold splash in the sky with cobwebs of southbound flights of ducks traced against it.

Dad is feeling discouraged. The price of butterfat has dropped 6¢ a pound. The price for No. I turkeys is only $4.00. That means $125.00 less in the money we had counted on to see us through until next fall. But the price of wheat is going up. Yesterday Dad went to Frank Gatlin's to borrow some wagons for threshing. Frank, still in bed, stuck his head out from under the covers and said, "Wheat sold at a dollar a bushel in Chicago yesterday. I've got 2,500 bushels of wheat stored on this place – and $11,000 worth of debts."

He pulled the covers over his head again.

June 14, 1932

Friday a cloudburst washed out the flax. Darn it! Flax is a good price and every year something happens to it.

Saturday evening Lyle asked me to go to the dance with him. I had been on the run all day and was too tired. He took Ethel.

Monday Dad was out in the potato field knocking potato bugs off the plants into a pail. He was going to kill them by pouring kerosene over them. When a sudden hailstorm came up, he set the pail down in the barnyard so he could help with the terrified horses. A horse kicked the bucket over. Several thousand of Dad's little jewels went back to the potato field.

April 25, 1934, Wednesday

Last weekend was the worst dust storm we ever had. We've been having quite a bit of blowing dirt every year since the drouth started, not only here, but all over the Great Plains. Many days this spring the air is just full of dirt coming, literally, for hundreds of miles. It sifts into everything. After we wash the dishes and put them away, so much dust sifts into the cupboards we must wash them again before the next meal. Clothes in the closets are covered with dust.

Last weekend no one was taking an automobile out for fear of ruining the motor. I rode Roany to Frank's place to return a gear. To find my way I had to ride right beside the fence, scarcely able to see from one fence post to the next.

Newspapers say the deaths of many babies and old people are attributed to breathing in so much dirt.

May 7, 1934, Monday

The dirt is still blowing. Last weekend Bud and I helped with the cattle and had fun gathering weeds. Weeds give us greens for salad long before anything in the garden is ready. We use dandelions, lamb's quarter, and sheep sorrel,

I like sheep sorrel best. Also, the leaves of sheep sorrel, pounded and boiled down to a paste, make a good salve.

Still no job. I'm trying to persuade Dad I should apply for rural school #3 out here where we went to school. I don't see a chance of getting a job in a high school when so many experienced teachers are out of work.

He argues that the pay is only $60.00 a month out here, while even in a grade school in town I might get $75.00. Extra expenses in town would probably eat up that extra $15.00. Miss Eston, the practice teaching supervisor, told me her salary has been cut to $75.00 after all the years she has been teaching in Jamestown. She wants to get married. School boards will not hire married women teachers in these hard times because they have husbands to support them. Her fiancé is the sole support of his widowed mother and can't support a wife, too. So she is just stuck in her job, hoping she won't get another salary cut because she can scarcely live on what she makes and dress the way she is expected to.

Dad argues the patrons always stir up so much trouble for a teacher at #3 some teachers have quit in mid-term. The teacher is also the janitor, so the hours are long.

I figure I can handle the work, kids, and patrons. My argument is that by teaching here I can work for my room and board at home, would not need new clothes, and so could send most of my pay to Ethel and Bud.

Source: Ann Marie Low, *Dust Bowl Diary* (Lincoln: University of Nebraska Press, 1984), pp. 49–52, 59–60, 67, 95–6.

3   John L. Spivak, Migrant Farm Workers, 1934

The Joad family from Steinbeck's Grapes of Wrath *abandoned their windswept Oklahoma farm to seek the American dream in the lush valleys of California. Like many of their real-life counterparts, they arrived to find the dream turned into a nightmare. Corporate farmers paid migrant pickers a pittance for long days of backbreaking labor. Although Steinbeck's famous novel captured many nuances of migrant life, it ignored the fact that the majority of farm workers were either Mexican or Filipino. These unfortunates lay for the most part beyond the help of New Dealers in Washington, and local unionization efforts produced minimal gains. In this article from the communist journal* New Masses, *author John L. Spivak uses a common Depression-era literary device, the letter to Franklin Roosevelt, to raise awareness of the horrible conditions these workers endured. Spivak casts his subjects as not just poor, but also as exiles from the national community. His references to "scarlet fever" echo Nathaniel Hawthorne's*

Scarlet Letter, *appropriating the earlier writer's symbol of unjust exclusion from a hypocritical society to build sympathy for his own teenage protagonist.*

What are the goals of this article? What did Spivak hope to achieve? What are the unnamed girl's goals? What barriers stand between her and her dreams?

A Letter from America

To President Roosevelt

Fresno, Calif.

Dear Mr. President:

I don't suppose you will ever see this but I am writing to you to keep a promise I made to a little fifteen-year-old Mexican girl. . . .

I cannot give you her name because when I told her I would write to you for her she became frightened and pleaded with me not to mention her name. She was afraid maybe you'd write the boss and her family would be denied the privilege of working in the fields all day for thirty-five cents. She said it was all right, so I'll tell you how to find her.

Just take the main highway from Fresno, Calif., to Mendota which is about thirty miles away and turn west at Mendota for about four miles. You can't miss it because you'll see a big sign "Land of Milk and Honey." When you've passed this sign you'll see against the horizon a cluster of houses and when you come to the sign "Hotchkiss Ranch – Cotton Pickers Wanted" turn up the side road a few hundred yards beyond the comfortable farm house with its barns and cotton shelters. There's a row of fifteen outhouses along the road. That is where the migratory workers and this little girl live, Mr. President.

There are two more outhouses a little away from these and those are the ones actually used for outhouses. You can tell that by the odor and the swarms of flies that hover around these two especially. This is a typical migratory workers' camp, only some have five outhouses for the workers and some have thirty. It depends upon the size of the farm.

You'll recognize a migratory workers' camp because each outhouse – "homes" they call them out here – is made of plain wooden boards, dried by years of tropical sun.

The little girl lives in the third house from the front as you approach. You can't miss it. It has a large sign: SCARLET FEVER.

But don't worry about that because the health authorities here are not worrying. They just tacked up the sign on this outhouse door and on that one there near the end of the row and went away. They didn't tell anyone to be careful about a contagious disease because that might have had the camp quarantined and the whole crop lost to the farmer, for all the cotton pickers and their children have been in that outhouse. I don't imagine it's very dangerous though for only two more children have caught it. If it had been dangerous I'm sure the health authorities would have warned them.

In this outhouse where a baby girl has scarlet fever you'll find an iron bedstead. That's where the baby sleeps, the one that's tossing around in fever while the mother tries to shoo the flies away. That's the only bed and it's one of the five in the whole camp, so you can't miss it. The other six in this family sleep on the floor huddled together; father, mother, two grown brothers, a little brother and the fifteen-year-old girl. They sleep like most everybody else in the camp: on the floor.

That barrel and rusty milk can in the corner of the room where everybody sleeps on the floor holds the water they bring from Mendota to cool the child's fever. It is four miles to Mendota and four miles back and eight miles costs a little for gas so they have to be very sparing with the water. That's why they all look so dirty – it's not because they don't like to wash. It's because it costs too much to get water – water needed for cooking and drinking. You can't waste water just washing yourself when it costs so much to get. After all, when you make thirty-five cents for a full day's work and spend some of that for gas to get water it leaves you that much less for food. . . .

Perhaps I had better tell you exactly how I found her and what we talked about so you can understand just what she wants. It would be a big favor, she said, and she would be very grateful.

She doesn't mind picking cotton bolls for thirty-five cents a day and she doesn't mind the filth and dirt and starvation but she is worried about that electric light in the shack. You noticed it, didn't you? The one with the dusty bulb right in the middle of the outhouse they live in? Well, you have to pay twenty-five cents a week if you want to use that electric light and twenty-five cents is a lot of money when you get only thirty-five cents a day and you need that twenty-five cents for food and for gas for the car so you can go get water.

It's not that she wants the light at night. She and her family get along without it but you see they've discovered that it's awfully hard to tend the sick baby in the darkness. And it's always dark when the baby seems to cry the most. And in addition, this little girl is worried about herself. She is going to have a baby and suppose it comes at night and there is no light? She is going to have a baby in this little outhouse where her mother and father and brothers live, this little outhouse with the sign SCARLET FEVER over its door.

What she wanted to ask you is if you could possibly get in touch with somebody and have them not charge them twenty-five cents for the use of the electric light – especially when somebody's sick or expecting a baby. It's not so bad when you're well, but it's awfully hard when you have a little sick sister tossing and crying and you yourself are expecting a baby. . . .

But I started to tell you what we talked about and here I've gone telling you what she wanted me to write. You see, when I walked out in the field there was this little girl dragging a huge sack along the furrow, and stuffing the brown bolls into it. She looked so tired, so weary and then I noticed that she was with child.

"How old are you?" I asked.

She looked up and smiled pleasantly.

"Fifteen."

"Working in the fields long?"

"Uh-uh."

"How old were you when you started?"

She shrugged shoulders. "Dunno. Maybe eight. Maybe nine. I dunno."

"What do you make a day?"

"Sometimes in first picking dollar and a half. We get seventy-five cents a hundred. Used to get sixty cents but red agitators got us fifteen cents raise. But for third picking get only forty cents a hundred and there ain't so much to pick."

You may be interested in her phrase "red agitators." That's what the Communists were called here by the newspapers, so now everybody calls a Communist a "red agitator." This little girl didn't know what a "red agitator" was; she knew only that "red agitators" got them a raise of fifteen cents on the hundred pounds by organizing them and calling a strike. . . .

Nobody else seemed to care for them, nobody ever tried to organize them until the "red agitators" came. Business men and bankers and farmers are terrified by "red agitators"; you understand, of course, why when you read this letter that the little girl wanted me to write you.

"Last year when 'red agitators' make strike in Tulare and get seventy-five cents a hundred so we get seventy-five cents here, too," she added laughing.

Her father, a tall, dark-skinned man with a week's growth of black beard saw me talking to her and came over.

"Somet'ing wrong, eh?" he asked.

"No. Nothing wrong. Just talking to your daughter. I want to find out how much you people make a week."

A slow smile spread over his features.

"We make nodding," he said definitely.

"How much?"

"Me, my wife, my girl here. Last week we work from Monday to Thursday night and make $2.50 – all of us."

"Your daughter is only fifteen. I thought there was a law against child labor."

He shrugged his shoulders. . . .

"Now that you've finished picking these acres what do you do?"

"Go to peas field. Everybody go in car or truck. We take everything except house. We get nodding but house when we come. When finished peas fields we come back for grapes." . . .

"Well, I got to go back pick bolls." He said something to the girl in Spanish. She flushed and started picking again.

"My father he say better work," she said.

"Yes; well, you go ahead and work while I walk alongside and talk to you. Are you married?"

She flushed again and shook her head.

"No. No marry."

"Looks like things are not so good for you people, eh?"

"Oh, they awright. Things gettin' better – everybody say. The President, he take care of poor people."

"Is he taking care of you?"

"No, sir. Not yet. Things very bad for us. But he got lots to do and he never hear about cotton pickers. I wanted write and tell him hurry up because I going to have a baby and things very bad for us. He do something for poor people if he know how things very bad, eh?"

"Why didn't you write to him, then?"

She blushed again.

"No got stamp."

"Oh," I said, "I'll give you a stamp."

"Thank you but no can write."

"Sure, you go ahead. The President will be glad to hear from you."

"No can write," she repeated. "No go school; work in fields all the time."

"If you'll tell me what you want to write, I'll do it for you."

She looked at me with a swift smile and giggled.

I took out a pencil and some paper and asked her name. A look of terror spread over her face.

"No! No! No write the President!" she begged.

"Why not? Didn't you want to write to him?"

"No! No! I just talk. Just talk."

"What are you afraid of?"

"No write the President, Mister, please." She straightened up and looked at me pleadingly. "If you write for me to the President my father get in trouble. Maybe the President get mad and my father, he no get no more work."

"I don't think so," I assured her. "But if you don't want me to tell who you are I can write to him and tell him about it without mentioning your name."

She looked up with a sudden hope.

"You do that?"

"Sure. I don't have to give your name. I'll just say a little Mexican girl in a cotton field four miles from Mendota."

She looked earnestly at me for a moment.

"Please, you write the President. Tell him my baby is coming," she said in a low tone. "I dunno when the baby come. Maybe at night and we got no light. Please, you tell the President things very bad. We no make maybe nothing. My little sister she sick and if baby come I no can have bed. I got to have baby on floor and if it come in night how I have baby?"

I nodded, unable to speak.

"You please tell the President maybe he tell boss here not charge us twenty-five cents a week for electric light so I can have my baby."

"I'll tell him exactly what you said," I promised.

"You no fool me?"

"No, I'm not fooling you, I promise."

Source: John L. Spivak, "A Letter from America to President Roosevelt," *New Masses* 10 (March 20, 1934): 9–10, 11.

4 Howard Kester, The Southern Tenant Farmers Union's "Ceremony of the Land," 1937

Many southern agriculturalists labored under the sharecropping system, whereby farmers rented small plots from landlords in exchange for a share of their produce. Landlords rigged the system in their own favor, often taking such a huge share that farmers received almost nothing for their toil. Founded in 1934 in Tyronza, Arkansas, the Southern Tenant Farmers Union (STFU) attempted to soften this unjust system. The biracial union infused members with a sense of pride as it encouraged them to view other farmers as brothers and sisters united in a noble cause. Local authorities responded with intimidation, eviction, and violence. STFU members often met in secret to evade armed deputies bent on upholding plantation owners' interests. As this document from the union's 1937 national convention in Muskogee, Oklahoma suggests, union leaders hoped to forge closer ties between scattered local chapters. STFU organizer Howard Kester penned a special "ceremony of the land" that served as the emotional high point of the proceedings. Delegates from around the farm belt joined in a poignant ritual that celebrated their collective strength while acknowledging their common woes.

What problems did STFU members face? Who did they blame for these problems? How did delegates hope to solve their problems?

READER:

> Bowed by the weight of centuries he leans
> Upon his hoe and gazes on the ground,
> The emptiness of ages in his face,
> And on his back the burden of the world.

AUDIENCE:

> Who made him dead to rapture and despair . . .
> Stolid and stunned, a brother to the ox?

READER:

> In Thy infinite wisdom and mercy, Thou O God,
> didst give unto Thy children "a good land; a land of
> brooks and waters that spring out of the valleys and
> hills; a land of wheat and barley, of vines and fig
> trees and pomegranates; a land of olive oil and honey"
> where on Thy children might live in freedom and security
> from want and injustice.

AUDIENCE:

> Thou didst establish the land and its fruit for all the
> people and Thou didst call us to be the Keepers of Thy
> good earth. We remember the ancient promise, "Here thou
> shall eat bread without scarceness; thou shalt not lack anything."

READER:

> What we lack, O God, is not of Thy doing but of man's. In
> man's greed for gold, he had destroyed the fruitfulness of the
> earth. In his lust for power and dominion he has brought misery
> upon us all. The land cries out against those who waste it. Thy
> children cry out against those who abuse and oppress them.

AUDIENCE:

> Greed has eaten up the land and poverty has swallowed the people.

READER:

> If the land is to be saved, men will have to bless it with
> intelligent labor and love.

AUDIENCE:

> If the land is to be saved only free men established in
> freedom and justice can save it.

READER:

> We would be free to till the soil as stewards of the Eternal God.
> We would be His tenants and not the tenants of other men.
> We would be free to build a brotherhood of the tillers of the soil.
> To live in trust upon it and amongst all those who till it.

AUDIENCE:

> We would be free to build a new kind of world – a world that
> Knows no hunger, no nakedness, no hate, no War.

READER:

> We have given freely of our labor. Our talents have been put to work for
> the good of humankind around the world. But of the good things of life,
> we have not shared. We have been oppressed by the strong and powerful.
> We have lived in the midst of plenty but we have often gone hungry. By
> sweat and tears we have labored to make America great, free and noble.

AUDIENCE:

> As America struggles to free the world from tyranny and slavery she will
> not forget us.

READER:

> We have been patient and long suffering but the promised day of
> freedom is at hand. When peace comes, it will come to our homes and
> firesides for America is awake – awake to the meaning of freedom of
> free men on free soil.

AUDIENCE:

> We covet no man's freedom, no man's fields, no man's houses or barns,
> only our share of the Eternal's earth.

READER:

> The land is the common heritage of the people.

AUDIENCE:

> The land shall not be sold in perpetuity.

READER:

> Let justice roll down as waters and righteousness as a mighty stream.

AUDIENCE:

> We face the future with all those who earn their bread by
> the sweat of their brow, who hate tyranny and oppression
> and who love justice, truth, freedom and beauty.

READER:

> By struggling eternally for one another, we shall dry up the wells of
> despair and hopelessness and bring healing to the land and its people.

AUDIENCE:

> To the disinherited belongs the future.

READER:

> Freedom, democracy; a free people, a free land. This is our dream.

AUDIENCE:

> The ancient promises will be fulfilled for America will not
> forget her children.

READER:

> Delegates to this convention of landless farmers, you may now
> march one by one to receive a portion of this soil brought by
> your brother delegates from the states in which they struggle
> for a better life. The soil is the nation's greatest resource.
> It is the basis of all life. When the soil is wasted, the people
> perish and the nation is destroyed. The soil is precious to us
> for by it we live. We have not lived well because we have not
> been at liberty to care for the soil as we desire: because we
> have not been free men, but tenants of another. America will be
> strengthened and made strong as she overcomes the evils of tenancy
> and establishes her tenants on land of their own. Take this earth
> as a symbol of the new day of freedom which is about to dawn for
> all men who till the soil. Take it as a symbol of our united
> struggle for freedom, peace and plenty on the land – in the cities
> throughout the world among all the sons and daughters of men.

CLOSING

READER:

> By means of this ceremony, we once again dedicate ourselves
> to the great struggle for freedom now going on throughout
> the world. As men are liberated from slavery elsewhere, let
> us be liberated from the evils of tenancy – of being farmers
> without land and homes and the rights of free men.

AUDIENCE:

> Land to the landless.

READER:

> The land is the common heritage of all.

ALL:

> Speed now the day when the plains and hills and all the
> wealth thereof shall be the people's own and free men shall
> not live as tenants of men on the earth which Thou hast
> given to all. Enable us humble and reverently, with clean
> hands and hearts to prepare ourselves for the day when we
> shall be Thy tenants alone and help us become faithful
> keepers of one another and of Thy good earth – our homes.

Source: Howard Kester, "Ceremony of the Land," *Papers of the Southern Tenant Farmers Union*, reel 4.

Discussion questions

1 What problems did rural Americans face during the 1930s?
2 How did Americans respond to the Depression?
3 If the Depression occurred today, how do you think Americans would respond? How would our actions compare with what you read in this chapter?

Chapter 10   The New Deal: Critics and Limitations

1   James P. Cannon, In Support of Unionization, 1934

Republican and Democratic administrations alike had long insisted that unions were responsible for spreading radical political ideologies, coerced workers into acting against their best interests, and deprived businessmen of the right to operate with minimal interference. Franklin Roosevelt rejected such animosity toward labor but saw putting Americans to work as a far higher priority than getting them into unions.

Union membership had been climbing since the Crash, and the June 1933 National Industrial Recovery Act gave labor an unexpected boost. Section 7(a) of the law guaranteed the right of workers to collective bargaining through a union. A burst of organization followed, and unions grew more aggressive in pursuing better lives for their members. Massive strikes rocked the United States during summer 1934. National Guardsmen clashed with protesters in Toledo, company-hired thugs brutalized agricultural workers in California's Imperial Valley, and San Francisco longshoremen persuaded sympathizers to declare a general work stoppage throughout the city. A wave of labor actions in Minnesota's Twin Cities prompted a violent response from the area's entrenched interests. Labor advocate James P. Cannon penned the following appeal in the midst of that turmoil.

According to Cannon, what are the benefits of unionization? How convincing would his arguments be to a Depression-era worker? Is Cannon a "radical"?

America Between the Wars, 1919–1941: A Documentary Reader, First Edition.
Edited by David Welky. Editorial material and organization © 2012 John Wiley & Sons, Inc.
Published 2012 by John Wiley & Sons, Inc.

The victory of unionism in our industry has already been won. In two great battles which stirred the whole country – first in the May strike and then in the strike just concluded – the drivers, helpers and inside workers of Minneapolis showed their determination to have a union of their own, free from the influence or coercion of the employers. Now there is to be an election to see if the workers really meant it. Very well. We shall have the election and go through the formality. Our big task now is to get ready for it, and to roll up such an overwhelming vote for the union that the question cannot be raised again.

There hasn't been a free and honest election held anywhere to our knowledge that did not result in a majority of the workers voting for a union of their own. . . .

The awakening workers of America, in every trade and industry, are moved by one common, overpowering impulse which can be expressed in a single word: UNIONISM! Every intelligent worker understands that that is the first step on the road to a better and freer life. "In almost every case", says *Labor*, "the paramount issue is the right of the workers to organize". Once that is accomplished, the worker, weak and helpless as an individual, becomes strong and independent. He has the confidence to demand improved conditions and better wages. And – united with his fellow workers – he has the strength to get them.

And that is just the point. In clinging to the idea of unionism, and fighting so doggedly for it, the workers are inspired by the thought of *what the union means*!

The union means bread and butter. The union is the weapon by which the workers wrest better wages from the profit-mad bosses. It means more and better food for the workingman's kids and a decent dress for his wife to wear. It means a few nickels in his own pocket to pay for a glass of beer or two if he feels that way. In fighting for a union, the worker in reality is fighting to improve his standard of life and to give his family a chance to live like human beings.

The union means protection and a certain degree of security in employment. Once a strong union appears on the scene the arbitrary powers of the employers over the lives of the workers are limited. The old system of hiring and firing according to the whim of the bosses gives way to seniority rights. The union is a protection to the individual worker against discrimination. In fighting for a union the worker is fighting for certain rights of "citizenship" in industry. He is fighting for the right to have something to say about his job. Without a union this is impossible.

The union means the beginning of independence. The unorganized worker has no rights whatever which the boss is obliged to respect. No matter how proud and sensitive the individual may be, he has to take what is offered and keep his mouth shut. Long hours, miserable wages, all kinds of abuse – the worker has to put up with all of that and has no comeback, no means of redress. The unorganized worker is as helpless as a slave.

The union man stands up on his feet and looks the world in the face. He has something behind him, a power to which he can appeal. The individual "bargain" between the worker and the boss, in which the worker is licked before he starts, is replaced by "collective bargaining" when the union is organized. That doesn't apply only to the question of wages. The union is the "collective" representative of the worker in any dispute he may have with the employer. Feeling that strength behind him, the worker gets more confidence in himself, more self respect, more of the sense of human dignity that befits a useful and productive member of society.

It is because the union means so much in the daily life of the workers that the movement for unionism is rising like a tidal wave. The workers want a new life and a better one, and the first step on this path is organization. . . .

Make Minneapolis a Union Town!

Source: James P. Cannon, "What the Union Means," *Organizer Daily Strike Bulletin*, August 23, 1934, in James P. Cannon, *Notebook of an Agitator* (Pathfinder Press, 1993). Copyright © 1958, 1973, 1993, by Pathfinder Press.

2 Huey Long, "Every Man a King," 1934

FDR's critics came from across the political spectrum. Dr. Francis Townsend attacked from the left with his call for monthly pensions to senior citizens, an idea later incorporated into the Social Security program. "Radio Priest" Charles Coughlin hit from the right as he combined a fascist-style cult of personality with paranoid isolationism and, eventually, rabid anti-Semitism. Senator Huey Long of Louisiana was the most colorful and politically dangerous of FDR's enemies. Known for his garish outfits and bombastic oratory, Long was a crafty political operator who seized control of Louisiana's state government before taking his show to the capital in 1933 (he won election to the Senate in 1930 but refused to step down as governor for over two years). Like FDR, Long used the radio to get his message directly to the people. His thick accent seeped through speakers like a mint julep. "Gowan and git yer neighbors," Long advised listeners. "I ain't gonna say nothin' important 'til ya'll git back." Long's naïve persona concealed an instinctive ability to rouse disaffected elements of the electorate. Although his proposals often made no economic sense and changed from speech to speech, he developed enough of a national following that FDR perceived him as a rival for the presidency, or at least as someone who could tip the 1936 election to the Republicans should he run as an independent. Roosevelt's aristocratic mother referred to Long as "that awful man."

Long jettisoned his initial support for Roosevelt partly because he found the president's recovery measures too timid and partly to further his own ambitions. He launched the Share Our Wealth Society in 1934 as a vehicle for his lofty dreams. The speech below articulates his political philosophy and, at least on this night, his platform. Around 5 million people joined Share Our Wealth clubs by spring 1935, the same year an assassin cut down Huey Long. His national network of clubs collapsed soon after.

How does Long craft his speech to appeal to his predominantly working-class and ill-educated followers? Who does he say is to blame for America's problems? What course of action does Long recommend? What is his attitude toward Franklin Roosevelt? Why does he see the New Deal as ineffective?

. . . I contend, my friends, that we have no difficult problem to solve in America, and that is the view of nearly everyone with whom I have discussed the matter here in Washington and elsewhere throughout the United States – that we have no very difficult problem to solve.

It is not the difficulty of the problem which we have; it is the fact that the rich people of this country – and by rich people I mean the super-rich – will not allow us to solve the problems, or rather the one little problem that is afflicting this country, because in order to cure all of our woes it is necessary to scale down the big fortunes, that we may scatter the wealth to be shared by all of the people. . . .

We have everything here that we need, except that we have neglected the fundamentals upon which the American government was principally predicated.

How many of you remember the first thing that the Declaration of Independence said? It said, "We hold these truths to be self-evident, that there are certain inalienable rights for the people, and among them are life, liberty, and the pursuit of happiness"; and it said, further, "We hold the view that all men are created equal."

Now, what did they mean by that? Did they mean, my friends, to say that all men were created equal and that that meant that any one man was born to inherit $10 billion and that another child was to be born to inherit nothing?

Did that mean, my friends, that someone would come into this world without having had an opportunity, of course, to have hit one lick of work, should be born with more than it and all of its children and children's children could ever dispose of, but that another one would have to be born into a life of starvation? . . .

Now, my friends, if you were off on an island where there were one hundred lunches, you could not let one man eat up the hundred lunches, or take the hundred lunches and not let anybody else eat any of them. If you did, there would not be anything else for the balance of the people to consume.

So, we have in America today, my friends, a condition by which about ten men dominate the means of activity in at least 85 percent of the activities that you own. They either own directly everything or they have got some kind of mortgage on it, with a very small percentage to be excepted. They own the banks, they own the steel mills, they own the railroads, they own the bonds, they own the mortgages, they own the stores, and they have chained the country from one end to the other until there is not any kind of business that a small, independent man could go into today and make a living, and there is not any kind of business that an independent man can go into and make any money to buy an automobile with; and they have finally and gradually and steadily eliminated everybody from the fields in which there is a living to be made, and still they have got little enough sense to think they ought to be able to get more business out of it anyway.

If you reduce a man to the point where he is starving to death and bleeding and dying, how do you expect that man to get hold of any money to spend with you? It is not possible.

Then, ladies and gentlemen, how do you expect people to live, when the wherewith cannot be had by the people? . . .

Both of these men, Mr. Hoover and Mr. Roosevelt, came out and said there had to be a decentralization of wealth, but neither one of them did anything about it. But, nevertheless, they recognized the principle. The fact that neither one of them ever did anything about it is their own problem that I am not undertaking to criticize; but had Mr. Hoover carried out what he says ought to be done, he would be retiring from the president's office, very probably three years from now, instead of one year ago; and had Mr. Roosevelt proceeded along the lines that he stated were necessary for the decentralization of wealth, he would have gone, my friends, a long way already, and within a few months he would have probably reached a solution of all of the problems that afflict this country today.

But I wish to warn you now that nothing that has been done up to this date has taken one dime away from these big fortune holders; they own just as much as they did, and probably a little bit more; they hold just as many of the debts of the common people as they ever held, and probably a little bit more; and unless we, my friends, are going to give the people of this country a fair shake of the dice, by which they will all get something out of the funds of this land, there is not a chance on the topside of this God's eternal earth by which we can rescue this country and rescue the people of this country. . . .

Now we have organized a society, and we call it "Share Our Wealth Society," a society with the motto "every man a king."

Every man a king, so there would be no such thing as a man or woman who did not have the necessities of life, who would not be dependent upon the whims and caprices and *ipse dixit* of the financial martyrs for a living. What do we propose by this society? We propose to limit the wealth of big men in the country. There is an average of $15,000 in wealth to every family in America. That is right here today.

We do not propose to divide it up equally. We do not propose a division of wealth, but we propose to limit poverty that we will allow to be inflicted upon any man's family. We will not say we are going to try to guarantee any equality, or $15,000 to families. No; but we do say that one third of the average is low enough for any one family to hold, that there should be a guaranty of a family wealth of around $5,000; enough for a home, an automobile, a radio, and the ordinary conveniences, and the opportunity to educate their children; a fair share of the income of this land thereafter to that family so there will be no such thing as merely the select to have those things, and so there will be no such thing as a family living in poverty and distress.

We have to limit fortunes. Our present plan is that we will allow no one man to own more than $50 million. We think that with that limit we will be able to carry out the balance of the program. It may be necessary that we limit it to less than $50 million. It may be necessary, in working out of the plans, that no man's fortune would be more than $10 million or $15 million. But be that as it may, it will still be more than any one man, or any one man and his children and their children, will be able to spend in their lifetimes; and it is not necessary or reasonable to have wealth piled up beyond that point where we cannot prevent poverty among the masses.

Another thing we propose is old-age pension of $30 a month for everyone that is sixty years old. Now, we do not give this pension to a man making $1,000 a year, and we do not give it to him if he has $10,000 in property, but outside of that we do.

We will limit hours of work. There is not any necessity of having overproduction. I think all you have got to do, ladies and gentlemen, is just limit the hours of work to such an extent as people will work only so long as is necessary to produce enough for all of the people to have what they need. Why, ladies and gentlemen, let us say that all of these labor-saving devices reduce hours down to where you do not have to work but four hours a day; that is enough for these people, and then praise be the name of the Lord, if it gets that good. . . .

Now that I have but a minute left, I want to say that I suppose my family is listening in on the radio in New Orleans, and I will say to my wife and three children that I am entirely well and hope to be home before many more days, and I hope they have listened to my speech tonight, and I wish them and all of their neighbors and friends everything good that may be had.

I thank you, my friends, for your kind attention, and I hope you will enroll with us, take care of your own work in the work of this government, and share or help in our Share Our Wealth Society.

Source: US Congress, Senate, *Congressional Record*, 73rd Cong., 2nd sess., pp. 3450–3.

3 Raymond E. Click to Franklin Roosevelt, The New Deal Means Socialism, 1935

Recent years have seen a revival of the same kinds of attacks once heaped on Franklin Roosevelt. Then as now, efforts to stabilize a struggling economy with federal dollars, regulate the financial sector, and strengthen the social safety net provoked charges of reckless government spending and raised fears of socialism or even dictatorship.

President Roosevelt spent little time worrying about conservative critics, who nevertheless comprised a large constituency in an America that still invested in the laissez-faire ideology of self help and small government. Many feared that FDR's liberalism would create a country of weak-hearted people dependent on government handouts. Roosevelt himself worried that job-relief programs might foster dependency but felt a political, economic, and moral need to put the unemployed back to work. His April 28, 1935 fireside chat highlighted the new Works Progress Administration (WPA), the largest of the New Deal job programs, while promoting two bills currently before Congress: the Social Security Act, and the Wagner Act, a proposal to continue federal support for unions made necessary after the Supreme Court ruled the National Industrial Recovery Act unconstitutional. As always, his address prompted responses from across the United States. The following letter illustrates many of the fears his administration spawned.

What problems does Mr. Click have with Roosevelt and his administration? What are the sources of those problems? Are his charges baseless or well grounded? What do you infer about Mr. Click's social status? What impact do you think that had on his opinions?

Sir:

Your latest piece of glorified propaganda – miscalled fireside chats – was disheartening and sickening. I must confess, I am ashamed that I once had some faith in you and your New Deal.

Prosperity? How you mock us. There can never be any true prosperity under your administration. Nothing but a vast destruction of wealth and hope, – a degrading and demoralizing of our national character.

Why not be perfectly frank with your people just once, and admit that you are engaged in a subtle and gigantic effort to ruin the investing classes, big and little. Why not come out in the open, and declare your unalterable and all too evident purpose to usher in government ownership of all important businesses and a Socialist state.

For the hypocricy [sic] of the New Deal is revolting.

Raymond E. Click
Prospect, Ohio

Source: Lawrence W. Levine and Cornelia R. Levine, *The People and the President: America's Conversation with FDR* (Boston: Beacon Press, 2002), p. 137.

4 The *Saturday Evening Post* Attacks Intrusive Government, 1935

Franklin Roosevelt was a perfect subject for reporters and publishers. He was charismatic, pithy, and always making news. Like other Americans, journalists worried that the economic downturn might lead to revolution or national collapse. They wanted reform and stability as much as everyone else, and accordingly skewed their coverage in Roosevelt's favor during his initial months in office. Many editors and columnists eventually broke with the administration over labor legislation, Roosevelt's perceived internationalism, efforts to regulate business and the economy, and fears that the activist president was creating a dictatorship. Two-thirds of daily newspapers favored FDR's opponent in the 1936 election, Kansas governor Alf Landon. The magazine industry also turned against the New Deal, as this 1935 article from the Saturday Evening Post *shows. With 3 million subscribers, the* Post *was a mainstay of the middle class. It consistently portrayed a warm, comfortable America where good-hearted businessmen extolled the merits of hard work and individual effort. Its editorial pages denounced New Dealers as "crack pot theorists" working to destroy American ideals through "drastic and experimental" legislation. In this case, it is the proposed Social Security bill that threatens old-fashioned values, traditions, and finances.*

How does the Post characterize the Roosevelt administration? Why does the Post oppose Social Security? What does its position suggest about its readership?

It sometimes happens that the most valuable, indeed, the most fascinating reading comes to one in dull gray form. Take, for example, a paper-bound volume of 1141 pages which has lately come to hand from the world's largest publisher, the Government Printing Office. It contains the hearings before the Committee on Ways and Means of the House of Representatives on H. R. 4120, which is known as "a bill to alleviate the hazards of old age, unemployment, and dependency, to establish a social insurance board in the Department of Labor, to raise revenue, and for other purposes." A perusal of these hearings will afford a clearer conception of the high handed, steam-roller methods of government now being pursued than could be gained from all the speeches, articles and editorials extant.

Here is provision for a basic, permanent change in American policy. It is in no sense whatever emergency legislation, as its principal features would not become operative for a matter of years. The legislation provides window dressing in the way of Federal aid to the states in such desirable matters as public and child health work, but it also sets up a vast Government scheme of old-age pensions and unemployment compensation. No European nation has ever adopted all these forms of security or social insurance at one time. Each subject is important enough to deserve separate and lengthy considera-tion: lumping them together and driving them through simply minimizes the careful scrutiny which each deserves.

In addition, this legislation would impose colossal new tax burdens upon industry. During the first ten years alone, the aggregate taxation would be more than $17,000,000,000, the bulk of it being derived from new pay-roll taxes from employers. Even as soon as January 1, 1937, nearly a billion dollars in taxes would be expected from employers and employees with far larger annual totals a few years later.

It is a grave question whether these new pay-roll taxes – the constitution-ality of which incidentally, is doubtful – would not seriously retard recovery by forcing some industries to close down entirely, to discharge employees or at least to adopt labor-saving machinery in their place. Just how social security can be attained by such methods is a frank puzzle to plain people whose old-fashioned thinking makes it difficult for them to reconcile increasing burdens upon industry with increasing employment. . . .

At the present writing, this legislation gives no credit or consideration to pension and unemployment-compensation plans built up by private industries, the total of which is very large, covering at least two million work-ers. Employers who have provided and who continue such plans will be forced to pay the tax, even though their own plan is more generous than the Government's.

Returning now to the 1141 pages of testimony before the Ways and Means Committee on this particular piece of legislation, it is highly sugges-tive to note that out of more than a hundred witnesses only an insignificant fraction represented what might be called the taxpaying industrial interests.

The legislation provides potentially for the greatest additional revenue in our history – in a sense, it is the biggest of all revenue measures to date – and yet those who pay the taxes were hardly heard at all.

Indeed, a careful study of the lengthy list of witnesses does not even disclose that any life-insurance company, or the life-insurance industry as such, made an appearance. It would seem as if a committee of Congress could hardly whip a vast new Government insurance-and-pension system into shape without the openly expressed views of those in charge of the institution of life insurance. If the life-insurance executives and trustees approve of this enormous new experiment in a field so similar to their own, their millions of policyholders are entitled to know it. If, on the other hand, those in charge of these great fiduciary institutions fear the effect upon their great and sacred trusts of the wholly experimental departure, the policyholders would like to know that too.

The pathetic part of the whole affair is that the possibly well-intentioned, but hasty, bull headed and quite autocratic manner in which so much New Deal legislation has been forced through, may eventually set back really worth-while social reforms, including such as may be practicable in the face of social insurance itself.

Source: "Bullheaded Government," *Saturday Evening Post* 207 (May 18, 1935): 26.

5 Cartoons Denouncing the Court-Packing Plan, 1937

Critics who charged Franklin Roosevelt with either aspiring to become a dictator or paving the way for a future dictator grew louder as actual dictatorships gained strength in Germany and Italy. It was in this tense climate that FDR made one of his few political missteps. In early 1937, with almost no prior consultation with congressional leadership, he announced a plan to expand the Supreme Court by six seats, one for every justice over the age of 70. The court had long irritated the president as its conservative majority struck down the Agricultural Adjustment Act, the National Recovery Administration, and other New Deal mainstays. Roosevelt feared that "nine old men" (the justices had an average age of 71) might sabotage his entire agenda. Congress and the public interpreted FDR's move as a bid to pack the court with sympathetic justices. This constituted an attack on judicial independence and, in the eyes of many, marked a blatant grab for power. Roosevelt's plan went down in flames. Although the court later upheld many key New Deal laws, FDR's defeat symbolized the end of his dominance over an increasingly conservative Congress ill-disposed to rubber stamp his legislative agenda.

What messages do these cartoons convey? How do they present the president, the Congress, and the court?

Figure 10.1 Cartoon denouncing the Court-Packing Plan. Editorial cartoon published Feb. 10, 1937, in the Columbus (Ohio) Dispatch. Reprinted with permission.

THE HANDS OF DICTATORSHIP!

Figure 10.2 Cartoon denouncing the Court-Packing Plan.

Source: *Los Angeles Times,* February 6, 1937.

Figure 10.3 Cartoon denouncing the Court-Packing Plan.

Source: *New York Herald-Tribune*, March 22, 1937.

Discussion questions

1 According to these critics, in what ways did the New Deal go too far? In what ways did it not go far enough?
2 Which side makes a more persuasive case: those who want the New Deal to do more, or those who want it to do less?
3 According to FDR's critics, what problems did the New Deal have? How valid are those criticisms?

Chapter 11 People of Color in the Age of Roosevelt

1 Herman J. D. Carter, An Injustice at Scottsboro, 1933

*Miscarriages of justice were common in the segregated South, but
no incident of discrimination captured the nation's attention like the
infamous Scottsboro case. Authorities near Scottsboro, Alabama yanked
nine black youths from a train in March 1931 and accused them of raping
two white women. The boys, who ranged in age from 12 to 19, professed
their innocence. An all-white jury nevertheless sentenced eight of the nine
"Scottsboro boys" to death by electrocution. A mob waiting outside the
courthouse cheered when a band played "There'll be a Hot Time in the
Old Town Tonight." A series of retrials stretched out the case for years.
Sympathy for the boys grew with every stop along the legal trail.*

*"No state in this union has a right to speak of justice as long as the
most friendless Negro child accused of a crime receives less than the best
defense that would be given its wealthiest white citizen," Theodore Dreiser
and other novelists wrote Alabama Governor Benjamin Miller. Writer
Herman J. D. Carter took up the boys' cause with a volume of poems
titled* The Scottsboro Blues. *Carter placed their miserable fate within the
larger context of African Americans' woes. Although his appeal had no
effect on the legal proceedings, new trials improved the boys' situation.
Heywood Patterson, whom Carter mentions in his work, had his sentence
commuted to life in prison, then escaped in 1948. He died in a Michigan
prison four years later. His co-defendants spent between six and nineteen
years in jail for a crime they did not commit.*

America Between the Wars, 1919–1941: A Documentary Reader, First Edition.
Edited by David Welky. Editorial material and organization © 2012 John Wiley & Sons, Inc.
Published 2012 by John Wiley & Sons, Inc.

*How would you describe the tone of this poem? Why do you think Carter
wrote it in "Negro dialect"? What theological argument does Carter make, and
how does that argument relate to his broader interpretation of black history?*

The Blacker Christ

"Jeezus,
God, or
Whutever yu iz,
Whut iz we done t' yu?
Ain' yu no good no mo'?
Iz yu daid or iz yu sleep
God?
Can yu see we'z po'ly fed,
Scourged, and framed t' die?
Yu ain' no just God
If
Yu don' turn yo' han's ni;
Man 'z done all dat he kin do.
If yu iz God, save me;
If yu don', away wid yu."

"Haywood, Haywood!"
Called a voice,
A voice from out the sky,
"I gave my son to man;
He died that you might
Live; but
You were again enslaved.
I sent Abe Lincoln
To set you free; again
You were enslaved.
My son died for you;
Lincoln died for you,–
Still my people are
Slaves.
Haywood, die!!!
Your people need
Your blood,
Then
Southern whites

Won't be so quick
To
Put a black in chains;
White women,
Before they scream
Will use their feeble brains.
Haywood, my son.
Die!!!
Your body will die, but
Not your soul, cause
You're my son,
The Blacker Christ.

Source: Herman J. D. Carter, *The Scottsboro Blues* (Nashville: Mahlon Publishing, 1933), pp. 10–11.

2 James R. Reid, Joe Louis: African American Hero, 1938

Joe Louis was the pre-eminent black hero of the interwar era. As a top-ranked fighter for much of the 1930s and as heavyweight champion from 1937 to 1949, Louis was the repository for the hopes, dreams, and desires of millions of fans who followed his every move with breathless devotion. Black newspapers referred to him simply as "Joe" – no last name necessary. Louis's 1938 rematch with German Max Schmeling, who had pummeled him in the ring two years earlier, was the decade's most anticipated fight. Political symbolism surrounded the event – fans believed a Louis victory would give the lie to Nazi racial propaganda. Democracy itself appeared to be on the line as America's champion battled Hitler's hero (an unfair depiction, as Schmeling quietly opposed the Nazi regime). Louis dominated the fight, dropping Schmeling to the canvas three times in two minutes before the German's corner threw in the towel. A crowd of 70,000 in Yankee Stadium cheered deliriously, as did a radio audience of millions. "With their faces to the night sky," novelist Richard Wright said of Harlemites that evening, "they filled their lungs with air and let out a scream of joy that it seemed would never end, and a scream that seemed to come from untold reserves of strength." James R. Reid, a journalist with the Chicago Defender, *a nationally distributed black newspaper, explained why the triumphant champion was a model for black Americans.*

Why do so many people perceive athletes as role models? What values are attached to modern-day sports figures? According to Reid, what qualities should the ideal African American display?

What has been the influence of Joe Louis upon Race youths in America? This article will attempt to answer that question but we realize it will not be an easy task, especially at this time – the time of such an important event as a championship fight.

When the calmer moments have stripped this event of the excitement that naturally gathers about such things, we believe the deep and abiding influences of the champion may be appreciated.

Ever-so-often in the affairs of men a human effort makes a story that defies the best craftsman in the art of story-telling.

This fight, of all fights, from the first gong to the final triumph told a story that bodes well to keep men, women and children in many lands agog with interest.

To plan a great adventure, to set about it, to achieve it definitely, completely, victoriously, before the eyes of the world – that falls to the lot of few men.

Joe Louis is fortunate, yes, he has achieved a success but in his rise to the championship he has displayed five unspectacular qualities, the lack of which may have taken some of the lustre from his triumphs.

They are MODESTY, CONFIDENCE, CLEAN LIVING, REVERENCE and BALANCED INTELLIGENCE.

Champions may come and go and Joe Louis' fame as a boxer may be lost in the limbo of forgotten has-beens, but we vouchsafe the guess that Louis' qualities of character will never he forgotten as long as Race babes prattle at the breasts of Race mothers.

It is not the purpose of this article to take from the glory of the championship for no honor could be higher and never has a crown set squarer upon the brows of any man, and an earthly king was never a worthier person than Louis.

But what we admire must about the champion are his traits of character that have done more to revolutionize the thinking of Race youth than any other thing in the history of the Race.

He has worn his laurels with a MODESTY that has elicited the admiration of the world – the true test of a great man.

He has shown a CONFIDENCE in the ring and out, has given our youth the courage to militantly fight all obstacles that would limit their accomplishments.

His examples of CLEAN LIVING have set a new high upon what may be achieved with a sound mind and a sound body.

REVERENCE – Louis' deep and abiding concern for the welfare of his mother and family and loyalty to his race has inspired us to feel proud that we are Race Americans.

His BALANCED INTELLIGENCE has kept him one of us and his wise investments have given him the security that we all seek.

Summed up, these qualities have instilled a new pioneering spirit in the youth of today and these twentieth century pathfinders have vowed to open avenues that lead to full social, political and economic emancipation.

Everytime Louis' glove has exploded on the chin of his opponent, he has likewise smashed into smithereens the false prophets of racial inequality. This if no more will furnish wells of inspiration for generations yet unborn.

What is Joe Louis to the youths of today? A martyr – a king – a saint – a champion – No. He is an inspiration – the spirit of a new age.

This spirit of Louis will never be stayed. Men cannot set limits to such a knightly adventurer and after his day is done, his spirit will stalk the world – everywhere black men shall dwell, carrying a message of inspiration to youths reminding them of their fine lineage and of one who sought right and justice for a race.

Louis has never coveted honor or distinction – his triumphs have come to him as a servant of his race.

Youth today is privileged. It has a greater vision because it can quaff at the fountain of Louis' inspiration and enter life endowed with a finer spirit of hope and confidence.

"Ethiopia shall stretch forth her hands," and press on to LIBERTY, HONOR and ACHIEVEMENT, because

Of the SPIRIT OF YOUTH – the spirit of JOE LOUIS.

Source: James R. Reid, "Reid Cites Qualities of Louis Which Have Inspired Race Youth," *Chicago Defender* (June 25, 1938).

3 John Collier on A New Deal for Native Americans, 1938

White conquerors had herded most Native Americans onto reservations decades before the New Deal began. The 1887 Dawes Act tried to "civilize" Native Americans by breaking communally held tribal lands into individual family lots, many of which were eventually sold to whites at discounted prices. Some 300,000 American Indians from around two hundred tribes scratched out a bleak existence on arid or poorly managed land during the 1930s. About one-third of them survived by begging. John Collier, appointed Commissioner of Indian Affairs in 1933, wanted to breathe new life into the reservations. Reversing decades of pressures to conform to white ways, Collier encouraged tribes to assert their own distinct culture by recapturing fading traditions and lifestyles. His greatest achievement came with the 1934 Indian Reorganization Act. The law encouraged the creation of tribal governments and enabled tribes to share land rather than divide it into individual parcels. Skeptical Native Americans mocked the law as a "back to the blanket" program designed to transform them into curiosities. he remained committed to increasing American Indians' autonomy throughout his 13 years in office. This period nevertheless saw his charges remain poor and marginalized. In the following report he describes the mistakes of the past and outlines his vision for a brighter future.

How does Collier's attitude toward Native Americans differ from that of previous generations? What are his goals for Native Americans? How would you characterize Collier's tone in this piece? Sympathetic? Condescending? Angry? Practical?

In all our colorful American life there is no group around which there so steadfastly persists an aura compounded of glamour, suspicion, and romance as the Indian. For generations the Indian has been, and is today, the center of an amazing series of wonderings, fears, legends, hopes.

Yet those who have worked with Indians know that they are neither the cruel, warlike, irreligious savages imagined by some, nor are they the "fortunate children of nature's bounty" described by tourists who see them for an hour at some glowing ceremonial. We find the Indians, in all the basic forces and forms of life, human beings like ourselves. The majority of them are very poor people living under severely simple conditions. We know them to be deeply religious. We know them to be possessed of all the powers, intelligence, and genius within the range of human endowment. Just as we yearn to live out our own lives in our own ways, so, too, do the Indians, in their ways.

For nearly 300 years white Americans, in our zeal to carve out a nation made to order, have dealt with the Indians on the erroneous, yet tragic, assumption that the Indians were a dying race – to be liquidated. We took away their best lands; broke treaties, promises; tossed them the most nearly worthless scraps of a continent that had once been wholly theirs. But we did not liquidate their spirit. The vital spark which kept them alive was hardy. . . .

Dead is the centuries-old notion that the sooner we eliminated this doomed race, preferably humanely, the better. No longer can we, with even the most generous intentions, pour millions of dollars and vast reservoirs of energy, sympathy, and effort into any unproductive attempts at some single, artificial permanent solution of the Indian problem. No longer can we naively talk of or think of the "Indian problem." Our task is to help Indians meet the myriad of complex, interrelated, mutually dependent situations which develop among them according to the very best light we can get on those happenings – much as we deal with our own perplexities and opportunities.

We, therefore, define our Indian policy somewhat as follows: So productively to use the moneys appropriated by the Congress for Indians as to enable them, on good, adequate lands of their own, to earn decent livelihoods and lead self-respecting, organized lives in harmony with their own aims and ideals, as an integral part of American life. Under such a policy, the ideal end result will be the ultimate disappearance of any need for government aid or supervision. This will not happen tomorrow; perhaps not in our lifetime; but with the revitalization of Indian hope due to the actions and attitudes of this government during the last few years, that aim is a probability, and a real one. . . .

So intimately is all of Indian life tied up with the land and its utilization that to think of Indians is to think of land. . . .

The Indian feels toward his land, not a mere ownership sense but a devotion and veneration befitting what is not only a home but a refuge. At least nine out of ten Indians remain on or near the land. When times are good, a certain number drift away to town or city to work for wages. When times become bad, home to the reservation the Indian comes, and to the comparative security which he knows is waiting for him. The Indian still has much to learn in adjusting himself to the strains of competition amid an acquisitive society; but he long ago learned how to contend with the stresses of nature. Not only does the Indian's major source of livelihood derive from the land but his social and political organizations are rooted in the soil.

A major aim, then, of the Indian Service is to help the Indians to keep and consolidate what lands they now have and to provide more and better lands upon which they may effectively carry on their lives. Just as important is the task of helping the Indian make such use of his land as will conserve the land, insure Indian self-support, and safeguard or build up the Indian's social life. . . .

In 1887, the General Allotment Act was passed, providing that after a certain trust period, fee simple title to parcels of land should be given to individual Indians. Individual proprietorship meant loss – a paradox in view of the Indian's love for the land, yet an inevitable result, when it is understood that the Indian by tradition was not concerned with possession, did not worry about titles or recordings, but regarded the land as a fisherman might regard the sea, as a gift of nature, to be loved and feared, to be fought and revered, and to be drawn on by all as an inexhaustible source of life and strength.

The Indian let the ownership of his allotted lands slip from him. The job of taking the Indian's lands away, begun by the white man through military expeditions and treaty commissions, was completed by cash purchase – always of course, of the best lands which the Indian had left. In 1887, the Indian had remaining 130 million acres. In 1933, the Indian had left only 49 million acres, much of it waste and desert.

Since 1933, the Indian Service has made a concerted effort – an effort which is as yet but a mere beginning – to help the Indian to build back his landholdings to a point where they will provide an adequate basis for a self-sustaining economy, a self-satisfying social organization.

Source: John Collier, "We Took Away Their Best Lands, Broke Treaties," *Annual Report of the Secretary of the Interior for the Fiscal Year Ended June 30, 1938* (Washington, DC: Government Printing Office, 1938), pp. 209–11.

4 Eva Lowe (Chen Junqi) Describes Chinese American Life during the Depression, 1982

Thousands of Chinese immigrated to the United States during the mid–nineteenth century. Most came to build railroads, toil in mines, or work on farms, physically demanding jobs that paid low wages. Native-born Americans and other immigrants accused them of working too cheaply and argued that they would never assimilate. Such hostility confined Chinese Americans to urban ghettos, where they gravitated toward businesses that required few language skills and little startup capital, including restaurants, shops, and laundries. Terrified that an "industrial army of Asiatic laborers" might drive white Americans into unemployment, Congress in 1882 passed the Chinese Exclusion Act. The law essentially barred Chinese from entering the United States and prevented those already in the country from becoming citizens. Congress repealed the ban in 1943.

Chen Junqi (also known as Eva Lowe) was born in the United States in 1909. She lived in China during the mid-1920s, then returned to attend high school in San Francisco. Chen spent the Depression years agitating for the rights of the unemployed and protesting foreign domination of China. In this interview with Genny Lim of the Chinese Women of America Research Project, she recalls the discrimination her people faced and her struggle to maintain both Chinese and American identities.

What special challenges did Chen Junqi face? How did she try to overcome those problems? In what ways did Chen embrace her Chinese heritage? How did she try to assimilate into American society?

. . . In Fort Bragg, my uncle knew lots of English, so we had American newspapers. I would always look at the cartoons. The Chinese were always drawn as very inferior, with a long pigtail. I had this feeling that I was not proud to be a Chinese because gee, the Chinese looked so bad in those cartoons. When I was in the first grade and we walked to school, the boys in my class called me "Ching Chong Chinaman." I had a straw hat with a brim around it and they threw horse manure all over it. One time my aunt was bathing me in one of those galvanized tubs (we didn't have a bathtub) and noticed my back was all bruised. She asked me, "What happened?" I said, "*Faan gwai jai*" – we always said *fan gwai jai* for foreign devil boys – "threw rocks at me." . . .

Gradually I wanted to learn Chinese. I was in Chinese school and I began to be proud [of being Chinese.]. . .

[W]hen my sister and brother-in-law took their family to China, I fought to go. My uncle and aunt told me not to go. "Don't go to China. You cannot come back. They're going to marry you in China." But I said I wanted to go because I wanted to learn Chinese. Afterward when I went to China, I went to Chinese school and I learned Chinese history; so many thousand years ago, the Tang dynasty and all kinds of dynasties until the end of the Qing dynasty and how the imperialist countries came over. Like Dr. Sun Yat-sen said, *gwa fun* [literally, a cut-up melon] – China was cut up like a watermelon and each imperialist European country had a part of it. I remember when I was in that class, I cried. You know, China used to be so strong and now it's [come to] this.

On the way back to America, I met this lady on the ship. She was a well-read woman and had brought lots of books from Shanghai to read. She explained to me what is socialism and opened my mind about inequality for women in China. She gave me lots of books to read, especially about women's rights and how Chinese women were oppressed. And then by golly, I thought about how my stepmother married my father with a rooster. You see, my father was in America. My mother [had] died. And right away my grandmother wanted a daughter-in-law to take care of her. She [her stepmother] never knew my father. It was a blind marriage and when she married, the rooster represented my father [in the ceremony]. . . .

When I was in high school, I was in that Chinese Students Club. At that time we had lots of memorial days. "5–30," May 30th, that's the day the British killed our students and workers in Shanghai. *Jai naam chaam on*, the Jinan [massacre]. On "6–23," *gwok chi* or "Humiliation Day," our student club would make speeches on the corner of Waverly [Place]. *Da do dai gwok jue yi*, down with imperialism! A lot of people gathered on the street and we would remind people about what the imperialists did on that day to the people of China. Several times I was the only girl [among the students]. Once I spoke over in Oakland, another time inside the Chinese Catholic Center on Stockton Street. My sister was there. She said, "You talk too loud." You see, my voice was strong even though I was konked out [over-tired]. (In school I was always second instead of first in class because I was a loudmouth.) I still remember coining the slogan "If you have money, give money. If you have muscles, give muscles. I have neither money or muscles, but I can lend my voice to the cause."

...We talked about what the foreign countries did to the Chinese. Nothing else. But they were labeling us Communists and all that. So my girlfriends got scared and quit. And I asked her, "Did we talk about communism? Did we talk about socialism?" "No." "What we talked about?" "Well, we talked about anti-imperialism." "Are you in favor of it?" "Yeah, I'm in favor of it." "But why are you scared?" (See, I'm a fighter.) "Well, my father said so.". . . So all my girlfriends quit except me. I believed in what they [the Chinese Students Club] did.

...During the depression years a lot of people had no work and they had a big march. There was a whole mass of people marching on Market Street, [shouting] we want work, we want work! I was the only Chinese woman watching these things. The Chinese would say I am a good fighter because I always like to do things for the underdog.

That depression year I saw an ad that said they wanted to hire a seamstress on Third Street. I remember I went over there and asked for the job. I had that ad from the newspaper and she said, "We don't hire Orientals." Not Chinese, but Orientals. I said, "You have the ad there." She told me, "Well, I don't mind, but I don't think the workers would be willing to work with you." Now you cannot say that. You'll be sued, right?

I was a waitress, but not in Chinatown. In Chinatown there were more men than women, so those women who waited on tables had to be very tough. This is what I heard, so I never worked in Chinatown. I would rather starve than work in Chinatown. I worked in a white place because the people treat you better. If anyone tried to get fresh with me, I just go tell my boss (I'm a tough lady), "You better wait on him." "What's the matter?" I said, "He caressed my hand." "That's nothing." I said, "If you want me to wait on him, I'll tell him to get out." This guy was a steady customer. He came every week to eat, so I never wait on him. When he comes in, I tell my boss, "Chan *suk* [uncle], he's yours." So one day Chan *suk* came out and said, "This man wants to talk to you." He apologized, "I'm sorry, will you wait on me from now on?" Which I did. You have to stand up for your rights. Nobody will give you anything for nothing.

You know, I was living with my Caucasian girlfriend. She didn't like living in Chinatown, so I compromised with her. She wanted to live in Nob Hill, so we went to rent an apartment there. She saw it first. She said, "I'll bring my girlfriend to see it." Sunday, we ring the manager's doorbell. She opened the door and said, "This is your girlfriend?" My Caucasian girlfriend said, "Yes." She said, "We don't rent to Orientals." Finally we found one up in

Russian Hill on Broadway [Street]. The landlord said to me, "If anybody asks about you, say 'I'm the maid.'" (*laughs*) But at that time, it hurt. Now when I tell people from Hong Kong about it, they can't believe it.

Source: Judy Yung, ed., *Unbound Voices: A Documentary History of Chinese Women in San Francisco* (Berkeley: University of California Press, 1999), pp. 368–70, 371–73.

5 Luisa Moreno, Latinos and American Identity, 1940

Anti-Mexican sentiment had prevailed throughout the American West and Southwest ever since the United States annexed those regions following the Mexican–American War of the 1840s. White newcomers snatched land from longtime Hispanic settlers who possessed shaky, often pre war documentation of ownership. Mexican Americans occupied the bottom rungs of the labor market, spending long hours in mines, mills, canneries, and corporate farms for little pay and with scant job security. Eager to maintain a tractable and inexpensive labor supply, employers launched campaigns to convince the public that Mexicans' alleged physical and mental limitations suited them for these onerous tasks. Conditions for Mexican Americans worsened in the 1930s due to increased competition for menial jobs, large-scale deportations, and New Deal programs that reduced the amount of cultivated land.

Guatemala-born Luisa Moreno emerged as a powerful voice of protest during these turbulent years. Moreno left a journalism career in Mexico for the United States in 1928. The wrenching poverty she witnessed in New York City's Spanish Harlem district radicalized her. She joined the Communist Party and began organizing local garment workers, then relocated to Florida to do the same for cigar rollers. In 1937 she signed up as a recruiter for the United Cannery, Agricultural, Packing, and Allied Workers of America. Her work led her to Los Angeles, where in 1939 she helped found the first national civil rights organization for Latinos, El Congreso de Pueblos de Hablan Española (the Spanish-Speaking Peoples' Congress). She advocated the preservation of a distinctive Hispanic culture within a tolerant, non-discriminatory America, a position at odds with Latinos who favored cultural assimilation.

Why does Moreno oppose cultural assimilation? What, according to Moreno, is the role of Latinos in the United States? What role would she like for them to play?

One hears much today about hemisphere unity. The press sends special correspondents to Latin America, South of the Border songs are wailed by the radio, educational institutions and literary circles speak the language of cultural cooperation, and, what is more important, labor unions are seeking the road of closer ties with the Latin American working people.

The stage is set. A curtain rises. May we ask you to see behind the scenery and visualize a forgotten character in this great theater of the Americas?

Long before the "grapes of wrath" had ripened in California's vineyards a people lived on highways, under trees or tents, in shacks or railroad sections, picking crops – cotton, fruits, vegetables – cultivating sugar beets, building railroads and dams, making a barren land fertile for new crops and greater riches.

The ancestors of some of these migrant and resident workers, whose home is this Southwest, were America's first settlers in New Mexico, Texas, and California, and the greater percentage was brought from Mexico by the fruit exchanges, railroad companies, and cotton interests in great need of underpaid labor during the early postwar period. They are the Spanish-speaking workers of the Southwest, citizens and noncitizens working and living under identical conditions, facing hardships and miseries while producing and building for agriculture and industry.

Their story lies unpublicized in university libraries, files of government, welfare and social agencies – a story grimly titled the "Caravans of Sorrow."

And when in 1930 unemployment brought a still greater flood of human distress, trainloads of Mexican families with children born and raised in this country departed voluntarily or were brutally deported. As a result of the repatriation drive of 1933, thousands of American-born youths returned to their homeland, the United States, to live on streets and highways, drifting unattached fragments of humanity. Let the annals of juvenile delinquency in Los Angeles show you the consequences.

Today the Latin Americans of the United States are seriously alarmed by the "antialien" drive fostered by certain un-American elements; for them, the Palmer days [referring to the mass arrests and expulsions of suspected Communist subversives conducted under the direction of Attorney General A. Mitchell Palmer during the height of the infamous "Red Scare" of 1919–20] have never ended. In recent years while deportations in general have decreased, the number of persons deported to Mexico has constantly increased . . . .

Let me state the simple truth. The majority of the Spanish-speaking peoples of the United States are victims of a setup for discrimination, be they descendants of the first white settlers in America or noncitizens.

I will not go into the reasons for this undemocratic practice, but may we state categorically that it is the main reason for the reluctance of Mexicans and Latin Americans in general to become naturalized. For you must know, discrimination takes very definite forms in unequal wages, unequal opportunities, unequal schooling, and even through a denial of the use of public places in certain towns in Texas, California, Colorado, and other Southwestern states. . . .

Another important factor concerning naturalization is the lack of documentary proof of entry, because entry was not recorded or because the immigrants were brought over en masse by large interests handling transportation from Mexico in their own peculiar way.

Arriving at logical conclusions, the Latin American noncitizens, rooted in this country, are increasingly seeing the importance and need for naturalization. But how will the thousands of migrants establish residence? What possibility have these people had, segregated in "Little Mexicos," to learn English and meet educational requirements? How can they, receiving hunger wages while enriching the stockholders of the Great Western Sugar Company, the Bank of America, and other large interests, pay high naturalization fees? A Mexican family living on relief in Colorado would have to stop eating for two and a half months to pay for the citizenship papers of one member of the family. Is this humanly possible?

But why have "aliens" on relief while the taxpayers "bleed"? Let me ask those who would raise such a question: what would the Imperial Valley, the Rio Grande Valley, and other rich irrigated valleys in the Southwest be without the arduous, self-sacrificing labor of these noncitizen Americans? . . . Has anyone counted the miles of railroads built by these same noncitizens? One can hardly imagine how many bales of cotton have passed through the nimble fingers of Mexican men, women, and children. And what conditions have they had to endure to pick that cotton? . . .

These people are not aliens. They have contributed their endurance, sacrifices, youth, and labor to the Southwest. Indirectly, they have paid more taxes than all the stockholders of California's industrialized agriculture, the sugar beet companies and the large cotton interests that operate or have operated with the labor of Mexican workers.

Surely the sugar beet growers have not been asked if they want to dispense with the skilled labor cultivating and harvesting their crops season after season. It is only the large interests, their stooges, and some badly misinformed people who claim that Mexicans are no longer wanted.

And let us assume that 1.4 million men, women, and children were no longer wanted, what could be done that would be different from the anti-Semitic persecutions in Europe? A people who have lived twenty and thirty years in this country, tied up by family relations with the early settlers, with American-born children, cannot be uprooted without the complete destruction of the faintest semblance of democracy and human liberties for the whole population. . . .

What then may the answer to this specific noncitizen problem be? The Spanish-Speaking Peoples' Congress of the United States proposes legislation that would encourage naturalization of Latin American, West Indian, and Canadian residents of the United States and that would nurture greater friendships among the peoples of the Western Hemisphere.

The question of hemispheric unity will remain an empty phrase while this problem at home remains ignored and is aggravated by the fierce "antialien" drive.

Legislation to facilitate citizenship to all natural-born citizens from the countries of the Western Hemisphere, waiving excessive fees and educational and other requirements of a technical nature, is urgently needed.

A piece of legislation embodying this provision is timely and important. Undoubtedly it would rally the support of the many friends of true hemispheric unity.

You have seen the forgotten character in the present American scene – a scene of the Americas. Let me say that, in the face of greater hardships, the "Caravans of Sorrow" are becoming the "Caravans of Hope." They are organizing in trade unions with other workers in agriculture and industry. The unity of Spanish-speaking citizens and noncitizens is being furthered through the Spanish-Speaking Peoples' Congress of the United States, an organization embracing trade unions and fraternal, civic, and cultural organizations, mainly in California. The purpose of this movement is to seek an improvement of social, economic, and cultural conditions, and for the integration of Spanish-speaking citizens and noncitizens into the American nation. The United Cannery, Agricultural, Packing, and Allied Workers of America, with thousands of Spanish-speaking workers in its membership, and Liga Obrera of New Mexico, were the initiators of the Congress.

This Congress stands with all progressive forces against the badly labeled "antialien" legislation and asks the support of this Conference for democratic legislation to facilitate and encourage naturalization. We hope that this Conference will serve to express the sentiment of the people of this country in condemnation of undemocratic discrimination practiced against any person of foreign birth and that it will rally the American people, native and foreign born, for the defeat of un-American proposals. The Spanish-speaking peoples in the United States extend their fullest support and cooperation to your efforts.

Source: Louisa Moreno, address delivered at the Panel of Deportation and Right of Asylum of the Fourth Annual Conference of the American Committee for Protection of the Foreign Born. (Washington, DC, March 3, 1940. Box 1, Folder 1,

Carey McWilliams Collection, University Research Library, Department of Special Collections, University of California, Los Angeles.)

Discussion questions

1 What issues did racial and ethnic minorities have in common during this period, and what issues separated them?
2 In what ways did black Americans' rhetoric in the 1930s resemble, and differ from, their rhetoric in the 1920s?
3 How does the minority experience of the 1930s compare with today's reality?

Chapter 12   Women in the New Deal Era

1 Babe Didrikson: Viking Girl, 1932

According to cultural stereotypes and the medical wisdom of the day, women who participated in strenuous athletics lost essential elements of their femininity. They grew ugly muscles, adopted mannish personality traits, and neglected their God-given roles as wives and mothers. Conflicting with this vision was the 1920s New Woman movement, which celebrated lithe, athletic females with short hair and rebellious spirits. Babe Didrikson, who won two gold medals and one silver medal in the 1932 Los Angeles Olympic Games, became a focal point for the Depression-era debate over women and physicality. She appeared during a moment of gender turmoil. Unemployed men were suffering from a loss of status, a feeling that they could no longer serve their traditional breadwinner roles. Women, in turn, compensated for hard times by assuming additional economic responsibilities. In this context, the brash, outspoken Didrikson came across as either an admirable example of modern, independent womanhood or as a dire omen of more upheaval to come.

In what ways does the press present Didrikson as a threat to traditional manhood? How does it then balance these fears by casting her as a "traditional" woman?

America Between the Wars, 1919–1941: A Documentary Reader, First Edition.
Edited by David Welky. Editorial material and organization © 2012 John Wiley & Sons, Inc.
Published 2012 by John Wiley & Sons, Inc.

'Twas a lucky day for American athletics when Ole Didrikson and his better half came over the Atlantic from rugged Norway.

Under the Texas sun they prospered and raised seven children. The sixth of these was a slim, wiry lass with the blue fire of sea-king ancestors in her eyes and the actinic alchemy of American sunshine in her system.

The Viking capacity for berserk rage in battle filtered down to the Texas maid as a disposition to attack the most prodigious feats with hot resolve and a soaring confidence in her own power of achievement.

Her name was Mildred, but she had another name – her mother vows it is not a nickname – that made her a rival of one of the most famous and popular Americans of history – Babe Ruth.

Yes, and Babe Didrikson, heroine of the Olympic Games, breaker of records, and winner of championships in an amazing variety of strenuous athletic sports, threatens to outdistance the home-run king as a figure of captivating interest to all the nations of the world.

"Perhaps," suggests one of her home-town papers, the Dallas *News*, "she supplies the proof that the comparatively recent turn of women to strenuous field sports is developing a new super-physique in womanhood, an unexpected outcome of suffragism which goes in for sports as well as politics, and threatens the old male supremacy even in the mere routine of making a living." . . .

Run with us over the tale of her Olympian feats in the Olympics, where she was, as Westbrook Pegler wrote for Chicago *Tribune* Press Service, "of all the remarkable characters, the one of whom you undoubtedly will be hearing the most in time to come."

It was the first full day of competition, but already the thousands upon thousands who jammed Los Angeles's great Olympic Stadium were groggy with the record-breaking spree. The spectators fall silent for a moment.

A leather-lunged announcer broke the hush. The name of Mildred Didrikson reverberated through the bowl.

A tall, powerful, graceful girl stept into the center of things, with a confident toss of her bobbed head. She held a javelin in her powerful hand. Babe, of Dallas, was ready for her first Olympic trial.

She took a running start to hurl the long, wooden, steel-tipped spear.

Then something happened she hadn't counted on. The javelin "slee-upped," to use the pronunciation with which Mr. Pegler credits her. It "slee-upped" out of her hand. And what a mighty "slee-upp" it was. That javelin just kept "slee-uppin" right along, and it didn't come down until it had traveled 143 feet and 4 inches.

The fans broke into a roar, writes Mr. [Grantland] Rice in one of his North American Newspaper Alliance accounts, the moment the javelin "struck and quivered in the green turf. The crowd knew a world record had been shattered without waiting for any announcer." The old record was 132 feet 7⅞ inches. . . .

Then, look at what Babe did in the eighty-meter hurdle trials.

"I'll smash this one, you see," Babe told her pals. . . .

"Bang! They were off. Miss Clark of South Africa led. Babe began to run a little faster. When they got to the fifth hurdle the Texas girl pulled up even with her rival. This wasn't enough for Babe. Not by a long shot. She didn't want to win – she wanted a world record. On she went, clipping the barriers with all the technique of an expert male. She hit the tape with all the fury of a Texas tornado. . . . And the time, of course a new world record, 11.8 seconds. The old record was 12.2 seconds.

"Babe may lower the mark again in the finals. She'll probably be disappointed if she doesn't."

And as a matter of fact, that's just what she did, bringing it down to 11.7 seconds. . . .

Is there anything in the athletic line that Miss Didrikson can't do? Enraptured sports writers tell of her prowess in running, jumping, hurdling, shot-putting, discus, javelin, baseball, tennis, golf, hockey, boxing, wrestling, riding, polo, billiards, pool, skating, football, fencing, basket-ball, swimming, diving, shooting.

But Westbrook Pegler detected her in one failure – "at a ping-pong table on the veranda of the Brentwood Country Club after eighteen holes of golf. She was too enthusiastic for ping-pong, and couldn't keep the ball on the table." Reading on in this Chicago *Tribune* Press Service account, we find her playing a golf game. Mr. Pegler writes:

"She showed up at the course looking much more feminine than she had seemed in her flannel track overalls at the Olympic Stadium, and as the round loafed along, the Babe belting long drives from most of the tees, but dubbing some of her iron shots, her personality became clearer. She hit a long one at the eighteenth, and turned around to say, 'Gee, I sure would like to learn to play this game.'". . .

Two years ago, Babe had "never competed in any athletic event." But one day, "in a sporting-goods store, shopping for a pair of gym shoes, she picked up a fifty-pound weight and did tricks with it. This caused talk, and was, she says, the first feat of her athletic career, as it brought her to the attention of one Melvin J. McCombs, the man who employs her. He had been an athlete himself, and now became her coach. Nobody else had anything to do with her athletic development. Several coaches have been admitting responsibility for this, lately, but the Babe disowns them all."

"Melvin J. McCombs was my only coach," she said [according to Mr. Pegler]. "If there is any credit in that, he is entitled to it."

"Can you sew?"

"You think you're foolin'?" the Babe said. "Yes, I can sew. I sewed me a dress with seven box pleats at the front and some more in back – a sport dress it was – that won first prize in the Texas State Fair at Austin, last year."

"Cook?"

"Cook some," she said. "Like gettin' dinner if I have to, and such cookin'. But I'm better at washin' dishes."

"Did you ever have any doubt of yourself in anything you try?"

"No, I generally know what I can do. I don't seem ever to get tired. Sleepy, but not dog-tired. I sleep more than most people."

The Babe weighs about 120 pounds, and her athletic style generally resembles that of the good male athletes in all the sports which she has tried. She is lean and flat, with big arms and leg muscles, large hands, and the rather angular jaw which the magazine illustrators have established as the standard for cowboys.

This chin of the Babe's, the thin, set lips, the straight, sharp profile, the sallow suntan, undisguised by rouge, regarded in connection with her amazing athletic prowess, at first acquaintance are likely to do her no justice. But the mouth can relax and the eyes smile, and the greatest girl athlete in the world just now, with a special liking for men's games, is as feminine as hairpins. She is a great competitor, come all of a sudden to prominence, who may yet add to her Olympic championships of the track and field and her sewing championship won in the Texas State Fair a title in the fancy dives and a national golf championship.

It's a mistake to think, however, that Mildred's talents are purely muscular, a mistake against which Muriel Babcock warns us in the Los Angeles *Times*. Take a tip from me, says Miss Babcock, continuing:

"The Babe can sew, and cook a mean meal. In the wardrobe that she brought with her from Dallas is a blue crepe party dress which she made herself."

The week-end before she left Dallas for Chicago tryouts, "Mama" (Mrs. Ole Didrikson of Beaumont) came to town to help Babe get ready.

As Babe told her sister, Mrs. C. F. Cole, Santa Monica:

"Ma thought I'd have to be sewed up and all my clothes mended. But I fooled her. Everything was all ready. We just visited."

Source: "The World-Beating Girl Viking of Texas," *Literary Digest* 114 (August 27, 1932): 26–7, 28.

2 Meridel Le Sueur, "I Was Marching," 1934

The Great Depression disrupted the United States' political, social, and cultural traditions as well as its economy. Large-scale upheavals unleashed a flood of socially conscious writings known collectively as proletarian literature. Proletarian writers offered radical, often Marxist, solutions to the deep structural problems within the American system. These authors were often amateurs who wrote in a clunky style that nevertheless conveyed penetrating immediacy. Michael Gold's Jews Without Money *(1930) took readers inside the immigrant slums. Grace Lumpkin's* To Make My Bread *(1932) followed Appalachian tenant farmers struggling to survive in the industrializing South. Meridel Le Sueur's short story "I Was Marching" exemplifies the strike narrative, a common theme of proletarian writers interested in exploring the sources and outcomes of labor dissent. Her fictionalized treatment of a brutal 1934 Teamsters Union strike in Minneapolis dramatized the need for women to play an active role in the burgeoning labor movement.*

How does Le Sueur create sympathy with striking workers? How does the role of women evolve as the strike continues?

I have never been in a strike before. . . . For two days I heard of the strike. I went by their headquarters. . . .

I saw cars leaving filled with grimy men, pickets going to the line, engines roaring out. I stayed close to the door, watching. I didn't go in. I was afraid they would put me out. After all, I could remain a spectator. . . .

I saw many artists, writers, professionals, even business men and women standing across the street, too, and I saw in their faces the same longings, the same fears.

The truth is I was afraid. Not of the physical danger at all, but an awful fright of mixing, of losing myself, of being unknown and lost. I felt inferior. I felt no one would know me there, that all I had been trained to excel in would go unnoticed. I can't describe what I felt, but perhaps it will come near it to say that I felt I excelled in competing with others and I knew instantly that these people were NOT competing at all, that they were acting in a strange, powerful trance of movement *together*. . . .

The next day, with sweat breaking out on my body, I walked past the three guards at the door. They said, "Let the women in. We need women." And I knew it was no joke.

At first I could not see into the dark building. I felt many men coming and going, cars driving through. . . .

Upstairs men sat bolt upright in chairs asleep, their bodies flung in attitudes of peculiar violence of fatigue. A woman nursed her baby. Two young girls slept together on a cot, dressed in overalls. The voice of the loudspeaker filled the room. The immense heat pressed down from the flat ceiling. I stood up against the wall for an hour. No one paid any attention to me. . . .

I found the kitchen organized like a factory. Nobody asks my name. I am given a large butcher's apron. I realize I have never before worked anonymously. At first I feel strange and then I feel good. The forewoman sets me to washing tin cups. There are not enough cups. We have to wash fast and rinse them and set them up quickly for buttermilk and coffee as the line thickens and the men wait. A little shortish man who is a professional dishwasher is supervising. I feel I won't be able to wash tin cups, but when no one pays any attention except to see that there are enough cups I feel better.

The line grows heavy. The men are coming in from the picket line. Each woman has one thing to do. There is no confusion. I soon learn I am not supposed to help pour the buttermilk. I am not supposed to serve sandwiches. I am supposed to wash tin cups. I suddenly look around and realize all these women are from factories. I know they have learned this organization and specialization in the factory. I look at the round shoulders of the woman cutting bread next to me and I feel I know her. The cups are brought back, washed and put on the counter again. The sweat pours down our faces, but you forget about it.

Then I am changed and put to pouring coffee. . . .

"Is your man here?" the woman cutting sandwiches asks me.

"No," I say, then I lie for some reason, peering around as if looking eagerly for someone, "I don't see him now."

But I was pouring coffee for living men.

For a long time, about one o'clock, it seemed like something was about to happen. Women seemed to be pouring into headquarters to be near their men. You could hear only lies over the radio. And lies in the paper. Nobody knew precisely what was happening, but everyone thought something would happen in a few hours. . . .

We kept on pouring thousands of cups of coffee, feeding thousands of men. . . .

The action seemed reversed. The cars were coming back. The announcer cried, "This is murder." Cars were coming in. I don't know how we got to the stairs. Everyone seemed to be converging at a menaced point. I saw below the crowd stirring, uncoiling. I saw them taking men out of cars and putting them on the hospital cots, on the floor. At first I felt frightened, the close black area of the barn, the blood, the heavy movement, the sense of myself lost, gone. But I couldn't have turned away now. A woman clung to my hand. I was pressed against the body of another. If you are to understand anything you must understand it in the muscular event, in actions we have not been trained for. Something broke all my surfaces in something that was beyond horror and I was dabbing alcohol on the gaping wounds that buckshot makes, hanging open like crying mouths. Buckshot wounds splay in the body and then swell like a blow. Ness, who died, had thirty-eight slugs in his body, in the chest and in the back. . . .

Men, women, and children are massing outside, a living circle close packed for protection. From the tall office building business men are looking down on the black swarm thickening, coagulating into what action they cannot tell.

We have living blood on our skirts.

That night at eight o'clock a mass-meeting was called of all labor. It was to be in a parking lot two blocks from headquarters. All the women gather at the front of the building with collection cans, ready to march to the meeting. I have not been home. It never occurs to me to leave. The twilight is eerie and the men are saying that the chief of police is going to attack the meeting and raid headquarters. The smell of blood hangs in the hot, still air. Rumors strike at the taut nerves. The dusk looks ghastly with what might be in the next half hour.

"If you have any children," a woman said to me, "you better not go." I looked at the desperate women's faces, the broken feet, the torn and hanging pelvis, the worn and lovely bodies of women who persist under such desperate labors. I shivered, though it was 96 and the sun had been down a good hour.

The parking lot was already full of people when we got there and men swarmed the adjoining roofs. An elegant café stood across the street with water sprinkling from its roof and splendidly dressed men and women stood on the steps as if looking at a show.

The platform was the bullet riddled truck of the afternoon's fray. We had been told to stand close to this platform, so we did, making the center of a wide massed circle that stretched as far as we could see. . . . The movements, the masses that I see and feel I have never known before. I only partly know what I am seeing, feeling, but I feel it is the real body and gesture of a future vitality. I see that there is a bright clot of women drawn close to a bullet riddled truck. I am one of them, yet I don't feel myself at all. It is curious, I feel most alive and yet for the first time in my life I do not feel myself as separate. I realize then that all my previous feelings have been based on feeling myself separate and distinct from others and now I sense sharply faces, bodies, closeness, and my own fear is not my own alone, nor my hope.

. . . There must be ten thousand people now, heat rising from them. They are standing silent, watching the platform, watching the cars being brought up. The silence seems terrific like a great form moving of itself. This is real movement issuing from the close reality of mass feeling. This is the first real rhythmic movement I have ever seen. My heart hammers terrifically. My hands are swollen and hot. No one is producing this movement. It is a movement upon which all are moving softly, rhythmically, terribly. . . .

We all watched carefully the placing of the cars. Sometimes we looked at each other. I didn't understand that look. I felt uneasy. It was as if something escaped me. And then suddenly, on my very body, I knew what they were doing, as if it had been communicated to me from a thousand eyes, a thousand silent throats, as if it had been shouted in the loudest voice.

THEY WERE BUILDING A BARRICADE.

Two men died from that day's shooting. Men lined up to give one of them a blood transfusion, but he died. Black Friday men called the murderous day. Night and day workers held their children up to see the body of Ness who died. Tuesday, the day of the funeral, one thousand more militia were massed downtown.

It was still over ninety in the shade. I went to the funeral parlors and thousands of men and women were massed there waiting in the terrific sun. One block of women and children were standing two hours waiting. I went over and stood near them. I didn't know whether I could march. I didn't like marching in parades. Besides, I felt they might not want me.

I stood aside not knowing if I would march. I couldn't see how they would ever organize it anyway. No one seemed to be doing much.

At three-forty some command went down the ranks. I said foolishly at the last minute, "I don't belong to the auxiliary – could I march?" Three women drew me in. "We want all to march," they said gently. "Come with us."

The giant mass uncoiled like a serpent and straightened out ahead and to my amazement on a lift of road I could see six blocks of massed men, four abreast, with bare heads, moving straight on and as they moved, uncoiled the mass behind and pulled it after them. I felt myself walking, accelerating my speed with the others as the line stretched, pulled taut, then held its rhythm. . . .

I felt my legs straighten. I felt my feet join in that strange shuffle of thousands of bodies moving with direction, of thousands of feet, and my own breath with the gigantic breath. As if an electric charge had passed through me, my hair stood on end. I was marching.

Source: Meridel Le Sueur, "I Was Marching," 1934. Copyright © 1948, 1956, 1966 Reprinted with permission of International Publishers Co. Inc.

3 Bruce Gould and Beatrice Blackmar Gould, A Modern Marriage, 1937

Mainstream Depression-era culture emphasized women's roles as wife, mother, and homemaker. In the world of Hollywood film, for example, career women secretly – and sometimes not so secretly – yearned for conventional married lives that freed them from the alleged burdens of working in the outside world. Women's magazines, which had vast and diverse readerships, tried to reach both "modern" and "traditional" women without alienating either side. The result was a paradoxical culture that reiterated Victorian notions of fragile and virtuous ladies even as it suggested that women could have careers and independence without sacrificing their femininity. The following article from Ladies' Home Journal, *at the time the world's most popular publication for women, demonstrates the difficulties of maintaining this contradictory message. In it, the husband-and-wife editing team of Bruce and Beatrice Blackmar Gould strain to offer a definition of modern marriage that also satisfied readers who believed that wives should be subordinate to their husbands.*

How do the Goulds characterize a successful marriage? How are the women here "modern"? How are they "traditional"?

We wonder if learning to dance well – we refer to modern ballroom dancing – isn't a pretty good training school for marriage – our modern twentieth-century marriage.

Consider two ballroom dancers.

The man leads. He chooses the pattern that their feet shall follow.

The woman must be guided by him. She must then be docile, she must submit herself to his guidance. But she must not be too docile. She must not lean. She must stand on her own feet, preserving in every intricate step her own balance, her own individuality as a separate, self-determined entity, subdued for the moment to his will. Even, she must resist a bit. Just a trifle, not too much – just enough to make the man aware that he is dancing with a partner, not alone. If she clings too closely, leans too heavily, follows too easily, the pleasure of dancing with her is lost, almost as surely as if she follows unwillingly, trying too strongly to guide their steps.

As we have said, it is the man who imposes his will. But how gently, how tactfully he must do it. Almost, it seems that they are guided by one impulse. And sometimes a pressure of her hand on his shoulder restrains him from stepping heavily backward on someone's toes. A holding back, a reluctance, warns him:

"Don't move in that direction."

The man has chosen the pattern that their feet follow. But he also submerges his will to something outside himself. He is controlled, guided by and submissive to, the demands of the music, which, like fate, permits him certain forms of expression, denies him others.

And so they move as one. Each of them is limited by the other's limitations, strong only where both are strong. Only as one, can they succeed. He choosing the pattern of their steps, within the circumscribed space of the dance floor, controlled by the tune, usually not of his own selecting, to which he must dance; imposing his will so lightly that it seems a mutual choice: she submissive to his leadership, but not too submissive, never losing her entity, her ability to balance perfectly on her own feet, influencing him subtly in her very docility – they move as one to the music which life has chosen for them.

Perhaps the lesson of the dance floor, perfectly learned, might lead to fewer divorces. Anyway, we think there's food for thought in the idea.

And we venture that our women readers, happily wedded, will agree that it's a good analogy. Or perhaps only just an illusion that we maintain.

Source: Bruce Gould and Beatrice Blackmar Gould, "The Dance of Life," *Ladies' Home Journal* 54 (October 1937): 4.

4 Eleanor Roosevelt, "My Day," 1937, 1939

"I'm just not the sort of person who would be any good at that job," Eleanor Roosevelt said as she prepared to become the first lady of the United States. Although she was the wife of one politician and the niece of another, former president Theodore Roosevelt, young Eleanor displayed an almost willful ignorance of politics and government. Her husband Franklin's battle with polio in the 1920s changed her perspective. With Franklin partially paralyzed, Eleanor traveled the country to maintain his extensive network of contacts and to gauge the public mood. As president, much of what FDR knew about the United States came filtered through Eleanor's compassionate eyes and ears. Although emotionally distant, the couple made a good political team – friends said that Eleanor focused on what should be done, while Franklin focused on what could be done.

Eleanor entered the White House resolved to maintain as much freedom as possible. She minimized the first lady's traditional hostess role in order to focus on travel and activism. Some saw her as a model for modern womanhood. Others thought her a symbol of the New Deal's break from traditional, time-tested American values. Eleanor associated with such causes as pacifism, workplace reform, and gender and racial equality. She shared her opinions through a daily syndicated column, "My Day." Initially intended as a daily digest of the first lady's doings, the column evolved into a forum for Eleanor to

voice her thoughts on whatever interested her at the moment – even when her
perspective clashed with the president's. This sampling of columns offer a taste
of Eleanor's writings on women during the Great Depression.

What does Eleanor Roosevelt advocate for women? How does her vision
reflect current realities for women? According to her columns, how did
readers respond to her ideas?

Washington, January 13, 1937

At the second of two teas yesterday afternoon, the couple who came through last paused a minute and the lady said: "Wouldn't it be very pleasant, Mrs. Roosevelt, to have a day without any hours in which you had to do prearranged things?"

At the moment I was thinking of how grateful I was that I had shaken hands with about five hundred-odd people and really didn't feel very tired, but the question started me thinking.

Of course, all of us want days when we can wake up in the morning and say, "I can do just as I like this whole day through." There are, however, comparatively few people in the world who have the chance to do this, except for short snatches of time, part of a day here and there.

Men have been able to do it more often than women because when they cast off business cares they may perhaps also cast off family cares. But women, many of them at least, when they have families dependent upon them, whether they are the daughters or the mothers, can very rarely lay aside their business cares and not be confronted with a constant succession of adjustments to the wants and pleasures of others.

Of course, there are families in which the father takes as much responsibility as the mother, but the fact remains that if he must have a rest, or feels that he must, the family won't fall to pieces as long as the mother or the responsible daughter is still on the spot.

Hyde Park, July 24, 1937

... The other day I received an appeal from an organization which has as its purpose the removal of any married woman, whose husband earns enough to support her, from all employment. Who is to say when a man earns enough to support his family? Who is to know, except the individuals themselves, what they need for daily living or what responsibilities are hidden from the public eye? There are few families indeed who do not have some members outside of their own immediate family who need assistance.

Added to this, who is to say whether a woman needs to work outside her home for the good of her own soul? Many women can find all the work they need, all the joy they need and all the interest they need in life in their own homes and in the volunteer community activities of their environment. Because of this I have received many critical letters from women complaining that other women who did not need paid jobs were taking them. That they were working for luxuries and not for necessities, that men who had families to support were being kept out of jobs by these selfish and luxury-loving creatures.

I have investigated a good many cases and find that, on the whole, the love of work is not so great. Those who are gainfully employed are usually working because of some real need. There are a few, however, who work because something in them craves the particular kind of work which they are doing, or an inner urge drives them to work at a job. They are not entirely satisfied with work in the home.

This does not mean they are not good mothers and housekeepers, but they need some other stimulus in life. Frequently they provide work for other people. If they suddenly ceased their activities many other people might lose their jobs. As a rule, these women are the creative type.

It seems to me that the tradition of respect for work is so ingrained in this country that it is not surprising fathers have handed it down to their daughters as well as to their sons. In the coming years, I wonder if we are not going to have more respect for women who work and give work to others than for women who sit at home with many idle hours on their hands or fill their time with occupations which may indirectly provide work for others but which give them none of the satisfaction of real personal achievement.

Hyde Park, August 13, 1937

I went this morning to the alumnae house at Vassar college to attend a meeting presided over by Miss Vera McCrea, president of the Business and Professional Women's clubs of New York State, and Miss Kathryn Starbuck. Representatives were present from various women's organizations interested in the service of women on juries.

One woman offered an important point: the accused is supposed to come before a jury of peers. In her experience, the better men of the community rarely served on juries and she was afraid the same would be the case with women. It would be unfortunate, she asserted, if only the ideal men and women qualified.

Another woman at once pointed out that this was just the reason why women should begin now to discuss the subject.

It seems important to me that men and women alike should realize that jury service is one of the responsibilities of citizenship. If you cannot serve because of illness or a business emergency, or some other valid reason, that excuses you.

But men have frequently invented excuses when, with a little effort, they might easily have performed jury service. Women will do the same thing, unless we can convince everyone that it is not fair to any government to accept all the privileges and shirk all the chores.

Jury schools, such as are proposed, would be open to women. I hope in every community they will be attended by both sexes.

Another woman brought up the point that her husband worked hard to keep a business going, which had labored through precarious times, and that her daughter was obliged to go to business. It was the housewife's job, the woman said, not to add to the family expenses and to see that all were well taken care of. She asked to know, then, how she could serve on a jury.

The answer is, of course, that the family as a whole must recognize the fact that jury service is a duty and, putting their heads together, find a solution. Someone could be brought in to cook the necessary meals – $3 a day is paid for jury service. Of course, it would be nice to keep that money but if this is a duty, it is worth doing well.

Perhaps the members of the household not serving on a jury might look in the icebox for sufficient food to keep them going, even to making themselves a cup of coffee and a boiled egg, if necessary.

It seems to me it is a question of whether you believe jury service is a job on a par with your other occupations in life. If it is, then you will surely find a way to perform it as you do all your serious responsibilities.

New York, June 16, 1939

There was one item in the paper yesterday which extremely interested me. It appears that Governor Herbert Lehman signed a bill introduced in the New York State Legislature this past term by Assemblyman Jane H. Todd, Republican, which makes it permissible to have equal representation of the sexes on all political committees.

This representation, so far as the Democratic party in New York State is concerned, has been acknowledged and considered advisable for a number of years. It is quite true that there have been cases where, on county committees and in other positions, certain gentlemen have objected to giving women equal representation and, therefore, in such places there have been few if any women active in the party. Since this bill is not mandatory, however, I cannot see how it really changes the present situation a great deal.

I feel quite sure that in the case of coveted positions on committees at state conventions, there will be considerable objection if any group of women attempt to obtain fifty-fifty representation! However, I suppose that having even a permissive law, rather than a party rule, is a step forward for the women, and I congratulate Miss Todd and the Governor on achieving this.

A number of people have written me in opposition to my stand that married women should be allowed the privilege of working. They plead with me to consider how cruel it is that these married women, with husbands well able to support them, should be taking jobs away from young people. They insist that most of these married women are simply doubling good incomes and acquiring luxuries for themselves. They think they are taking the bread out of the mouths of single women who are helping to support members of their families.

It sounds a bit hysterical, so let us consider the question calmly. Basically, is it wise to begin to lay down laws and regulations about any particular group? If we begin to say that married women cannot work, why shouldn't we say next that men with an income of more than a certain sum shall not work, or that young people whose parents are able to support them have no right to look for jobs? It seems to me that it is the basic right of any human being to work.

Many women, after marriage, find plenty of work in the home. They have no time, no inclination or no ability for any other kind of work. The records show that very few married women work from choice, that they are working only because a husband is ill or has deserted them, or there are special expenses caused by illness or educational requirements in the home. There may even be fathers, mothers, sisters or brothers to be supported. It seems to me that it is far more important for us to think about creating more jobs than it is for us to worry about how we are going to keep any groups from seeking work.

Source: Rochelle Chadakoff, ed., *Eleanor Roosevelt's My Day: Her Acclaimed Columns, 1936–1945* (New York: Pharos Books, 1989), pp. 43–4, 66–7, 69–70, 126–7.

5 Letters from African American Women to the Federal Government, 1935–41

African Americans had traditionally voted for Republican candidates, a testament to enduring memories of Abraham Lincoln and emancipation, but in 1932 a majority voted for Franklin Roosevelt, the Democratic

*candidate. In 1936 Roosevelt won over 70 percent of the black vote. African
Americans made only incremental gains under Roosevelt. The president
allowed most job programs to operate on a segregated basis. New Deal
agricultural reforms often hurt black sharecroppers. Lynching remained
tragically common. At the same time, FDR gave African Americans
unprecedented influence within his government. With prodding from Eleanor,
he nominated the first black federal judge and established a circle of black
advisors, known as the "black cabinet," that informed him on minority
affairs. Even so, as this collection of letters to various federal departments
indicates, African Americans, particularly women, faced daunting challenges
in their everyday lives.*

   *What special problems did African Americans face during the Depression?
What did whites expect from African Americans? Why did these women
write to the federal government? What did they hope to accomplish?
What could the federal government have done to improve the status of
black southern women?*

Millen, Ga.
R 1, Box 31
February 4, 1935

United States Department of Agriculture
Extension Service
Office of Cooperative Work
Washington, D.C.
Dear Friends:

I am a widow woman with seven head of children, and I live on my place
with a plenty of help. All are good workers and I wants to farm. I has no
mule, no wagon, no feed, no grocery, and these women and men that is controlling the Civil Work for the Government won't help me.

   Because I am a woman. I wants to ask you all to please help me to
make a crop this year and let me hear from you on return mail. Yours for
business.

Mosel Brinson
Please answer me on return mail.

P.S.   These poor white people that lives around me wants the colored
people to work for them for nothing and if you won't do that they goes
down to the relief office and tell the women – "don't help the colored

people, we will give them plenty of work to do, but they won't work." That is the reason the poor colored people can't get any help, these poor white people going down to the relief office telling lies. Now I am living on my own land and I am got a plenty of children to make a farm, and all I wants is a chance, and I am not in debt. I wants a mule and feed, and gear and plows, and a little groceries and guano. Please help a poor widow woman one year. Please help me to get a start, I will try to keep it.

Fort Valley, Ga.
March 11, 1935

Mr. Harry Hopkins
Dear Sir:

I am asking you to please help me and my poor husband, we are old and well on in years. I am 60 years old and my husband is 85 or older, *he was a plough boy in slavery time.* He been sick here almost four years down helpless as a baby and these relief people will not give me any help. I wrote Mrs. Gay B. Shepperson of Atlanta and she wrote these people here and sent them the letter I wrote her and they disliked it very much and talked very hard to me because I am in my own house. It just a 3 room house me and my husband worked and paid for when we could work and every time we ask for help they tell me we have our own house and they can't help us, and they say they don't help old people nohow, they help young people who is able to work, but there are plenty of people who are much better off than I will ever be. I thought I would apply to you all for help. My husband is bare for clothes and also for food. I have only one child, she is grown and married but her husband is dead and she do all she can for me and my husband but she only make $3.00 per week cooking at a boarding house 3 meals a day but she cannot keep us all on that. My husband work for the city of Fort Valley 22 years and they give him a little money for a few weeks and stop that and I can't get him on the county or get help any way. When I go to them for help they talk to me like I was a dog. My husband have a stroke of paralysis was brought home three times from the streets where he worked. I have high blood pressure. Looking to hear from you at once,

Sarah Young

117 Ash St.
Greenwood, Miss.
Dec. 23, 1936

President Roosevelt
Dear Sir:

We are wondering what is going to become of this large number of widow women with and without children. These white women at the head of the PWA is still letting we colored women when we go to the office to be certified for work to go hunt washings. . . .

I was in the office a few days ago. A woman was there she had five children and a husband not able to work. They told her to go hunt washings. . . . The white people dont pay anything for their washing. She cant do enough washing to feed her family. I was reading an article in the paper enquiring why colored men did not show up on WPA projects in some places. You all are not down here. So you has to take these white people word. . . .

I know we have had men here in Greenwood to walk [to the relief office] several weeks then white women and men would tell them come back tomorrow come back Monday. Finally they would say what are you Nigers [sic] keep on coming up here for. We cant take on any more go hunt you some work. Then they will write you all our men and women cant be found. Good many of our men have told me they would eat grass like a cow and drink water before they would go back to any of the relief offices, let them white people dog them again. We have old people cant get any help. If the old people go they will say go to your children if the children go to the relief they will tell them we cant take on any more. Like my father is old. Last week he came to me for help. He is on relief but cant get nothing. He lives in Carroll County.

. . . I cant get work. I could not help him and he cant help me. . . .

I visit my sick people because I feel like it is my duty. The white woman got mad with me because she thought I was taking note of how they was being treated. Come to my house to raise a fuss. Told me I better not take any note of the sick people she visit, if I did, what she was going to do.

That why many of our people are gone to untimely graves. Poor white people is nothing but Negro haters. If you all would please let the colored people look after the colored people old sick and the white look after white that will keep down confusion and save many of our lives if we cant have colored home visators we dont want any. We have been slaves for them all our lives and dont need them standing around over us telling us how to sweep the floor, writeing down how many people visit the sick room and what they brought.

Respectifully
Pinkie Pilcher

New Orleans, Louisiana
April 18, 1941

Mrs F.D. Roosevelt
Dear Mrs.

I'm a Negro girl of 25 yrs. I'm sick. I been sick 4 months. I'm in need of food and closes. I don't have any relative at all so help me. I hop I'm not asking so much of you, but I hop you would help me, Mrs. Roosevelt. I'm righting you this morning I dont have food for the day. I gose to the hospital. The dr say all my sickes is from not haveing food.

I was working on the NYA [National Youth Administration]. . . . I work there 10 month. They lad me off because I was sick and diden give me nothing to live off after tune me off. . . . They was so hard every time I get a job I get sick but I try to keep them anyway but after all I lose them. Mrs. Roosevelt I'm rooming with a old lade she dont have a husban. She give me food when she have it but she dont have it all the time. I own her 5 month rent right now. She have to pay rent her silf. She was asking me when I was going to pay her. If I dont be able to pay her in 2 week she going to put me out. I dont have nobody to go to for help and no where to go what I going to do if she put me out.

Could you do something for me help me to fine something. Tell me what to do if you could give me some to do in the hospitial or in a hotel or any where I will do it. I will take a day job are a night job anything. Please help me. You can see I'm in need of help Mrs. Roosevelt. Will you please help me I can live much longer without food – have lot of micine to take I do take it but it wont do me any good without food and if the lady put me out I just no I will die because I dont have no where to go. . . . Mrs. Roosevelt if you can get me a job in the post office anywhere it will do. Please wright at once as soon as you can. I be looking for a letter from you.

Please do what every you can for me. I'm in need of help bad. . . . Thank you. Your kindes will never be foregoting. Yours sincerely.

Mabel Gilvert
1225 Poydres St. New Orleans, La.

Please do some thing for me at once any thing. Pleasanywhere pleas.

Woodland Park Biteley, Mich.
April 23, 1941

President Roosevelt
Dear Sir:

We are the colored women Democrat club. We are sending in a plea for help for our people of our community. Our men are out of work and have ben for sometimes.

We can't get any Welfare help unless we sign our homes over to the welfare. We do not want to be beggers. Our men would work if they could only get work to do. We have helped in every way we could to help make your third election a success. We had some hard things to undergo during the time we were campaigning but the victory was well worth the pain. Our club were and are still for you and all of your supporters, one hundred percent. . . .

We here in this community are having a tuff way to go just now. There were a lay off just after Jan. and our men were laid off. Any time anything happens like this our group are always the first ones to get the first blow. We have tried to get work. We are sending our plea to you feeling sure you will and can help us in our needy condition. We aren't getting a fair deal. Some of our boys are being drafted for service for our country and here we are in a free land are not aloud to work and make a living for their wives and childrens. You are the Father of this country and a Father are suppose to look out for all of his children so we are depending on you.

From the Colored Womens Democrat Club. We are hoping to hear from you soon.

Yours truly
Lutensia Dillard

Source: Gerda Lerner, ed., *Black Women in White America: A Documentary History* (New York: Pantheon, 1972), pp. 399–404, 405.

6 Dorothea Lange, Photos of Women Surviving Hard Times, 1939

Almost half of American women lived in rural areas during the 1930s. Life for farm women had always been hard. Now, with the Depression savaging an already brutalized agricultural economy, life was even harder. Women either struggled to keep the family farm going or suffered the dislocation of migrating to more promising lands. Photographer Dorothea Lange captured some of these difficulties when she toured the United States in 1939 on behalf of the Farm Security Administration. Four of the thousands of images she captured are included below. The first shows a grandmother in a California migrant camp. The second is of a woman who, with her husband, farmed a few acres of vegetables in North Carolina. The third presents a family living in a shack in Oregon that the unseen head of the household purchased with his Works Progress Administration salary. The final image shows a mother and daughter who fled their drought-stricken Colorado farm for a homestead in Washington.

What do these images say about rural women's lives during the 1930s? What obstacles do they face? How would you characterize their material lives? What do these photographs suggest about their subjects' characters?

Figure 12.1   Stanislaus County, California, 1939.

Source: Library of Congress, Prints & Photographs Division, LC-USF34-019475-C.

Figure 12.2   Caroline Atwater, 1939.

Source: Library of Congress, Prints & Photographs Division, LC-USF34-019902-E.

Figure 12.3   Near Klamath Falls, Oregon, 1939.

Source: Library of Congress, Prints & Photographs Division, LC-USF34-021000-E.

Figure 12.4   The Adolph family, living in the Yakima Valley, Washington, 1939.

Source: Library of Congress, Prints & Photographs Division, LC-USF34-020397-C.

Discussion questions

1   What would the word "feminism" mean to the subjects of these pieces?
2   How did discussions of womanhood change and remain constant between the
     1920s and 1930s?
3   What do you think was the most important cause of the revolution in gender
     roles in the twentieth century?

Chapter 13   Raising the Walls in Turbulent Times

1 Henry Cabot Lodge Denounces the Proposed League of Nations, 1919

The idealistic, moralistic Woodrow Wilson believed that World War I would forever transform humanity. He spoke in grand terms of a war to end all wars and of making the world safe for democracy. Achieving those noble goals meant concluding the conflict with a wise treaty. In an unprecedented move, Wilson traversed the Atlantic to represent the United States personally at the Paris peace talks. He brought with him his Fourteen Points, an ambitious slate of proposals designed to create a freer, more open, and more democratic postwar world. His agenda faced stiff resistance from Britain and France, wartime allies now bent on protecting and expanding their overseas empires and on punishing defeated Germany. "Even the good Lord contented Himself with only ten commandments," French Prime Minister Georges Clemenceau sniffed upon hearing his American counterpart's plan. Although intense opposition whittled away most of Wilson's points, the president refused to budge on his central demand: a League of Nations capable of arbitrating future disputes before they erupted into pointless wars.

Wilson conceded that the Treaty of Versailles was an imperfect document but was hopeful that the League could correct its flaws. First he had to persuade a reluctant Senate to ratify it. Opponents coalesced around Massachusetts Senator Henry Cabot Lodge, a longtime Wilson foe whose positions as Senate majority leader and chair of the Senate Foreign Relations Committee gave him considerable say over the treaty's fate. Lodge held

America Between the Wars, 1919–1941: A Documentary Reader, First Edition.
Edited by David Welky. Editorial material and organization © 2012 John Wiley & Sons, Inc.
Published 2012 by John Wiley & Sons, Inc.

grave reservations about the nebulous new League. The treaty left it unclear as to whether the League's rules superseded American laws or whether American soldiers might be called to fight on the organization's behalf. Wilson's unwillingness to compromise contributed to the treaty's failure to win ratification. The United States signed separate peace treaties with Germany and Austria in 1921. Wilson was by then out of office, and the country he had led into war was eager to turn away from overseas affairs. The United States never joined the League of Nations, which collapsed after proving incapable of controlling the tension that led to World War II.

Why does Lodge oppose the treaty? How does his perception of the United States and its role in the world influence his position? How persuasive is Lodge's argument? Do you think the world would have been better off had the United States joined the League? What role should the United States play in world affairs?

The question and the only question before us here is how much of our sovereignty we are justified in sacrificing. In what I have already said about other nations pulling us into war I have covered one point of sovereignty which ought never to be yielded – the power to send American soldiers and sailors everywhere, which ought never to be taken from the American people or impaired in the slightest degree. Let us beware how we palter with our independence. We have not reached the great position from which we were able to come down into the field of battle and help to save the world from tyranny by being guided by others. Our vast power has all been built up and gathered together by ourselves alone. We forced our way upward from the days of the Revolution, through a world often hostile and always indifferent. We owe no debt to anyone except to France in that Revolution, and those policies and those rights on which our power has been founded should never be lessened or weakened. It will be no service to the world to do so and it will be of intolerable injury to the United States. We will do our share. We are ready and anxious to help in all ways to preserve the world's peace. But we can do it best by not crippling ourselves.

I am as anxious as any human being can be to have the United States render every possible service to the civilization and the peace of mankind. But I am certain that we can do it best by not putting ourselves in leading strings, or subjecting our policies and our sovereignty to other nations. The independence of the United States is not only more precious to ourselves, but to the world, than any single possession. . . . Contrast the United States with any country on the face of the earth today and ask yourself whether the situation of the United States is not the best to be found. I will go as far as anyone in world service, but the first step to world service is the maintenance of the United States. You may call me selfish, if you will, conservative or reactionary, or use any other harsh adjective you see fit to apply, but an American I was born, an American I've remained all my life. I can never be anything else but an American, and I must think of the United States first. And when I think of the United States first in an argument like this, I am thinking of what is best for the world, for if the United States fails the best hopes of mankind fail with it. I have never had but one allegiance – I can not divide it now. I have loved but one flag and I can not share that devotion and give affection to the mongrel banner invented by a league. Internationalism, illustrated by the Bolshevik and by the man to whom all countries are alike provided they can make money out of them, is to me repulsive. National I must remain, and in that way I like all other Americans can render the amplest service to the world. The United States is the world's best hope, but if you fetter her in the interests and quarrels of other nations, if you tangle her in the intrigues of Europe, you will destroy her power for good and endanger her very existence. Leave her to march freely through the centuries to come, as in the years that have gone. Strong, generous, and confident, she has nobly served mankind. Beware how you trifle with your marvelous inheritance, this great land of ordered liberty. For if we stumble and fall, freedom and civilization everywhere will go down in ruin.

We are told that we shall "break the heart of the world" if we do not take this league just as it stands. I fear that the hearts of the vast majority of mankind would beat on strongly and steadily and without any quickening if the league were to perish altogether. If it should be effectively and beneficently changed the people who would lie awake in sorrow for a single night could be easily gathered in one not very large room but those who would draw a long breath of relief would reach to millions.

We hear much of visions and I trust we shall continue to have visions and dream dreams of a fairer future for the race. But visions are one thing and visionaries are another, and the mechanical appliances of the rhetorician designed to give a picture of a present which does not exist and of a future which no man can predict are as unreal and short-lived as the steam or canvas clouds, the angels suspended on wires and the artificial lights of the stage. They pass with the moment of effect and are shabby and tawdry in the daylight. . . .

Ideals have been thrust upon us as an argument for the league until the healthy mind which rejects cant revolts from them. Are ideals confined to this deformed experiment upon a noble purpose, tainted, as it is, with bargains and tied to a peace treaty which might have been disposed of long ago to the great benefit of the world if it had not been compelled to carry this rider on its back? . . . .

No doubt many excellent and patriotic people see a coming fulfillment of noble ideals in the words "League for Peace." We all respect and share these aspirations and desires, but some of us see no hope, but rather defeat, for them in this murky covenant. For we, too, have our ideals, even if we differ from those who have tried to establish a monopoly of idealism. Out first ideal is our country, and we see her in the future, as in the past, giving service to all her people and to the world. Our ideal of the future is that she should continue to render that service of her own free will. She has great problems of her own to solve, very grim and perilous problems, and a right solution, if we can attain to it, would largely benefit mankind. We would have our country strong to resist a peril from the West, as she has flung back the German menace from the East. We would not have our politics distracted and embittered by the dissensions of other lands. We would not have our country's vigor exhausted, or her moral force abated, by everlasting meddling and muddling in every quarrel, great and small, which afflicts the world. Our ideal is to make her ever stronger and better and finer because in that way alone, as we believe, can she be of the greatest service to the world's peace and to the welfare of mankind. [Prolonged applause in the galleries.]

Source: US Congress, Senate, *Congressional Record*, 66th Cong., 1st sess., p. 3784.

2 Harry Elmer Barnes, World War I Was a Mistake, 1926

The Senate's rejection of the Treaty of Versailles provided a nebulous ending to a war few people – even those who fought in it – could explain. Always suspicious of overseas adventures, Americans concluded that the war was a pointless waste of life. They had fought for nothing and gained nothing. Popular culture, an enthusiastic supporter of Wilson's wartime policies, changed its tune with the return of peace. Motion pictures such as The Big Parade *(1925),* The Dawn Patrol *(1930), and* Men Must Fight *(1933) lamented the senseless slaughter. Novels, including* Three Soldiers *(1920),* The Sun Also Rises *(1926), and* All Quiet on the Western Front *(1929), shared their disgust. Conventional wisdom held that wily European propagandists and greedy arms dealers had tricked gullible Americans into entering the conflict. Columbia University historian Harry Elmer Barnes gave these arguments a measure of scholarly credibility in 1926 when he published* The Genesis of the World War, *a project funded in part by the German Foreign Ministry. Although much of the book focuses on the war's European origins, Barnes saves some of his harshest rhetoric for his section on American intervention.*

According to Barnes, what forces conspired to pull the United States into the war? What does his position suggest about how he views the world and America's place in it? What impact do you think these impressions of the World War might have once Europe went to war again in 1939?

The alleged reason why the United States entered the War was, of course, the resumption of unlimited German submarine warfare, but to have any understanding of the deeper causes we must get at the reasons for the German submarine warfare in general, as well as its resumption in January, 1917. Here we are on firm ground. There is no doubt that the German submarine warfare was developed as a counter movement against the English violation of international law in regard to blockade, contraband and continuous voyage. By practically destroying, in these respects, the rights of neutrals, which had been worked out in a century of the development of international law, Great Britain was virtually able to shut off all imports into Germany from foreign countries, not only directly but also through neutral ports. It was to retaliate against this that Germany initiated her submarine warfare, which certainly cannot be regarded as in any sense more atrocious in fact or law than those English violations of neutral rights which had produced the submarine campaign. By practically acquiescing in these British violations of international law we not only lost most of what we had gained in the past in the way of establishing neutral rights on the seas, but also set a precedent which will prove an extremely nasty and embarrassing stumbling-block in the course of future negotiations in the event of war.

In addition to these English violations of international law which vitally affected Germany as well as neutrals, there were many special examples of British lawlessness, such as the interception of our mails, the use of the American flag on British ships, the seizure and search of United States officials below the rank of minister while traveling to and from their continental posts, and the capture of ships like the *Dacia* (by the French at the instigation of Page and the British), which had been legally transferred from enemy countries to American owners. If the United States had held England strictly to international law upon the threat of severance of diplomatic relations or even war, as we did in the case of Germany and as we unquestionably should have done in the case of England, the German submarine warfare would not have been necessary and probably would not have been utilized. So we may say with absolute certainty that it was the unneutrality, lack of courage, or maladroitness of the Washington authorities in regard to English violations of international law which produced the German submarine warfare that actually led us into war. It must be remembered, however, that the resumption of German submarine warfare, like the Belgian question in England, was the excuse and not the real reason for our entering the War. President Wilson and Colonel House had decided that we would come in at least a year before the submarine warfare was resumed by Germany. . . .

Next we should note the powerful pressure of the great American financial interests and their subsidized press. From the beginning the international banking houses of the United States had taken a distinctly unneutral attitude, favoring investment in the bonds of the Allied countries, and discouraging or refusing investment in the paper of the Central Powers. This immediately gave us a strong financial stake in the cause of the Entente, and this stake grew larger with each year of the war. Likewise, American industry inevitably became violently pro-Ally. This was due to the fact that the British illegal blockade unlawfully cut off our sales of war materials to the Central Powers and made our enormous war profits dependent upon the purchases made by Great Britain, France, Russia and Italy . . . .

This favorable attitude of the American press toward the Entente Powers was an enormous advantage to the latter. We were made to feel that the Entente was fighting the cause of the small and weak nations against the ruthlessness of a great bully. We were inevitably led to believe that the War had been started through the deliberate determination of Germany to initiate her alleged long-cherished plan to dominate the planet, while the Entente had proposed diplomatic settlement from the beginning and had only taken up arms in self-defense with the utmost reluctance. This theory of the German provocation of the War and the German lust for world dominion was played up in the newspapers and distributed in pamphlets of the National Security League and the American Defense Society until the danger from Germany struck terror into the hearts of Americans, and citizens of Peoria, Illinois, and Council Bluffs, Iowa, lived in daily dread of a German submarine attack; as a few years later they searched under their beds nightly for the Bolshevik there secreted.

Then, the United States was peculiarly at the mercy of the falsified atrocity pictures and other propaganda poured into this country by the Allies, who were at the same time able to keep from public knowledge the German counter-propaganda as well as German proofs of the falsity of these atrocity pictures, recently so conclusively demonstrated. These circumstances made it much easier for the pro-Ally groups to inflame American opinion and swing the country for war. . . .

A very important element in adequately debunking us of wartime illusions is a consideration of the actual results for the world of the American entry into the World War. We have conventionally believed that it was a great boon to civilization and that it saved the world from German domination and the imposition of German militarism and tyranny upon the planet as a whole. The facts are almost exactly the reverse of this picture. In 1916 and 1917 Germany was ready for peace on very moderate and constructive terms, certainly terms far more fair and more to the advantage of the world at large than those imposed at Versailles two years later. In fact, if the American papers had been able or willing to get hold of and print the full German terms of peace and to portray accurately the state of the German mind in 1916 and 1917, there is no likelihood that Mr. Wilson or any one else could have forced the United States into the World War. There is little probability that Germany could have crushed the Allies if America had not intervened. What the American entry did was to encourage the Allies in the wastes and savagery which led to Versailles, the blockade of Germany after the Armistice, and the outrages in the Ruhr. The highly precarious foundation upon which Europe stands today with almost a sure guaranty of future war, as well as the outbreak of Bolshevism, which was due to the prolongation of the War after the Russian people desired to withdraw, may both be traced to the results of American intervention. Our entry was, thus, a menace to both the "Reds" who met punishment as a result of the Palmer inquisition, and the conservatives who were thrown into a panic by Bolshevism. . . .

Added to the material and financial expenditures of the United States, due to our participation in the World War, are the political corruption and incompetence which it has generated, the raids upon American liberty by Palmer and his associates and successors, and the general decline of morale in American public and private life which has been unparalleled by any earlier developments in the history of our country. Democracy did not cure war, but the War cured democracy in the United States – an outcome foreseen with eager anticipation by the American plutocrats in 1917. . . .

If we honestly face the facts we shall probably have to agree that the entry of the United States into the World War was an almost unmitigated disaster, not only to us but to Europe.

3 Calvin Coolidge, Address to Congress Regarding the Invasion of Nicaragua, 1927

*Americans had thought of the Western Hemisphere as off limits to
Europeans ever since President James Monroe issued his famous 1823
doctrine. A succession of administrations extended the United States'
regional dominance. Teddy Roosevelt, for example, fomented a revolution
in the Colombian state of Panama when Colombia's national government
refused to ratify a treaty granting the United States the right to dig a canal
across its territory. The newly independent Republic of Panama quickly
signed the document. Roosevelt later sent marines into Cuba. Woodrow
Wilson in 1917 ordered a force into Mexico. These interventions bred
distrust of American bullying among Latin Americans but struck American
policymakers as necessary to defending their interests. Widespread
disenchantment with overseas affairs after the World War did not cause
Americans to relinquish their far-flung Caribbean and Pacific empire,
which included Puerto Rico, Guam, and the Philippines. In addition to its
formal colonies, Cuba, the Dominican Republic, Haiti, Nicaragua, and
Panama remained so closely aligned with the United States as to be nearly
protectorates.*

*The 1920s-era Harding and Coolidge administrations attempted to
improve hemispheric relations. They remained willing, however, to dispatch
troops to impose their priorities. Such a moment occurred in 1927 when
President Coolidge sent 5,000 marines to Nicaragua to prop up American
puppet Adolfo Díaz against a Mexican-backed liberal rebellion that
threatened to make Juan Batista Sacasa, whom Díaz had deposed, president.
The Coolidge administration eventually negotiated a complex power sharing
agreement that marines spent the next six years enforcing. President Herbert
Hoover removed the force in 1933.*

*On what basis does Calvin Coolidge justify his actions? Based on the
argument presented here, was it right for the United States to intervene
in Nicaragua?*

It is well known that in 1912 the United States intervened in Nicaragua
with a large force and put down a revolution, and that from that time to
1925 a legation guard of American marines was, with the consent of the
Nicaraguan Government, kept in Managua to protect American lives and
property. In 1923 representatives of the five Central American countries,
namely, Costa Rica, Guatemala, Honduras, Nicaragua, and Salvador, at the
invitation of the United States, met in Washington and entered into a series
of treaties. These treaties dealt with limitation of armament, a Central
American tribunal for arbitration, and the general subject of peace and

amity. The treaty last referred to specifically provides in Article II that the Governments of the contracting parties will not recognize any other government which may come into power in any of the five Republics through a *coup d'état* or revolution and disqualifies the leaders of such coup d'état or revolution from assuming the presidency or vice presidency. . . .

The United States was not a party to this treaty, but it was made in Washington under the auspices of the Secretary of State, and this Government has felt a moral obligation to apply its principles in order to encourage the Central American States in their efforts to prevent revolution and disorder. . . .

Immediately following the inauguration of President Diaz and frequently since that date he has appealed to the United States for support, has informed this Government of the aid which Mexico is giving to the revolutionists, and has stated that he is unable solely because of the aid given by Mexico to the revolutionists to protect the lives and property of American citizens and other foreigners. . . .

At the end of November, after spending some time in Mexico City, Doctor Sacasa went back to Nicaragua, landing at Puerto Cabezas, near Bragmans Bluff. He immediately placed himself at the head of the insurrection and declared himself President of Nicaragua. He has never been recognized by any of the Central American Republics nor by any other Government, with the exception of Mexico, which recognized him immediately. As arms and munitions in large quantities were reaching the revolutionists, I deemed it unfair to prevent the recognized Government from purchasing arms abroad, and, accordingly, the Secretary of State has notified the Diaz Government that licenses would be issued for the export of arms and munitions purchased in this country. It would be thoroughly inconsistent for this country not to support the Government recognized by it while the revolutionists were receiving arms and munitions from abroad. . . .

For many years numerous Americans have been living in Nicaragua developing its industries and carrying on business. At the present time there are large investments in lumbering, mining, coffee growing, banana culture, shipping, and also in general mercantile and other collateral business. All these people and these industries have been encouraged by the Nicaraguan Government. That Government has at all times owed them protection, but the United States has occasionally been obliged to send naval forces for their proper protection. In the present crisis such forces are requested by the Nicaraguan Government, which protests to the United States its inability to protect these interests and states that any measures which the United States deems appropriate for their protection will be satisfactory to the Nicaraguan Government.

In addition to these industries now in existence, the Government of Nicaragua, by a treaty entered into on the 5th day of August, 1914, granted in perpetuity to the United States the exclusive proprietary rights necessary and convenient for the construction, operation, and maintenance of an oceanic canal. . . .

There is no question that if the revolution continues American investments and business interests in Nicaragua will be very seriously affected, if not destroyed. . . .

I am sure it is not the desire of the United States to intervene in the internal affairs of Nicaragua or of any other Central American Republic. Nevertheless it must be said that we have a very definite and special interest in the maintenance of order and good government in Nicaragua at the present time, and that the stability, prosperity, and independence of all Central American countries can never be a matter of indifference to us. The United States can not, therefore, fail to view with deep concern any serious threat to stability and constitutional government in Nicaragua tending toward anarchy and jeopardizing American interests, especially if such state of affairs is contributed to or brought about by outside influences or by any foreign power. It has always been and remains the policy of the United States in such circumstances to take the steps that may be necessary for the preservation and protection of the lives, the property, and the interests of its citizens and of this Government itself. In this respect I propose to follow the path of my predecessors.

Consequently, I have deemed it my duty to use the powers committed to me to insure the adequate protection of all American interests in Nicaragua, whether they be endangered by internal strife or by outside interference in the affairs of that Republic.

Source: *Papers Relating to the Foreign Relations of the United States, 1927* (Washington, DC: Government Printing Office, 1942), vol. 3, pp. 288–9, 294–5, 297–8.

4 The Sinking of the *Panay*, 1937

Americans' desire to withdraw from international entanglements continued into the Depression decade. Choosing to ignore the Depression's global impact most people insisted that the United States must tend to its own affairs. The country paid little attention to Japan's 1931 invasion of Manchuria and Italy's unprovoked 1935 attack on Ethiopia. A series of Neutrality Acts, the first passed weeks before the Italo-Ethiopian War began, codified America's relationship with this troubled world. Under the Acts, American businesses could not sell weapons to countries at war, send trading vessels into war zones, or extend credit to warring nations. The Acts also

*gave President Roosevelt the power to warn citizens that they traveled
into war zones at their own risk, and that the government assumed no
responsibility for their safety.*

Japan's 1937 sinking of the Panay, *an American gunboat gathering
intelligence from its base on China's Yangtze River, challenged this
neutrality. Japanese pilots bombed the vessel, apparently on their own
authority, then strafed survivors swimming to safety. Two Americans died
and 30 were wounded in the attack. The strike could not have been a
mistake, as the* Panay *displayed two large American flags on its deck. This
deliberate assault outraged President Roosevelt, who considered blockading
Japan before allowing cooler heads to prevail. He accepted Japan's apology
but quietly ordered the military to update its battle plans for a possible
Pacific conflict. Rather than inspire war cries, as was the case when the* USS
Maine *exploded in 1898 and when a German U-Boat sunk the* Lusitania *in
1915, the* Panay *incident raised calls for the United States to remove itself
from a dangerous region. The following article from* Christian Century,
a liberal Protestant journal, captures the national spirit of retreat.

*According to the article, in what ways does the United States deserve
blame for the* Panay *incident? What do you think would be the American
response should a comparable incident happen today? What does that say
about the similarities or differences between 1937 and the present?*

Nothing that has happened during the fighting in China has so shocked the
rest of the world as the sinking of the United States gunboat Panay on
December 12. . . .

For the gunboat was not only a vessel in the American navy. It was a naval
vessel engaged in humanitarian service, its nationality as plainly marked
as was possible, its position officially communicated to the Japanese authorities, and its safety supposedly guaranteed by the Japanese command.
That Japanese aviators should not only have "fired on the flag," but have done
so under such circumstances, has astounded the American public.

Japan has recognized from the first the seriousness of the situation.
Nothing has been left undone that could be done to assure this country of a
desire to make such amends as are possible. The complete official apology,
with its offer of full reparations and its promise of punishment for the aviators involved in the bombing, was actually made before the American
ambassador at Tokyo had time to present the demands of his government.
And much more impressive than all the efforts of diplomats and army and
navy officers to express their nation's regret is the news from Tokyo of the
virtual abandonment of popular celebrations of the capture of Nanking.

Apparently, the Japanese people are more stunned than any others by this sinking of an American warship and by contemplation of what might be involved in the incident.

If a bright spot is to be discerned in so dark a picture, it has undoubtedly been furnished by the poise of the American people. Seriously as the incident is viewed in this country, there has hardly been the slightest trace of such frenzied excitement as followed the sinking of the Maine and of the Lusitania. Comment in Congress has been notable in its restraint. The most belligerent utterance which the Japophobe Hiram Johnson, senator from California, could work up was prefaced by the avowal: "I want no war. I will go to any length to prevent a war of any kind." Senator Pittman, chairman of the foreign relations committee, took a truculent line, intimating that the sinking of the Panay must have been deliberate. But even the Pittman speech went no further than to demand an apology and reparations.

Shocked as the American public has been by the sinking of a naval vessel flying the American flag, an encouraging segment of opinion has raised the question: What was the gunboat doing in the midst of the war zone? . . . China is the only country in which other nations have quartered their armed forces. The Yangtze patrol, of which the Panay formed a part, is a relic of a type of imperialistic policy which survives nowhere else in the world and will not survive the present war in China, whether China or Japan wins.

The patrol of the Yangtze by gunboats from the United States, the European powers and Japan dates back to the series of treaties extracted from China after her defeat by Great Britain in the war of 1858. The excuse given for the maintenance of naval forces on the interior waters of a supposedly sovereign and friendly state has been the danger to the lives of foreigners from riots. . . .

Secretary Hull, in reply to a formal inquiry made in the House of Representatives by Congressman Francis H. Case of South Dakota, recently wrote that these army and navy forces are maintained in China "for the general purpose of providing protection to American nationals (including the embassy personnel) and, in case of emergency calling for evacuation, making available an armed escort." It is frequently declared that one of the principal reasons for keeping such large forces – about one soldier to every two Americans is the present proportion – in Chinese territory is to safeguard missionaries and mission property. . . . Yet readers of The Christian Century are well aware of the strenuous efforts which missionaries have been making for years past to rid themselves of this embarrassing "gunboat protection."

Since the present hostilities broke out, the obvious fact has been that the concentration of American fighting forces in China has operated in such a way as to make it far more likely that America would be dragged into trouble than that Americans would be kept out. The cocky attitude of many Japanese officers and troops, flushed with victory, has been reciprocated in some instances by a chip-on-shoulder aggressiveness of American troop and skip commanders. In the early days of the fighting, clashes were narrowly avoided between the invading Japanese and the American troops stationed at Tientsin. The case has been much worse at Shanghai. So fraught with possibilities of evil has the situation become that demands have mounted in Congress for a general withdrawal of American forces from all fighting zones. Only a few days before the Panay was sunk, the government announced that such withdrawal was about to begin.

The sinking of the Panay provides a deeply ironical comment on the contention of the state department that China is a special case, different from any else in the world, and that this fact requires the maintenance of armed forces in the interior of a friendly country and in a war zone as a means of protecting and giving safe escort to American citizens. Tested by events, the theory has failed to work. The Americans "rescued" from Nanking on the Panay have been subjected to deadly peril of their lives; it may be that some of them have been killed. The Americans who persisted in their refusal to board the gunboat and took chances inside the besieged capital have not only come through the ordeal unscathed but have been a means – by organizing the so-called "neutral zone" in the city – of saving thousands of Chinese lives and adding immeasurably to American prestige among the Chinese.

Great numbers of Americans had come to believe, weeks before the sinking of the Panay, that a wise policy on the part of this government would order the immediate withdrawal of all American armed forces from the Far Eastern fighting zones. As the Panay affair is studied, we expect that this public demand for official extrication from the war peril will be increased. . . .

It is impossible wholly to guard against tragic accidents in the inferno of battle. No doubt the Japanese will do their best to see that no more such accidents as the sinking of the Panay occur. Nevertheless, the presence of American warships and of American troops where fighting is going on or where a military occupation is in progress is a constant tempting of fate. The gunboats, the regulars and the marines should be withdrawn before a worse catastrophe befalls.

Source: "The Sinking of the Panay," *Christian Century* 54 (December 22, 1937): 1582–3.

Discussion questions

1 Explain the arguments for and against isolationism.
2 What impact did World War I have on American foreign policy during the
   1920s and 1930s?
3 Do you agree or disagree with the ideas of isolationism?

Chapter 14   The Great Debate: America Encounters World War II

1   Franklin Roosevelt's Neutrality Message, 1939

Most Americans disliked the Nazis and their charismatic leader, Adolf Hitler, but showed little concern for Germany even after its provocative remilitarization of the Rhineland, its annexation of Austria, and its absorption of the Czechoslovakian Sudetenland. Memories of World War I ran deep in a country accustomed to remaining aloof from European affairs. President Roosevelt was no isolationist. Facing a skeptical electorate, an increasingly hostile Congress, and the restrictive Neutrality Acts, however, he could do little to discourage Axis expansion or to encourage the French and British to oppose it.

Hitler swallowed the rest of Czechoslovakia in March 1939 and began menacing Poland, Germany's neighbor to the east. Roosevelt's hopes for peace ended when the telephone by his bed rang at 3 a.m. on September 1. Ambassador to France William Bullitt was on the line. "Mr. President," Bullitt said, "several German divisions are deep in Polish territory." "Well, Bill," FDR responded, "it has come at last. God help us all." FDR chose his words carefully when he addressed the nation two days later. He tried to calm isolationists convinced he would drag them into a war while alerting his countrymen to the potential for disaster should the United States ignore the conflict. Many listeners penned letters voicing their opinions on the president's speech. One of those notes appears below.

How did FDR want Americans to respond to the onset of war? What role should the United States play in the fight? In what ways did Roosevelt try to

America Between the Wars, 1919–1941: A Documentary Reader, First Edition.
Edited by David Welky. Editorial material and organization © 2012 John Wiley & Sons, Inc.
Published 2012 by John Wiley & Sons, Inc.

prepare listeners for the prospect of the United States becoming more involved in the conflict in the future? What arguments and assumptions do the Taylors make in their letter?

Tonight my single duty is to speak to the whole of America. Until 4:30 o'clock this morning I had hoped against hope that some miracle would prevent a devastating war in Europe and bring to an end the invasion of Poland by Germany.

For four long years a succession of actual wars and constant crises have shaken the entire world and have threatened in each case to bring on the gigantic conflict which is today unhappily a fact.

It is right that I should recall to your minds the consistent and at times successful efforts of your government in these crises to throw the full weight of the United States into the cause of peace. In spite of spreading wars I think that we have every right and every reason to maintain as a national policy the fundamental moralities, the teachings of religion and the continuation of efforts to restore peace – for some day, though the time may be distant, we can be of even greater help to a crippled humanity.

It is right too, to point out that the unfortunate events of these recent years have been based on the use of force or the threat of force. And it seems to me clear, even at the outbreak of this great war, that the influence of America should be consistent in seeking for humanity a final peace which will eliminate, as far as it is possible to do so, the continued use of force between nations.

It is, of course, impossible to predict the future. I have my constant stream of information from American representatives and other sources throughout the world. You, the people of this country, are receiving news through your radios and your newspapers at every hour of the day. . . .

At the same time, as I told my press conference on Friday, it is of the highest importance that the press and the radio use the utmost caution to discriminate between actual verified fact on the one hand and mere rumor on the other.

I can add to that by saying that I hope the people of this country will also discriminate most carefully between news and rumor. Do not believe of necessity everything you hear or read. Check up on it first.

You must master at the outset a simple but unalterable fact in modern foreign relations. When peace has been broken anywhere, peace of all countries everywhere is in danger.

It is easy for you and me to shrug our shoulders and say that conflicts taking place thousands of miles from the continental United States, and indeed, the whole American Hemisphere, do not seriously affect the Americas, and that all the United States has to do is to ignore them and go about our own business.

Passionately though we may desire detachment, we are forced to realize that every word that comes through the air, every ship that sails the sea, every battle that is fought does affect the American future.

Let no man or woman thoughtlessly or falsely talk of America sending its armies to European fields. At this moment there is being prepared a proclamation of American neutrality. This would have been done even if there had been no neutrality statute on the books, for this proclamation is in accordance with international law and with American policy. . . .

I cannot prophesy the immediate economic effect of this new war on our nation but I do say that no American has the moral right to profiteer at the expense either of his fellow-citizens or of the men, women and children who are living and dying in the midst of war in Europe.

Some things we do know. Most of us in the United States believe in spiritual values. Most of us, regardless of what church we belong to, believe in the spirit of the New Testament – a great teaching which opposes itself to the use of force, of armed force, of marching armies and falling bombs. The overwhelming masses of our people seek peace – peace at home, and the kind of peace in other lands which will not jeopardize peace at home.

We have certain ideas and ideals of national safety and we must act to preserve that safety today and to preserve the safety of our children in future years.

That safety is, and will be, bound up with the safety of the Western Hemisphere and of the seas adjacent thereto. We seek to keep war from our firesides by keeping war from coming to the Americas.

This nation will remain a neutral nation, but I cannot ask that every American remain neutral in thought as well. Even a neutral has a right to take account of facts. Even a neutral cannot be asked to close his mind or his conscience.

I have said not once but many times that I have seen war and that I hate war. I say that again and again.

I hope the United States will keep out of this war. I believe that it will. And I give you assurances that every effort of your government will be directed toward that end.

Source: *Vital Speeches of the Day* 5 (September 15, 1939): 712–13.

Dear Mr. President,

My wife and I have just heard your great speech over the radio. We cannot refrain from expressing our deepest appreciation of your statement that you and the rest of our great government will do everything possible to keep this country neutral in this horrible struggle. I, personally, was a medical officer in the World War in 1918 in France. Though a member of the Society of Friends [Quakers], I believed then, mistakenly, that it was a war to end war and a war to make the world safe for democracy, and while I could not conscientiously go to take life, I felt I could go in such a noble cause to save life. Now I know there is no such thing, and we all know it.

The light of reason has gone out over a large part of Europe and will be replaced by hate and fury. May God uphold your powerful arm in keeping that light burning steadily, clearly and brightly in this country, and keep you firm in your resolve that millions of our young men will not be condemned to death because of selfish Old World diplomacy that is bringing a large part of mankind to death and destruction.

On behalf of our two sons, on behalf of all the people of this great nation, on behalf of humanity, and in the name of Him who said, "Father, forgive them for they know not what they do", we thank you for your great stand which you have voiced this day.

Most sincerely yours, with deep gratitude,

Frederick R. Taylor, M.D.
Rachel F. Taylor
High Point, N.C.

Source: Lawrence W. Levine and Cornelia R. Levine, *The People and the President: America's Conversation with FDR* (Boston: Beacon Press, 2002), p. 276.

2. Charles Lindbergh, America is Drifting toward War, 1940

Poland surrendered just weeks after Germany's September 1939 invasion. Denmark, Norway, Holland, and Luxembourg fell in spring 1940. Nazi legions entered Paris in mid-June, leaving Great Britain alone in opposing the Axis. Franklin Roosevelt had by then persuaded Congress to repeal the arms embargo provision of the Neutrality Acts, a move that enabled a trickle of weapons to cross the U-boat-infested Atlantic. Tentative as they were, the Roosevelt administration's efforts to strengthen ties with Great Britain aroused fears that the president intended to drive the United States to war. Most prominent among the isolationists was the famous aviator Charles Lindbergh, whose conviction that entering the war would mean disaster for the United States trumped his reluctance to draw media attention.

*Lindbergh's 1938 visit to Germany had impressed him. "I have come
away with a great feeling of admiration for the German people," he noted.
In contrast, he saw Britain and France as too corrupt and weak to
counter Hitler's aggression. He viewed the war as a European squabble
over resources and influence rather than as a clash that might determine the
fate of the entire world. Lindbergh gave numerous public addresses
supporting American neutrality throughout the winter of 1939–40,
including this one, which he offered to a national radio audience the day
after Paris fell.*

*Why does Lindbergh believe that the United States needs to remain
neutral? What should the United States do in response to the war?*

I believe that we, in America, are drifting toward a position of far greater seriousness to our future than even this present war. There is an attempt to becloud the issue that confronts us. It is not alone an issue of building an adequate defense for our country. That must and can be done. Our people are solidly behind an adequate military preparedness, and no one believes in it more than I.

But we must not confuse the question of national defense with the question of entering a European war. And it is just as important not to confuse this present war with the type of war we have to wage if we fought against Germany. Arming for the defense of America is compatible with normal life, commerce and culture. It is an integral part of the destiny of our nation. But arming to attack the continent of Europe would necessitate that the lives and thoughts of every man, woman and child in this country be directed toward war for the next generation, probably for the next several generations.

We cannot continue for long to follow the course our government has taken without becoming involved in war with Germany. There are some who already advocate our entry into such a war. There are many perfectly sincere men and women who believe that we can send weapons to kill people in Europe without becoming involved in war with these people. Still others believe that by gestures and applause we can assist France and England to win without danger to our own country.

In addition to these, however, there are men among us of less honesty who advocate stepping closer and closer to war, knowing well that a point exists beyond which there can be no turning back. They have baited the trap of war with requests for modest assistance. This latter group is meeting with success at the moment. . . .

This dabbling we have been doing in European affairs can lead only to failure in the future as it has in the past. It is not a policy that we can continue to follow and remain a great nation. Let us look at our position today. Our leaders have lost the influence we could have exerted as the world's greatest neutral nation.

The driblets of munitions we have sold to England and France have had a negligible effect on the trend of the war, and we have not sufficient military strength available to change that trend.

We demand that foreign nations refrain from interfering in our hemisphere, yet we constantly interfere in theirs. And while we have been taking an effective part in the war abroad, we have inexcusably neglected our defenses at home. In fact we have let our own affairs drift along until we have not even a plan of defense for the continent of North America. . . .

There is still very little understanding of what our entrance into the European war would mean. When we talk of such a war, we must realize that we are considering the greatest struggle the world has yet known, a conflict between hemispheres, one half of the white race against the other half. Before allowing ourselves to become further involved, we should consider the conditions which may exist by the time we are ready for military action. If we enter a war at all, we should prepare to meet the worst conditions rather than the best.

It is useless to talk of sending American troops to Europe now, for we would need months of preparation before we could train and equip even a small army, and small efforts do not effect great movement – witness Norway, Holland and Belgium.

We must face the fact, regardless of how disagreeable it is to us, that before we can take effective action in a European war the German armies may have brought all Europe under their control. In that case Europe will be dominated by the strongest military nation the world has ever known, controlling a population far larger than our own. If we decide to enter [the] war we must be prepared to attack that nation. We must prepare to invade a continent which it controls.

No people ever had a greater decision to make. We hold our children's future in our hands as we deliberate, for if we turn to war the battles will be hard fought and the outcome not likely to be decided in our lifetime. This is a question of mortgaging the lives of our children and our grandchildren. Every family in the land would have its wounded and its dead.

We start at a disadvantage because we are not a military nation. Ours is not a land of guns and marching men. If we decide to fight then the United States must prepare for war for many years to come, and on a scale unprecedented in all history. In that case we must turn to a dictatorial government, for there is no military efficiency to be lost. . . .

But whatever our decision may be in regard to Europe, we must start now to build our own defenses. We must stop these gestures with an empty gun. In this we are a united nation. The only question that arises concerns how our defense can best be built. . . .

We must be willing to do more than pay taxes and make appropriations. Military strength cannot be purchased by money alone. Strength is a thing of spirit, of preparation and of sacrifice extending over years of time. The men of our country must be willing to give a year of their lives to military training, more if necessary. And our capitalists as well as our soldiers should be willing to serve without personal profit. We must have a nation ready to give whatever is required for its future welfare and leaders who are more interested in their country than in their own advancement.

With an adequate defense, no foreign army can invade us. Our advantage in defending America is as great as our disadvantage would be in attacking Europe. From a military geographical standpoint, we are the most fortunate country in the world. There is no other nation in this hemisphere strong enough to even consider attacking us, and the Atlantic and Pacific Oceans separate us from the warring armies of Europe and Asia.

Shall we submerge our future in the endless wars of the Old World?

Or shall we build our own defenses and leave European war to European countries? . . .

Source: *Vital Speeches of the Day* 6 (July 1, 1940): 549–50, 551.

3 Franklin Roosevelt, Fireside Chat on "An Arsenal of Democracy," 1940

Otto von Bismarck, the principal architect of the modern German state, said in 1898 that the most vital fact in world diplomacy was that Americans spoke English. The United States' longstanding cultural link with Great Britain deepened during 1940 into a strategic alliance. That year, after months of intensive bombing, Hitler cancelled Germany's planned invasion of Great Britain, and British Prime Minister Winston Churchill's eloquent promises of a fight to the bitter end convinced a sizable minority of Americans that the island nation could survive the war. Even so, the British situation was desperate, and Churchill begged Roosevelt for more help. FDR, however, was locked in a tight election campaign and had to tread lightly lest he arouse isolationist ire. Fortunately, his Republican opponent, Indiana attorney and businessman Wendell Willkie, also supported military preparedness and greater assistance for Britain. Willkie's position gave

Roosevelt political cover to push a peacetime draft through Congress and to issue an executive order that gave 50 aged destroyers to Britain in exchange for long-term leases on British bases in the Caribbean.

Churchill needed more. By late 1940 his country could no longer afford to purchase American military supplies. After winning his third-term victory, Roosevelt designed a program to circumvent this obstacle. Lend-lease, he explained to reporters on December 17, abolished "the silly, foolish old dollar sign." The proposal would enable the United States to loan military goods to Britain in exchange for vague promises of future repayment. "Lending war equipment is a good deal like lending chewing gum," Republican Senator and administration critic Robert Taft observed. "You don't want it back."

FDR used his 16th fireside chat to sell lend-lease. Employing some of his most anti-Axis language to date, he urged Americans to accept that they had a stake in the war. His speech, while stopping short of calling for American intervention, unnerved isolationist listeners. Lisette Wessel's response to the president rejected Churchill's assertion that "the English-speaking democracies, the British Empire and the United States, will have to be somewhat mixed up together in some of their affairs for mutual and general advantage." Congress nevertheless passed lend-lease in January 1941. America was on its way toward involvement in World War II.

What did Roosevelt mean when he called upon America to become the "arsenal of democracy"? Why does Roosevelt believe that the Axis posed a threat to the United States? Do you believe that, in December 1940, FDR wanted the United States to enter the war? How does Roosevelt's rhetoric resemble, and differ from, his 1939 neutrality speech? How does Wessel's perspective on global affairs differ from Roosevelt's?

This is not a fireside chat on war. It is a talk on national security; because the nub of the whole purpose of your President is to keep you now, and your children later, and your grandchildren much later, out of a last-ditch war for the preservation of American independence and all the things that American independence means to you and to me and to ours. . . .

Never before since Jamestown and Plymouth Rock has our American civilization been in such danger as now.

For, on September 27, 1940, by an agreement signed in Berlin, three powerful nations, two in Europe and one in Asia, joined themselves together in the threat that if the United States of America interfered with or blocked the expansion program of these three nations – a program aimed at world control – they would unite in ultimate action against the United States.

The Nazi masters of Germany have made it clear that they intend not only to dominate all life and thought in their own country, but also to enslave the whole of Europe, and then to use the resources of Europe to dominate the rest of the world. . . .

In view of the nature of this undeniable threat, it can be asserted, properly and categorically, that the United States has no right or reason to encourage talk of peace, until the day shall come when there is a clear intention on the part of the aggressor nations to abandon all thought of dominating or conquering the world. . . .

Some of our people like to believe that wars in Europe and in Asia are of no concern to us. But it is a matter of most vital concern to us that European and Asiatic war-makers should not gain control of the oceans which lead to this hemisphere. . . .

Does anyone seriously believe that we need to fear attack anywhere in the Americas while a free Britain remains our most powerful naval neighbor in the Atlantic? Does anyone seriously believe, on the other hand, that we could rest easy if the Axis powers were our neighbors there?

If Great Britain goes down, the Axis powers will control the continents of Europe, Asia, Africa, Australasia, and the high seas – and they will be in a position to bring enormous military and naval resources against this hemisphere. It is no exaggeration to say that all of us, in all the Americas, would be living at the point of a gun – a gun loaded with explosive bullets, economic as well as military.

We should enter upon a new and terrible era in which the whole world, our Hemisphere included, would be run by threats of brute force. To survive in such a world, we would have to convert ourselves permanently into a militaristic power on the basis of war economy. . . .

Frankly and definitely there is danger ahead – danger against which we must prepare. But we well know that we cannot escape danger, or the fear of danger, by crawling into bed and pulling the covers over our heads. . . .

There are those who say that the Axis powers would never have any desire to attack the Western Hemisphere. That is the same dangerous form of wishful thinking which has destroyed the powers of resistance of so many conquered peoples. The plain facts are that the Nazis have proclaimed, time and again, that all other races are their inferiors and therefore subject to their orders. And most important of all, the vast resources and wealth of this American Hemisphere constitute the most tempting loot in all the round world.

Let us no longer blind ourselves to the undeniable fact that the evil forces which have crushed and undermined and corrupted so many others are already within our own gates. Your Government knows much about them and every day is ferreting them out.

Their secret emissaries are active in our own and in neighboring countries. They seek to stir up suspicion and dissension to cause internal strife.

They try to turn capital against labor, and vice versa. They try to reawaken long slumbering racial and religious enmities which should have no place in this country. They are active in every group that promotes intolerance. They exploit for their own ends our natural abhorrence of war. These trouble-breeders have but one purpose. It is to divide our people into hostile groups and to destroy our unity and shatter our will to defend ourselves.

There are also American citizens, many of them in high places, who, unwittingly in most cases, are aiding and abetting the work of these agents. I do not charge these American citizens with being foreign agents. But I do charge them with doing exactly the kind of work that the dictators want done in the United States. . . .

The experience of the past two years has proven beyond doubt that no nation can appease the Nazis. No man can tame a tiger into a kitten by stroking it. There can be no appeasement with ruthlessness. There can be no reasoning with an incendiary bomb. We know now that a nation can have peace with the Nazis only at the price of total surrender. . . .

The British people and their allies today are conducting an active war against this unholy alliance. Our own future security is greatly dependent on the outcome of that fight. Our ability to "keep out of war" is going to be affected by that outcome.

Thinking in terms of today and tomorrow, I make the direct statement to the American people that there is far less chance of the United States getting into war, if we do all we can now to support the nations defending themselves against attack by the Axis than if we acquiesce in their defeat, submit tamely to an Axis victory, and wait our turn to be the object of attack in another war later on. . . .

The people of Europe who are defending themselves do not ask us to do their fighting. They ask us for the implements of war, the planes, the tanks, the guns, the freighters which will enable them to fight for their liberty and for our security. Emphatically we must get these weapons to them in sufficient volume and quickly enough, so that we and our children will be saved the agony and suffering of war which others have had to endure.

Let not the defeatists tell us that it is too late. It will never be earlier. Tomorrow will be later than today. . . .

There is no demand for sending an American Expeditionary Force outside our own borders. There is no intention by any member of your Government to send such a force. You can, therefore, nail any talk about sending armies to Europe as deliberate untruth.

Our national policy is not directed toward war. Its sole purpose is to keep war away from our country and our people.

Democracy's fight against world conquest is being greatly aided, and must be more greatly aided, by the rearmament of the United States and by sending every ounce and every ton of munitions and supplies that we can possibly spare to help the defenders who are in the front lines. It is no more unneutral for us to do that than it is for Sweden, Russia and other nations near Germany, to send steel and ore and oil and other war materials into Germany every day in the week.

We are planning our own defense with the utmost urgency; and in its vast scale we must integrate the war needs of Britain and the other free nations which are resisting aggression. . . .

This Nation is making a great effort to produce everything that is necessary in this emergency – and with all possible speed. This great effort requires great sacrifice. . . .

If our capacity to produce is limited by machines, it must ever be remembered that these machines are operated by the skill and the stamina of the workers. As the Government is determined to protect the rights of the workers, so the nation has a right to expect that the men who man the machines will discharge their full responsibilities to the urgent needs of defense.

The worker possesses the same human dignity and is entitled to the same security of position as the engineer or the manager or the owner. For the workers provide the human power that turns out the destroyers, the airplanes and the tanks.

The Nation expects our defense industries to continue operation without interruption by strikes or lock-outs. It expects and insists that management and workers will reconcile their differences by voluntary or legal means, to continue to produce the supplies that are so sorely needed. . . .

We must be the great arsenal of democracy. For us this is an emergency as serious as war itself. We must apply ourselves to our task with the same resolution, the same sense of urgency, the same spirit of patriotism and sacrifice as we would show were we at war. . . .

We have no excuse for defeatism. We have every good reason for hope – hope for peace, hope for the defense of our civilization and for the building of a better civilization in the future.

Source: B. D. Zevin, ed., *Nothing to Fear: The Selected Addresses of Franklin Delano Roosevelt, 1932–1945* (Freeport, NY: Books for Libraries Press, 1946), pp. 248–9, 250, 251, 252–5, 257.

Having listened to your speech of Dec. 29th most carefully, I, (with millions of other mothers I am sure), am filled with horror and dread, that you are surely and unremittedly driving us into a war, that is not our making.

We have broken almost every law of neutrality that ever existed and if the tables were turned and Italy and Germany had done to us, what we have insistently and continuously done against them, we would have declared war against them long ago.

Why all this solicitation for England? Why not America first, last and always? We haven't even begun to prepare ourselves for defense!

What has England ever done for us, that we owe her such enormous consideration? And what would England do for us, should we ever cry for help?

I am a widow with one son, and he is all the world to me. If war came to our shores, my son, would fight for *his* country, with the best of them; but I absolutely refuse to sanction any move that might mean his leaving the United States to fight the battles of *foreign countries. . . .*

Yours most respectfully

(Mrs. F. Wm.) Lisette M. Wessel
New York, N.Y.

Source: Lawrence W. Levine and Cornelia R. Levine, *The People and The President: America's Conversation with FDR* (Boston: Beacon Press, 2002), p. 331.

4 A. Philip Randolph Calls for a March on Washington, 1941

America's military buildup raised unexpected social, economic, and cultural issues. Most of the nation focused on expanding aid to Great Britain and on tightening economic sanctions against the Axis. In contrast, many African Americans viewed the global crisis as an opportunity to win equality. Beyond lingering injustices such as segregation and lynching, they objected to widespread discrimination in hiring practices among defense plants and to the military's policy of relegating black soldiers to kitchen duty, janitorial work, and service roles. FDR disliked the unequal treatment but feared that taking steps against it might alienate white southerners, create social unrest, and derail his preparedness program.

Socialist labor leader A. Philip Randolph was determined to force the president's hand. A longtime agitator for black rights and head of the all-black Brotherhood of Sleeping Car Porters, Randolph issued an appeal in January 1941 for a march on Washington to pressure FDR into abolishing discriminatory hiring practices and treatment of recruits. At first he called for 10,000 black marchers to descend upon the capital then, as the proposed July 1 date for the event approached, predicted that 100,000 would show up. Randolph postponed the demonstration after FDR issued Executive Order

*8802, forbidding government contractors from using race as a criteria
in hiring, a sequence of events that was surely more than coincidental.
Randolph continued his work as a civil rights leader and is perhaps best
known for organizing the 1963 March on Washington that featured
Martin Luther King, Jr.'s "I Have a Dream" speech.*

   *On what grounds does Randolph justify his agenda? How do Randolph's
tone and demands compare with W. E. B. Dubois's 1919 "Returning Soldiers,"
featured in chapter 1? Some would argue that activists should not push for
social change during times of national crisis. Do you agree or disagree?*

Negroes are not getting anywhere with National Defense. The whole
National Defense setup reeks and stinks with race prejudice, hatred, and
discrimination. It is obvious to anyone who is not deaf, dumb and blind that
the south, with its attitude that the Negro is inferior, worthless, and just
simply don't count, is in the saddle. It is a matter of common knowledge that
the Army, Navy, and Air Corps are dominated and virtually controlled by
southerners.

   But the southerners are not alone responsible for the fact that Negroes are
being brutally pushed around. The north, east and west are also to blame,
because they wink, connive at and acquiesce in this practice of discriminating
against Negroes.

   But regardless of who is responsible for the raw deal Negroes are getting,
the big bald fact is they are getting it.

   Responsible committees of Negroes who seek to intercede in behalf of the
Negro being accorded the simple right to work in industries and on jobs
serving National Defense and to serve in the Army. Navy, and Air Corps are
being given polite assurances that Negroes will be given a fair deal. But it all
ends there. Nothing is actually done to stop discriminations.

   It seems to be apparent that even when well-meaning, responsible, top
government officials agree upon a fair and favorable policy, there are loopholes, and subordinate officers in the Army, Navy, and Air Corps, full of race
hatred, who seek its contravention, nullification, and evasion.

   This is why upstanding, independent, able and intelligent Negroes should
be in responsible posts of every department of the government. They must
be there to stimulate, suggest and initiate the formulation of certain policies
favorable to the Negro, and they must be there to help police these policies
in the interest of their fair and consistent execution. . . .

   But they are helpless without the collective, mass support of the Negro
people. Aggressive, articulate, determined, mass support will strengthen
their hands.

It is not enough for Negroes to want jobs in the factories, mills, mines, and offices, they must diplomatically and undiplomatically, ceremoniously and unceremoniously, cry out in no uncertain terms their demand for work and their rightful places in every department of the Army, Navy, and Air Corps, based of course, upon recognized qualifications.

Evidently, the regular, normal and respectable method of conferences and petitions, while proper and ought to be continued as conditions may warrant, certainly don't work. They don't do the job. . . .

Just a casual analysis and survey of the dynamics and mechanics of modern movements, legislation, administration and execution, show that only power can effect the enforcement and adoption of a given policy, however meritorious it may be. The virtue and rightness of a cause are not alone the condition and cause of its progress and acceptance. Power and pressure are at the foundation of the march of social justice and reform.

Now power and pressure do not reside in the few, the intellegentsia, they lie in and flow from the masses. Power does not even rest with the masses as such. Power is the active principle of only the organized masses, the masses united for a definite purpose.

Hence, Negro America must bring its power and pressure to bear upon the agencies and representatives of the Federal Government to exact their rights in National Defense employment and the armed forces of the country. No real, actual, bonafide, definite and positive pressure of the Negro masses has ever been brought to bear upon the executive and legislative branches of the city, state, and national governments.

Now, as to a practical program:

I suggest that 10,000 Negros march on Washington, D. C., the capital of the nation, with the slogan: WE LOYAL NEGRO-AMERICAN CITIZENS DEMAND THE RIGHT TO WORK AND FIGHT FOR OUR COUNTRY.

Our demand would be simple, single and central; namely, jobs in National Defense and placement as soldiers and officers of all ranks we are qualified for, in the armed forces.

No propaganda could be whipped up and spread to the effect that Negroes seek to hamper defense. No charge could be made that Negroes are attempting to mar national unity. They want to do none of these things. On the contrary, we seek the right to play our part in advancing the cause of national defense and national unity. But certainly, there can be no true national unity where one-tenth of the population are denied their basic rights as American citizens.

Such a pilgrimage of 10,000 Negroes would wake up and shock Official Washington as it has never been shocked before. Why? The answer is clear. Nobody expects 10,000 Negroes to get together and march anywhere for anything at any time. Negroes are supposed not to have sufficient iron in their blood for this type of struggle. In common parlance, they are supposed to be just scared and unorganizable. Is this true? I contend it is not.

What an impressive sight 10,000 Negroes would make marching down Pennsylvania Avenue in Washington, D.C., with banners preaching their cause for justice, freedom and equality.

One thing is certain and that is if Negroes are going to get anything out of this National Defense which will cost the nation 30 or 40 billions of dollars that we Negroes must help pay in taxes as property owners and workers and consumers, WE MUST FIGHT FOR IT AND FIGHT FOR IT WITH GLOVES OFF.

Source: *Pittsburgh Courier*, January 25, 1941.

5 Franklin Roosevelt Declares an Unlimited National Emergency, 1941

Lend-lease marked an important step toward a formal Anglo-American alliance, and relations between the two governments grew closer over the first half of 1941. American military planners met in secret with their British counterparts to hammer out a unified war strategy. American warships ranged far into the Atlantic to alert British vessels to German threats. In April the United States occupied the Danish colony of Greenland. It did the same with Iceland two months later. Convinced that the Nazis wanted either to conquer the world or, at the very least, isolate the United States, Roosevelt had all but resigned himself to war. Roosevelt knew that the public remained profoundly isolationist even though most Americans disliked the Nazis. His inability to convince his countrymen that Hitler posed a serious threat frustrated him. "Less than 1 per cent of our people" really understood the war, he fumed in a moment of private angst. The slow pace of rearmament further irritated Roosevelt. Increased defense appropriations – federal spending far beyond anything seen in the New Deal – were lifting the economy from depression. Manufacturers sensing a return to prosperity hesitated to convert production from consumer to military goods. Hoping to galvanize the nation without provoking isolationist or pacifist elements, FDR took to the airwaves in May 1941 to explain his reasons for declaring an unlimited national emergency.

According to FDR, why did Hitler pose a threat to the United States? How successful is he in conveying this danger? Does the president lay out a clear agenda in his speech? What should the American people do now that their country is in an "unlimited national emergency?"

WHEREAS on September 8, 1939, because of the outbreak of war in Europe a proclamation was issued declaring a limited national emergency and directing measures "for the purpose of strengthening our national defense within the limits of peacetime authorizations,"

WHEREAS a succession of events makes plain that the objectives of the Axis belligerents in such war are not confined to those avowed at its commencement, but include overthrow throughout the world of existing democratic order, and a worldwide domination of peoples and economies through the destruction of all resistance on land and sea and in the air, AND

WHEREAS indifference on the part of the United States to the increasing menace would be perilous, and common prudence requires that for the security of this Nation and of this hemisphere we should pass from peacetime authorizations of military strength to such a basis as will enable us to cope instantly and decisively with any attempt at hostile encirclement of this hemisphere, or the establishment of any base for aggression against it, as well as to repel the threat of predatory incursion by foreign agents into our territory and society,

Now, THEREFORE, I, Franklin D. Roosevelt, President of the United States of America, do proclaim that an unlimited national emergency confronts this country, which requires that its military, naval, air, and civilian defenses be put on the basis of readiness to repel any and all acts or threats of aggression directed toward any part of the Western Hemisphere.

I call upon all the loyal citizens engaged in production for defense to give precedence to the needs of the Nation to the end that a system of government that makes private enterprise possible may survive.

I call upon all our loyal workmen as well as employers to merge their lesser differences in the larger effort to insure the survival of the only kind of government which recognizes the rights of labor or of capital.

I call upon loyal State and local leaders and officials to cooperate with the civilian defense agencies of the United States to assure our internal security against foreign directed subversion and to put every community in order for maximum productive effort and minimum of waste and unnecessary frictions.

I call upon all loyal citizens to place the Nation's needs first in mind and in action to the end that we may mobilize and have ready for instant defensive use all of the physical powers, all of the moral strength, and all of the material resources of this Nation.

Source: Samuel I. Rosenman, ed., *The Public Papers and Addresses of Franklin D. Roosevelt* (New York: Russell & Russell, 1950), vol. 10, pp. 194–5.

Discussion questions

1 How did the national debate over involvement in World War II shift between 1939 and 1941?
2 How did Franklin Roosevelt's rhetoric and arguments change during the first years of World War II?
3 In what ways are the debates over involvement in World War II similar to and different from debates over American involvement in subsequent international events?

Chapter 15   Popular Culture and the Great Debate

1 Will Hays, *The Motion Picture in a Changing World*, 1940

*Hollywood exerted a powerful influence on public tastes and attitudes.
Movie making was a multi-billion-dollar industry that needed the
goodwill of both domestic and foreign audiences to survive. On the
whole, major movie studios took a wait-and-see approach to the
outbreak of war. Studio heads, nearly all of them Jewish, loathed Hitler.
They also knew that most Americans opposed involvement in the conflict.
Producers worried that addressing wartime themes might cause them to
lose access to foreign markets even as it turned off domestic patrons.
Complicating matters was the fact that ignoring the war would make
Hollywood seem out of touch with contemporary events. Films perceived
as anti-Nazi or pro-war, on the other hand, might antagonize a
Roosevelt administration hoping to maintain at least an image of
neutrality. In his annual summary of industry affairs, Will Hays, the
powerful head of the Motion Picture Producers and Distributors
Association, reflected studio heads' desire to please everyone while
irritating no one.*

*What does Hays see as the industry's role during wartime? How does this
parallel contemporary attitudes toward the war, as revealed in the previous
chapter? What are Hays's primary concerns?*

America Between the Wars, 1919–1941: A Documentary Reader, First Edition.
Edited by David Welky. Editorial material and organization © 2012 John Wiley & Sons, Inc.
Published 2012 by John Wiley & Sons, Inc.

The succession of exceptional pictures now flowing from our studios is particularly noteworthy in view of the discouraging and difficult conditions under which it was achieved. American pictures have been gauged to a world market. The war has seriously affected our leading export fields and and no man can know even the immediate future.

With crumbling foreign markets on one flank and the need of sharp and effective production economies on the other, producers did the proper and courageous thing – they advanced in the center, making pictures of even higher artistic and entertainment appeal. Whatever obstacles may still arise – and no world industry can be out of the woods at this critical period – this is the direction in which they can be met and overcome. There is no saturation point in the demand for good entertainment, particularly important under the tensions of the present day.

In applying the yardstick of social values to motion picture progress, those who write the history of our times are not likely to ignore the contributions of the films in exposing the tragedy of war to the youth of our country. The answer as to whether certain war pictures produced by the industry "glorified" war or laid bare its horrors lies in the fact that the pressure of youth in our own country is towards peace not involvement. The romance of war has been punctured. . . . Only the screen, through news-reels and dramatic films can picture war as it is with sufficient vividness to impress the mind of youth. It is significant that many American pictures were banned abroad because in the judgment of foreign government censors they were anti-militaristic.

Hand in hand with such pictures were many patriotic films that aroused interest in our defense problems, showed the efficiency of our various national services and the dangers of propanganda with which we are faced. Youth in America today is clear-headed and clear-eyed with regard to the futility of war; and pictures, more than words, have tended to bring this result. Whatever satisfaction we may derive from the artistic and social progress made by the screen during the year under review, this is no time for complacency. Much of our business is subject to the misfortunes of war, and the obstacles still before the industry may be graver today than at any time in its history. . . .

The shock of the European war, coming at a time when foreign receipts were a most important factor in the planning of production schedules by many of our companies here, was made doubly serious by the investments and undertakings of American producers for the production of pictures in England. On one day the banks in England were closed, holdings of foreign currency were called in, and export of bank notes, gold securities or foreign currency was prohibited without special permission. All theatres in the United Kingdom were closed by Government order.

Later theatres gradually reopened but the loss in the first few weeks was necessarily severe. . . .

In France, the needs of mobilization, involving trained theatre operatives as well as others, caused the closing of numerous theatres during the first weeks, but the French Government from the beginning requested that theatres be kept open, if possible. . . .

In other foreign markets, too, American films must continue to thread their way through a maze of trade restrictions, tariffs, embargoes, quotas, import licenses, exchange controls and numerous other devices for preventing imports.

Duties and import taxes have been raised in the Argentine, Australia, Bolivia and England. Quota restrictions have been increased in Estonia, the Italian African Colony and Japan. New quota laws have been passed in Australia, Brazil, Greece, Mexico, Spain and Switzerland. New interior taxes have been adopted in Algeria, the Argentine, Brazil, Canada, Egypt, England, India, Siam, and Spain.

It is fortunate that our Government has recognized the importance of our films not only as a part of our total exports, but as the messengers of American commerce everywhere. As a result of the trade agreements concluded by the State Department, our industry has been definitely and favorably affected by the opportunities to negotiate against exactions, barriers and restraints in certain countries.

Source: Will H. Hays, *The Motion Picture in A Changing World: Annual Report to the Motion Picture Producers and Distributors of America, Inc.* (March 25, 1940), pp. 3–5, 6–7.

2 Henry R. Luce, America and the War, 1940

The great debate over America's role in World War II ricocheted through popular culture. Motion pictures steered clear of the discussion as best they could. Many magazines, however, plunged in with both feet. Periodicals reached fewer people than movies and had little financial exposure to the overseas market. Appearing either weekly or monthly, they were expected to provide more up-to-date takes on global affairs than movies, which took months to assemble. Except for some hysterical and, from the perspective of 1940, embarrassingly pro-war films made during World War I, movies had little history of speaking out on controversial subjects. Magazine publishers felt more freedom to speak their minds. Henry Luce, who directed Time, Life, *and* Fortune *magazines, had strong opinions on Nazism and the war.* Life, *the most popular periodical of the era, promoted the American defense*

effort, pushed for additional aid to Britain, and criticized the Nazis
throughout the late 1930s. In mid-1940, after spending a month in Europe,
Luce returned to the United States determined to rally people to his cause.
He spoke on a national NBC radio hookup against a dire backdrop.
Germany's forces had moved into Norway, Denmark, Belgium, Luxembourg,
and the Netherlands in recent weeks. Hitler had been close to capturing
much of Britain's military at Dunkirk. Although Luce did not know it, the
invasion of France was just days away.

As Luce sees it, what are the stakes in this war? How well does he define
"the America I want to fight for?" How does his rhetoric compare to what
FDR was saying around the same time?

America is now confronted by a greater challenge to its survival as a land of liberty than any it has had to face in 80 years.

When I sailed for Europe in April, the American people were not willing to face the challenge. I believe they are willing to face it now.

What precisely is this challenge? The fundamental truth is very simple. Let us not be distracted by ifs and buts. The truth, fully attested by every competent observer of world events I know, is simply this: that the American way of life is bitterly opposed by mighty and ruthless military nations. And the fundamental truth is, further: that nothing will stop these mighty and ruthless military nations – not money or cajolery or friendship – nothing but superior force. . . .

If Great Britain and France fail, we know that we and we only among the great powers are left to defend the democratic faith throughout the world. And if Great Britain and France succeed by a miracle of heroism in beating off the enemy, we know that Great Britain and France, weakened with loss of blood and treasure, will need our ungrudging co-operation in order to restore in half the world a peace of justice and humanity. We may never fight side by side, comrades in arms of France and Britain. But we know now that, fundamentally, their struggle is our struggle.

The frame of mind of the American people has changed amazingly in the last few weeks. I am amazed to find an attitude almost amounting to one of intense alarm. Now if the alarm is like the alarm on an alarm clock reminding us what time of day it is – then that's fine. But there is no occasion for the kind of alarm that gives way to panic.

What is the actual situation? It is this. Certain stupefying events have happened in Europe. And we realize we have to cake action. What we have to do I would summarize under two heads. First we have to arm ourselves. We have to prepare ourselves to meet force with force – to meet force with *superior* force. That is a colossal job. The second thing we have to do is to make up our minds what we are willing to fight for. That for us, as for all free peoples, is an even harder job.

The job of arming America physically is a job which we all agree cannot be delayed. To this I would add the following points:

First, armaments are expensive – the most terribly expensive things in the world. They are a sheer and appalling economic waste. That means that all of us are going to be a lot poorer than we otherwise might have been. But we will not cry about that. Along with all other democracies, we will take our full share of the blame for not having done our share toward creating a better world and for not having erected stronger bulwarks against monstrous aggression.

Secondly, the arming of America must in itself be the first practical test of our ability to act as a united people. For many years we have been anything but a united people. We have been a very expensively divided nation. The arming of America must be our first great act of national unity.

Thirdly, the arming of America must get fully under way now under the leadership of our President. Franklin Roosevelt is in many respects a very great leader. But he has his faults. Who hasn't? There are two faults – two of the defects of his virtues perhaps – which we want him to guard against now. One fault is his tolerance of incompetent people. A very nice fault – but one we cannot afford just now. The other fault is his intolerance of extremely able people who don't happen to agree with him. During the last few years Franklin Roosevelt hasn't got on at all well with most of our ablest industrialists. It may have been their fault or it may have been his. Never mind. Today we need the services of the ablest industrialists in America for the most efficient arming of America. . . .

Fourthly, let us constantly remember that appropriations are not armaments. Adolf Hitler is not afraid of big dollar signs in the newspapers. Hitler will only be afraid of actual airplanes, actual tanks, actual guns – and actual pilots and actual gunners. Hitler knows right now just how many actual airplanes, tanks, guns, pilots, gunners we have – and he'll keep on knowing every step of the way. During some possible lull in the European scene you may lose interest in the arming of America but Hitler won't. The price of military domination is eternal vigilance – and it is also the price of liberty.

Finally, let us face frankly the handicaps of democracies in their inevitable contests with autocracies. Autocracies foster above all else the will to fight, even the love of fighting – what is called the martial spirit. And except on rare occasions, democracies just do not foster the will to fight. That is a very great military handicap. Billions and billions of dollars worth of airplanes and tanks and guns aren't worth the trouble of dumping them into the sea – unless there are men who have the will and the courage and the daring to use them. For many young men and women, who have grown up in a period of great revulsion against war, this is a very unpleasant truth. For seven long years Hitler and all his storm-trooping henchmen have been sneering at us democrats because, they say, we are soft and effeminate and self-indulgent and greedy for comfort and pleasure. There is, I fear, only too much truth in that sneering indictment.

But of course democracies have fought wars and they have won wars. Otherwise they wouldn't exist today in this very imperfect world. Good peace-loving democrats have fought with supreme courage and skill. For what do they fight?

This question brings us to the second thing which the American people have to do. We have to make up our minds what we are willing to fight *for*. . . .

What I am willing to fight for is, of course, America but not America as a geologic mass, not for its mountains and plains and rivers, greatly though I love them and much though they have concerned me. The America I want to fight for is the America of freedom and justice, the America which has stood throughout the world for the hope of progress in the democratic way of life and for faith in the ultimate brotherhood of man. America belongs to us, the lucky 130,000,000 people who are living here today. But America does not belong entirely to us. A little of America belongs to every man and woman everywhere who has had faith in democracy and hope in a world of peace and justice. We the living who control the destiny of America today are the heirs of a great inheritance from men who lived and from men who died to make men free. What they meant by America is what I would wish to mean by America. And for that America I am willing to fight. And I am the more willing to fight because if I know anything I know that that America, the America we love, has small chance of surviving the tyranny and chaos which everywhere advances unless those who love America make it plain that they are willing and ready to fight.

If something like this is the answer which will be given in the coming weeks and months by the American people, then I for one am completely willing to trust our leaders, whoever they may be at any time, in the White House, in the State Department and in Congress to decide exactly where and when and how the American people shall take their stand at Armageddon.

Source: Henry R. Luce, "America and Armageddon," *Life* 8 (June 3, 1940): 40, 100.

3 Edward R. Murrow, *This is London*, 1940

Like motion pictures, radio was by 1940 a hugely popular entertainment medium. Listeners depended upon it for sports coverage, dramatic and comedic programming, and news. Surveys revealed that Americans were not only laying down their newspapers in favor of radio news, but also that they trusted radio reporters more than newspaper journalists. Unlike the newspaper, radio reports transported audiences to far away places with audio pictures that print sources could never emulate. The rise of broadcasting networks made the radio, and radio news, truly national.

Hitler's militarism and the outbreak of World War II offered a proving ground for an up-and-coming generation of newsmen. Edward R. Murrow, CBS radio's chief European correspondent, seized the opportunity. His wartime broadcasts elevated him from an unknown to an internationally famous journalist. Murrow was a relative novice who made his first on-air appearance during Germany's 1938 annexation of Austria. He proved an innovative reporter with a gift for capturing the essence of a situation in a few well-turned phrases. Murrow headquartered in London in autumn 1940 as German bombers pummeled Britain, presumably in preparation for a full-scale invasion. Speaking from rooftops and deserted streets, his voice steady as bombs burst around him, Murrow provided a first hand description of the Nazi war machine and humanized the British people. Although he could not directly state his views on the air, Murrow supported giving additional American aid to Great Britain.

How does Murrow present the British? What characteristics do they possess? How do his reports make them sympathetic figures?

September 3, 1940

This is London, three-thirty in the morning. A year ago tonight the weather was warm and muggy. It's the same tonight. Twelve months ago tonight we had a violent thunderstorm. As lightning streaked the sky and thunder rode down these crooked streets, I saw white-faced people running for air-raid shelters. If there should be a similiar storm tonight, there would be no panic: nerves are much steadier, London is not as black tonight as it was on that first night, when darkness settled over Europe. Now we have dim little street lights and shaded automobile headlights. . . .

The cost of living has gone up. Taxes have gone up. Automobile showrooms have closed. The number of balloons overhead has increased. So has the number of fire engines and ambulances. A few houses on the outskirts of London have been smashed by bombs.

But, in spite of all these changes, the face of London has altered little during the first year of this war. This year, which has brought an unending succession of disaster and disappointment to London, has left few visible signs. The real transformation can only be sensed; it can't be seen. For example, the little brick house in that blind alley known as Downing Street looks just as it did, but there's a new man living at No. 10, and certainly one of the greatest changes of the year occurred when Mr. Chamberlain moved out and Mr. Churchill moved in.

In September, 1939, the talk was of the Navy, the ring of steel that was to starve the Germans. Today the Royal Air Force has captured the respect and admiration which has traditionally been given to the Royal Navy.

On the day war was declared any man who predicted that after a year of war, including only ten weeks of battle, Britain would be without effective allies and faced with the prospect of invasion would have been considered mad. Invasion is now one of the favorite topics of conversation. These Londoners know what they're fighting for now – not Poland or Norway – not even for France, but for Britain.

Men who scoffed at the idea of parachute troops now spend their nights watching for them. No longer do we hear the sound of church bells on Sunday morning. They will be rung only to announce the arrival of airborne troops.

There were no seaside holidays for Londoners this year. The beaches are being reserved and prepared for fighting. Newspapers and magazines have been reduced in size. The publication of serious books has decreased. Night clubs are doing a roaring business. The intellectual – the man who can write and talk – now counts for even less than he did a year ago; the man who can run a lathe, fly a plane, or build a ship counts for more.

The King and Queen are two of the busiest people in these islands. They go about inspecting ships, guns, canteens, factories, and nearly everything else. The King spends considerable time decorating his soldiers, sailors, and airmen.

But one thing has happened to London or, rather, to Londoners which can only be appreciated by one who has spent considerably more than a year in this sprawling city beside the Thames: they've become more human, less reserved; more talkative and less formal. There's almost a small-town atmosphere about the place. Sometimes strangers speak to you in the bus or subways. I've even heard conversation between total strangers in a railway car – something which was unthinkable in peacetime. There's been a drawing together, particularly during the last two months. Part of that is the result of air raids. Class distinction, dignity, and even financial prestige are hard to maintain in an air-raid shelter at three o'clock in the morning.

And so, as this second year of this war opens, we find the world's greatest army opposing the most powerful navy in the world, with most of the fighting taking place in the air. Europe has suffered much this last twelve months. The next year and the years after that will twist and torture minds and bodies. Reporting Europe will not be a pleasant task. One feels very small and humble. We can only continue to give you the news and the atmosphere in which it happens. You must reach your own conclusions.

September 10, 1940 – 6:45 p.m.

When you hear that London has been bombed and hammered for ten to twelve hours during the night, you should remember that this is a huge, sprawling city, that there is nothing like a continuous rain of bombs – at least, there hasn't been so far. Often there is a period of ten or twenty minutes when no sound can be heard, no searchlights seen. Then a few bombs will come whistling down. Then silence again. A hundred planes over London doesn't mean that they were all here at the same time. They generally come singly or in pairs, circle around over the searchlights two or three times, and then you can hear them start their bombing runs, generally a shallow dive, and those bombs take a long time to fall.

After three nights of watching and listening, these night attacks are assuming something of a pattern for me. The Germans come over as soon as it's dark, a few minutes earlier each night. For the first few hours they drop very little heavy stuff, seem to concentrate on incendiaries, hoping to start fires to act as beacons for the high explosives later on. For the last three nights the weight of the attacks developed around midnight. As you know, the damage has been considerable. But London has suffered no more than a serious flesh wound. The attack will probably increase in intensity, but things will have to get much worse before anyone here is likely to consider it too much to bear.

We are told today that the Germans believe Londoners, after a while, will rise up and demand a new government, one that will make peace with Germany. It's more probable that they'll rise up and murder a few German pilots who come down by parachute. The life of a parachutist would not be worth much in the East End of London tonight.

The politicians who called this a "people's war" were right, probably more right than they knew at the time. I've seen some horrible sights in this city during these days and nights, but not once have I heard man, woman, or child suggest that Britain should throw in her hand. These people are angry. How much they can stand, I don't know. The strain is very great. The prospect for the winter, when some way must be found to keep water out of the shelters and a little heat inside, is not pleasant. Nor will it be any more pleasant in Germany, where winters are generally more severe than on this green island. After four days and nights of this air *Blitzkrieg*, I think the people here are rapidly becoming veterans, even as their Army was hardened in the fire of Dunkerque.

Many people have already got over the panicky feeling that hit everyone in the nerve centers when they realized they were being bombed. Those people I talked to in long queues in front of the big public shelters tonight were cheerful and somewhat resigned. They'd been waiting in line for an hour or more, waiting for the shelters to open at the first wail of the sirens. They had no private shelters of their own, but they carried blankets to throw over the chairs in this public underground refuge. Their sleep tonight will be as fitful as you could expect in such quarters without beds. Of course, they don't like the situation, but most of them feel that even this underground existence is preferable to what they'd get under German domination.

All the while strong efforts are being made to remind the British subjects who live underground that RAF bombers are flying in the other direction and that the Germans are having rather a rough time of it, too.

December 24, 1940

This is London, reporting all clear. There was a single German aircraft over East Anglia this afternoon, but there are no reports of German raiders over Britain tonight. Whether this inactivity is due to good will or bad weather, I don't know, nor do we know whether the RAF bombers are flying tonight. Christmas Day began in London nearly an hour ago. The church bells did not ring at midnight. When they ring again, it will be to announce invasion. And if they ring, the British are ready. Tonight, as on every other night, the rooftop watchers are peering out across the fantastic forest of London's chimney pots. The antiaircraft gunners stand ready. And all along the coast of this island, the observers revolve in their reclining chairs, listening for the sound of German planes. The fire fighters and the ambulance drivers are waiting, too. The blackout stretches from Birmingham to Bethlehem, but tonight over Britain the skies are clear.

This is not a merry Christmas in London. I heard that phrase only twice in the last three days. This afternoon as the stores were closing, as shoppers and office workers were hurrying home, one heard such phrases as "So long, Mamie," and "Good luck, Jack," but never "A merry Christmas." It can't be a merry Christmas, for those people who spend tonight and tomorrow by their firesides in their own homes realize that they have bought this Christmas with their nerves, their bodies, and their old buildings. Their nerve is unshaken; the casualties have not been large, and there are many old buildings still untouched. Between now and next Christmas there stretches twelve months of increasing toil and sacrifice, a period when the Britishers will live hard. Most of them realize that. Tonight's serious Christmas Eve is the result of a realization of the future, rather than the aftermath of hardships sustained during the past year. The British find some basis for confidence in the last few months' developments. They believe that they're tearing the Italian Empire to pieces. So far shelter life has produced none of the predicted epidemics. The nation's health is about as good now as it was at this time last year. And above all they're sustained by a tradition of victory.

Tonight there are few Christmas parties in London, a few expensive dinners at famous hotels, but there are no fancy paper hats and no firecrackers. Groups determined to get away from the war found themselves after twenty minutes inspecting the latest amateur diagram of the submarine menace or the night bombers. A few blocks away in the underground shelters entire families were celebrating Christmas Eve. Christmas carols are being sung underground. Most of the people down there don't know that London is not being bombed tonight. Christmas presents will be unwrapped down underground before those people see daylight tomorrow. Little boys who have received miniature Spitfires or Hurricanes will be waking the late sleepers by imitating the sound of whistling bombs, just as we used to try to reproduce the sound of a locomotive or a speeding automobile. . . .

I should like to add my small voice to give my own Christmas greetings to friends and colleagues at home. Merry Christmas is somehow ill-timed and out of place, so I shall just use the current London phrase – so long and good luck.

Source: Elmer Davis, ed. *This Is London* (New York: Simon & Schuster, 1941), pp. 150, 151–3, 162–4, 221–4.

4 War and Consumerism: Advertisements from *Time* Magazine, 1941

America's defense buildup was a topic of everyday conversation by late 1941, when these four advertisements appeared in Time. *Movies, radio dramas, and magazine fiction all addressed the war, the draft, and the need to sacrifice for national defense. Many corporations mirrored this sense of muscular patriotism in order to attract investors or sell merchandise. Although none of them dared take a concrete position on overseas events or hint at American intervention, they all strove to suggest that their product somehow played a part in ensuring the nation's safety.*

How do these advertisements connect products with American patriotism? How successful are they? Can you think of contemporary ad campaigns that exploit flag waving?

AMERICA MAINTAINS ITS MOST *FAMOUS TRADITION*

IT was a young America which established its great tradition of the Freedom of the Seas. It was the World's newest nation which voiced the courageous words, "Millions for defense, but not one cent for tribute." Now building is the greatest fleet the world has ever known, for America is more determined than ever its famous tradition shall continue. ¶ In this task American industry and engineering genius are playing a leading role. And with it Auto-Lite's engineering laboratories and 18 great production plants are rendering effective aid to the nation. ¶ Spark plugs, batteries, instruments, wire and cable, complete ignition systems, are being supplied for crash boats, flashing pursuit ships, mighty bombers, trucks and reconnaissance cars. Auto-Lite builds a wide range of other defense material, too — mess kits and map cases, trigger arm assemblies, gun-firing solenoids, boosters, fuses and projectiles. ¶ In this national emergency we have enlisted our plants and our personnel. Both have demonstrated their ability to meet the extraordinary demands of the defense program while maintaining Auto-Lite standards of service to the customers who have helped build our business.

SPARK PLUGS · BATTERIES
ETCHED, EMBOSSED
AND LITHOGRAPHED NAMEPLATES
WIRE AND CABLE · IRON CASTINGS
ALUMINUM AND ZINC DIE CASTINGS
STARTING, LIGHTING AND IGNITION

AUTO·LITE

AIRCRAFT AND OTHER INSTRUMENTS
AND GAUGES
LAMP ASSEMBLIES · METAL STAMPINGS
HORNS AND SIGNAL DEVICES
PLASTIC PRODUCTS · LEATHER GOODS
STAINLESS STEEL KITCHEN UTENSILS

TIME, October 27, 1941   59

Figure 15.1   War and consumerism: Auto-Lite advertisement.

Source: *Time* 38 (October 27, 1941): 59.

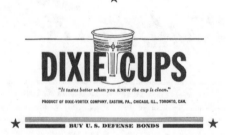

FIGHT BACK at this THREAT!

EMPLOYEE ILLNESS, and its spread through contagion, must be fought. Common colds, influenza and other illnesses ... so easily spread through indirect mouth-to-mouth contact by the common drinking vessel ... cannot be tolerated now!

The nation is under pressure to *produce*. Plants not directly on defense work are doubly active in substituting for those that are. Neither the individual shop or business — nor America at large — can now afford any loss of man-hours of productive effort.

Take heed to your water coolers, your drinking fountains, the soda bars — wherever drinking is done in public. DIXIE CUPS banish the threat of mouth-to-mouth contamination, simply and easily. For DIXIES are used but once and then destroyed.

This winter must be epidemic free ... in the national interest.

DIXIE CUPS

"It tastes better when you KNOW the cup is clean."

PRODUCT OF DIXIE-VORTEX COMPANY, EASTON, PA., CHICAGO, ILL., TORONTO, CAN.

BUY U. S. DEFENSE BONDS

Figure 15.2   War and consumerism: Dixie Cups advertisement.

Source: *Time* 38 (November 24, 1941): 112.

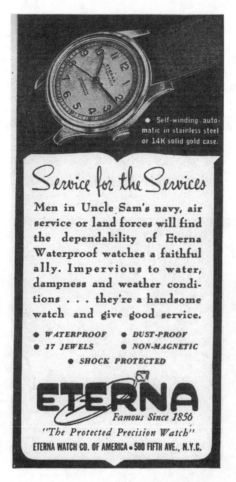

Figure 15.3   War and consumerism: Eterna Watch advertisement.

Source: *Time* 38 (November 24, 1941): 54.

Plowing a
1600-mile furrow
for defense

THE nation's transcontinental telephone facilities are being more than doubled—in a hurry!

Telephone crews now are working west from Omaha. Others soon will start east from Sacramento. When they meet, their tractor-hauled "plow trains" will have buried two Long Distance telephone cables three feet underground, in a furrow 1600 miles long!

Together, these twin cables provide for more than 500 *new* telephone talking channels — plus facilities for radio, teletype and telephoto. Protected against all weather hazards, they make it unlikely that America's coast-to-coast communications will ever be broken.

Big as it is, this job is only a small part of the Bell System's share in national defense.

LONG DISTANCE helps unite the nation
"THE TELEPHONE HOUR" *is broadcast every Monday evening over the N.B.C. Red Network*

Here's the new cable route—from Omaha to Cheyenne, to Denver, to Salt Lake City, to Sacramento. The special plow in the picture cuts a deep, narrow trench, lays two cables, and refills, in one continuous operation. Each plow can cover several miles a day under favorable conditions.

TIME, October 27, 1941   11

Figure 15.4   War and consumerism: Bell Telephone (plowing for defense).

Source: *Time* 38 (October 27, 1941): 11.

5 Harry Warner's Testimony to a Senate Subcommittee on War Propaganda in Film, 1941

Hollywood's anti-Nazism intensified through 1940 and 1941. Groups such as the Hollywood Anti-Nazi League staged star-studded events designed to expand opposition to Hitlerism. The Fighting 69th *(1940),* Sergeant York *(1941) , and other films presented World War I as a brutal yet ennobling conflict that preserved democracy and forged a stronger union.* Confessions of a Nazi Spy *(1939) and* The Mortal Storm *(1940) probed the brutalities of Hitlerism. Isolationists saw little chance of getting out their message in the face of mighty Hollywood's apparent (and overstated) ideological unity. "The silver screen has been flooded with picture after picture designed to rouse us to a state of war hysteria," North Dakota Senator Gerald Nye thundered. Along with allies in the Senate, Nye organized hearings intended to expose movie producers as propagandists, warmongers, and possibly subversives. Supporters stressed industry executives' Jewish heritage and foreign backgrounds in order to draw their "Americanness" into question. One of the highlights of the hearings came when Harry Warner, president of Warner Bros., the most virulently anti-Nazi studio, testified. His defiant attitude embodies the cultural shift that had occurred since Will Hays offered his tepid report less than two years earlier.*

How does Warner defend himself against charges of warmongering? How does his argument differ from Will Hays's? Is it appropriate for movies to take positions on controversial issues? Is popular culture powerful enough to drown out opposing viewpoints?

MR. WARNER. I am opposed to nazism. I abhor and detest every principle and practice of the Nazi movement. To me, nazism typifies the very opposite of the kind of life every decent man, woman, and child wants to live. I believe nazism is a world revolution whose ultimate objective is to destroy our democracy, wipe out all religion, and enslave our people – just as Germany has destroyed and enslaved Poland, Belgium, Holland, France, and all the other countries. I am ready to give myself and all my personal resources to aid in the defeat of the Nazi menace to the American people. . . .

Shortly after Hitler came to power in Germany I became convinced that Hitlerism was an evil force designed to destroy free people, whether they were Catholics, Protestants, or Jews. I claim no credit as a prophet. Many appraised the Nazis in their true role, from the very day of Hitler's rise to power.

I have always been in accord with President Roosevelt's foreign policy. In September 1939, when the Second World War began, I believed, and I believe today, that the world struggle for freedom was in its final stage. I said publicly then, and I say today, that the freedom which this country fought England to obtain, we may have to fight with England to retain.

I am unequivocally in favor of giving England and her allies all supplies which our country can spare. I also support the President's doctrine of freedom of the seas, as recently explained to the public by him.

Frankly, I am not certain whether or not this country should enter the war in its own defense at the present time. The President knows the world situation and our country's problems better than any other man. I would follow his recommendation concerning a declaration of war.

It Hitler should be the victor abroad, the United States would be faced with a Nazi-dominated world. I believe – and I am sure that the subcommittee shares my feeling – that this would be a catastrophe for our country. I want to avoid such a catastrophe, as I know you do.

I have given my views to you frankly and honestly. They reduce themselves to my previous statement: I am opposed to nazism. I abhor and detest every principle and practice of the Nazi movement. I am not alone in feeling this. I am sure that the overwhelming majority of our people and our Congress share the same views.

While I am opposed to nazism, I deny that the pictures produced by my company are "propaganda," as has been alleged. Senator Nye has said that our picture *Sergeant York* is designed to create war hysteria. Senator Clark had added *Confessions of a Nazi Spy* to the isolationist blacklist. John T. Flynn, in turn, has added *Underground*. These witnesses have not seen these pictures, so I cannot imagine how they can judge them. On the other hand, millions of average citizens have paid to see these pictures. They have enjoyed wide popularity and have been profitable to our company. In short, these pictures have been judged by the public and the judgment has been favorable.

Sergeant York is a factual portrait of the life of one of the great heroes of the last war. If that is propaganda, we plead guilty. *Confessions of a Nazi Spy* is a factual portrayal of a Nazi spy ring that actually operated in New York City. If that is propaganda we plead guilty.

So it is with each and every one of our pictures dealing with the world situation or with the national defense. These pictures were carefully prepared on the basis of factual happenings and they were not twisted to serve any ulterior purpose.

Apparently our accusers desire that we change our policy of picturing accurately world affairs and the national defense program. This, Warner Bros. will never do. This, I am sure the Congress would not want us to do. This, I am certain the public would not tolerate.

As I have said, reckless and unfounded charges have been made before your committee against Warner Bros. and myself. These charges are so vague that, frankly, I have great difficulty in answering them. However, they have been widely disseminated and may be believed by the uninformed. I have tried to summarize the charges. They seem to divide into four allegations, as follows:

1. That Warner Bros. is producing a type of picture relating to world affairs and national defense for the purpose allegedly of inciting our country to war.

    This, we deny. Warner Bros. has been producing pictures on current affairs for over 20 years and our present policies are no different than before there was a Hitler menace. The pictures complained of were prepared under similar studio routine to all Warner Bros. productions.

2. That the Warner Bros. pictures concerning world affairs and national defense are inaccurate and are twisted for ulterior purpose.

    This, we deny. The pictures complained of are accurate. They were all carefully researched. They show the world as it is.

3. That Warner Bros. is producing pictures that the public does not wish to see and will not patronize.

    The proof of the pudding is in the eating. All of the productions complained of have been profitable. To the point is *Sergeant York*, which, I believe, will gross more money for our company than any other picture we have made in recent years.

4. That, in some mysterious way, the Government orders us to make this or that type of picture.

    This, we deny. We receive no orders, no suggestion – direct or indirect – from the administration. It is true that Warner Bros. has tried to cooperate with the national-defense program. It is true that Warner Bros., over a period of 8 years, has made feature pictures concerning our Army, Navy, and air force. It is true that we have made a series of shorts portraying the lives of American heroes. To do this, we needed no urging from the Government and we would be ashamed if the Government would have to make such requests of us. We have produced these pictures voluntarily and proudly. . . .

I am an American citizen, and I bow to no one in my patriotism and devotion to my country. Our country has become great because it is, in truth, a land of freedom. No one can take these freedoms from the American people. The United States has always been a united nation of free people living in tolerance and faith in each other. We have been able to achieve this unity because of the freedoms of the individual.

In conclusion, I tell this committee honestly, I care nothing for any temporary advantage or profit that may be offered to me or my company. I will not censor the dramatization of the works of reputable and well-informed writers to conceal from the American people what is happening in the world. Freedom of speech, freedom of religion, and freedom of enterprise cannot be bought at the price of other people's rights. I believe the American people have a right to know the truth. You may correctly charge me with being anti-Nazi. But no one can charge me with being anti-American.

Thank you, gentlemen, for your courtesy in listening to me. [Applause.]

Source: United States Senate, 77th Cong., 1st sess., *Hearings Before a Subcommittee of the Committee on Interstate Commerce on S. Res. 152, September 9 to 26, 1941* (Washington DC: Government Printing Office, 1942), pp. 338–40, 347–8.

Discussion questions

1   What do you think accounts for the varying messages coming from American popular culture regarding the war?
2   In what ways does popular culture follow or vary from the arguments Franklin Roosevelt made about America's role in the conflict?
3   How should popular culture address controversial issues of national importance?

Bibliography

Introduction

Paul Carter, *The Twenties in America*, 2nd ed. (Arlington Heights, IL: Harlan Davidson, 1975).

Lynn Dumenil, *The Modern Temper: American Culture and Society in the 1920s* (New York: Hill & Wang, 1995).

David M. Kennedy, *Freedom from Fear: The American People in Depression and War, 1929–1945* (New York: Oxford University Press, 2001).

David E. Kyvig, *Daily Life in the United States, 1920–1940: How Americans Lived Through the Roaring Twenties and the Great Depression* (Chicago: Ivan R. Dee, 2004).

William E. Leuchtenberg, *Franklin D. Roosevelt and the New Deal* (New York: Harper, 1963).

Robert S. McElvaine, *The Great Depression: America, 1929–1941* (New York: Crown, 1984).

Nathan Miller, *New World Coming: The 1920s and the Making of Modern America* (New York: Da Capo, 2004).

Michael Parrish, *Anxious Decades: America in Prosperity and Depression, 1920–1941* (New York: W. W. Norton, 1994).

America Between the Wars, 1919–1941: A Documentary Reader, First Edition.
Edited by David Welky. Editorial material and organization © 2012 John Wiley & Sons, Inc.
Published 2012 by John Wiley & Sons, Inc.

1　Challenges to Postwar Readjustment

Eliot Asinof, *Eight Men Out: The Black Sox and the 1919 World Series* (New York: Henry Holt, 1977).

John M. Barry, *The Great Influenza: The Story of the Deadliest Pandemic in History* (New York: Penguin, 2005).

David Brody, *Labor in Crisis: The Steel Strike of 1919* (Urbana: University of Illinois Press, 1987).

Stanley Coben, *A. Mitchell Palmer: Politician* (New York: Columbia University Press, 1963).

Ann Hagedorn, *Savage Peace: Hope and Fear in America, 1919* (New York: Simon & Schuster, 2008).

David M. Kennedy, *Over Here: The First World War and American Society* (New York: Oxford University Press, 1980).

Margaret Macmillan, *Paris 1919: Six Months that Changed the World* (New York: Random House, 2002).

David Mitchell, *1919: Red Mirage, Year of Desperate Rebellion* (New York: Macmillan, 1970).

David Montgomery, *The Fall of the House of Labor: The Workplace, the State, and American Labor Activism, 1865–1925* (New York: Cambridge University Press, 1987).

Robert K. Murray, *The Politics of Normalcy: Governmental Theory and Practice in the Harding-Coolidge Era* (New York: W. W. Norton, 1973).

Robert K. Murray, *Red Scare: A Study in National Hysteria, 1919–1920* (Minneapolis: University of Minnesota Press, 1955).

David Pietrusza, *1920: The Year of the Six Presidents* (New York: Basic Books, 2008).

Grif Stockley, *Blood in Their Eyes: The Elaine Race Massacres of 1919* (Fayetteville: University of Arkansas Press, 2001).

2　Social Battles of the 1920s

Norman H. Clark, *Deliver Us from Evil: An Interpretation of American Prohibition* (New York: W. W. Norton, 1976).

Roger Daniels, *Guarding the Golden Door: American Immigration Policy and Immigrants Since 1882* (New York: Hill & Wang, 2004).

David J. Goldberg, *Discontented America: The United States in the 1920s* (Baltimore: Johns Hopkins University Press, 1999).

John Higham, *Strangers in the Land: Patterns of American Nativism, 1865–1925*, 2nd ed. (Piscataway, NJ: Rutgers University Press, 1988).

Kenneth T. Jackson, *The Ku Klux Klan in the City, 1916–1930* (New York: Oxford University Press, 1967).

Desmond King, *Making Americans: Immigration, Race, and the Origins of the Diverse Democracy* (Cambridge: Harvard University Press, 2000).

Edward J. Larson, *Summer for the Gods: The Scopes Trial and America's Continuing Debate over Science and Religion* (Cambridge: Harvard University Press, 1998).

Nancy MacLean, *Behind the Mask of Chivalry: The Making of the Second Ku Klux Klan* (New York: Oxford University Press, 1994).

Leonard J. Moore, *Citizen Klansmen: The Ku Klux Klan in Indiana, 1921–1928* (Chapel Hill: University of North Carolina Press, 1997).

Daniel Okrent, *Last Call: The Rise and Fall of Prohibition* (New York: Scribner, 2010).

Bruce Watson, *Sacco and Vanzetti: The Men, The Murders, and the Judgment of Mankind* (New York: Viking, 2007).

3 The New Negro

Davarian L. Baldwin, *Chicago's New Negros: Modernity, the Great Migration, and Black Urban Life* (Chapel Hill: University of North Carolina Press, 2007).

A'Lelia Bundles, *On Her Own Ground: The Life and Times of Madam C. J. Walker* (New York: Scribner, 2001).

St. Clair Drake and Horace A. Cayton, *Black Metropolis: A Study of Negro Life in a Northern City* (Chicago: University of Chicago Press, 1993).

Philip Dray, *At the Hands of Persons Unknown: The Lynching of Black America* (New York: Random House, 2003).

James R. Grossman, *Land of Hope: Chicago, Black Southerners and the Great Migration* (Chicago: University of Chicago Press, 1991).

Nathan Irvin Huggins, *Harlem Renaissance* (New York: Oxford University Press, 1971).

Nicholas Lehman, *The Promised Land: The Great Black Migration and How It Changed America* (New York: Vintage, 1991).

David Levering Lewis, *When Harlem Was in Vogue* (New York: Oxford University Press, 1981).

Mary G. Rolinson, *Grassroots Garveyism: The United Negro Improvement Association in the Rural South, 1920–1927* (Chapel Hill: University of North Carolina Press, 2007).

Judith Stein, *The World of Marcus Garvey: Race and Class in Modern Society* (Baton Rouge: Louisiana State University Press, 1986).

Joe William Trotter, ed., *The Great Migration in Historical Perspective: New Dimensions of Race, Class, and Gender* (Bloomington: Indiana University Press, 1991).

4 New Trends in Literature

Houston A. Baker, Jr., *Modernism and the Harlem Renaissance* (Chicago: University of Chicago Press, 1989).

Malcolm Cowley, *Exile's Return: A Narrative of Ideas* (New York: W. W. Norton, 1934).

Michel Fabre, *From Harlem to Paris: Black American Writers in France, 1840–1980* (Urbana: University of Illinois Press, 1993).

Ernest Hemingway, *A Moveable Feast: The Restored Edition* (New York: Scribner, 2009).

Alain Locke, *The New Negro: Voices of the Harlem Renaissance* (New York: Touchstone, 1999).

Craig Monk, *Writing the Lost Generation: Expatriate Autobiography and American Modernism* (Iowa City: University of Iowa Press, 2008).

Roderick Nash, *The Nervous Generation: American Thought, 1917–1930* (Chicago: Ivan R. Dee, 1990).

Joan Shelley Rubin, *The Making of Middlebrow Culture* (Chapel Hill: University of North Carolina Press, 1992).

Cheryl A. Wall, *Women of the Harlem Renaissance* (Bloomington: Indiana University Press, 1995).

Steven Watson, *The Harlem Renaissance: Hub of African-American Culture, 1920–1930* (New York: Pantheon, 1995).

David Welky, *Everything Was Better in America: Print Culture in the Great Depression* (Urbana: University of Illinois Press, 2008).

5 Women in the 1920s

Susan Porter Benson, *Household Accounts: Working-Class Family Economies in the Interwar United States* (Ithaca, NY: Cornell University Press, 2007).

Dorothy Brown, *Setting a Course: American Women in the 1920s* (Boston: Twayne, 1987).

Ellen Chesler, *Woman of Valor: Margaret Sanger and the Birth Control Movement in America* (New York: Simon & Schuster, 1992).

Nancy F. Cott, *The Grounding of Modern Feminism* (New Haven: Yale University Press, 1987).

Paula Fass, *The Damned and the Beautiful: American Youth in the 1920s* (New York: Oxford University Press, 1977).

Kathy Lee Peiss, *Hope in a Jar: The Making of America's Beauty Culture* (New York: Metropolitan, 1998).

Jennifer Scanlon, *Inarticulate Longings: The Ladies' Home Journal, Gender and the Promise of Consumer Culture* (New York: Routledge, 1995).

Winifred Wandersee, *Women's Work and Family Values, 1920–1940* (Cambridge: Harvard University Press, 1981).

6 Mass Culture

Charles C. Alexander, *Breaking the Slump: Baseball in the Great Depression Era* (New York: Columbia University Press, 2002).

A. Scott Berg, *Lindbergh* (New York: Putnam, 1998).

Stanley Coben, *Rebellion Against Victorianism: The Impetus for Cultural Change in 1920s America* (New York: Oxford University Press, 1991).

Michael Denning, *The Cultural Front: The Laboring of American Culture in the Twentieth Century* (London and New York: Verso, 1997).

Susan J. Douglas, *Listening In: Radio and the American Imagination* (New York: Times Books, 1999).

Melvin Patrick Ely, *The Adventures of Amos 'n' Andy: A Social History of An American Phenomenon* (New York: Free Press, 1991).

Lewis Erenberg, *Swingin' the Dream: Big Band Jazz and the Rebirth of American Culture* (Chicago: University of Chicago Press, 1999).

Roland Marchand, *Advertising the American Dream: Making Way for Modernity, 1920–1940* (Berkeley: University of California Press, 1985).

Lary May, *The Big Tomorrow: Hollywood and the Politics of the American Way* (Chicago: University of Chicago Press, 2002).

Barbara Melosh, *Engendering Culture: Manhood and Womanhood in New Deal Public Art and Theater* (Washington, DC: Smithsonian Institution Press, 1991).

Richard H. Pells, *Radical Visions and American Dreams: Culture and Social Thoughts in the Depression Years* (New York: Harper & Row, 1973).

Murray Sperber, *Shake Down the Thunder: The Creation of Notre Dame Football* (New York: Henry Holt, 1993).

Warren I. Susman, *Culture as History: The Transformation of American Society in the Twentieth Century* (New York: Pantheon, 1985).

7 The Onset of the Great Depression

Michael A. Bernstein, *The Great Depression: Delayed Recovery and Economic Change in America, 1929–1939* (New York: Cambridge University Press, 1987).

Michael D. Bordo, Claudia Goldin, and Eugene N. White, eds., *The Defining Moment: The Great Depression and the American Economy in the Twentieth Century* (Chicago: University of Chicago Press, 1998).

Barry Eichengreen, *Golden Fetters: The Gold Standard and the Great Depression, 1919–1939* (New York: Oxford University Press, 1992).

John A. Garraty, *The Great Depression: An Inquiry Into the Causes, Course, and Consequences of the Worldwide Depression of the Nineteen-Thirties* (New York: Harcourt, 1986).

John Kenneth Galbraith, *The Great Crash, 1929* (Boston: Houghton Mifflin, 1963).

Charles Kindleberger, *The World in Depression, 1929–1939*, rev. ed. (Berkeley: University of California Press, 1986).

Maury Klein, *Rainbow's End: The Crash of 1929* (New York: Oxford University Press, 2003).

Gene Smiley, *Rethinking the Great Depression* (Chicago: Ivan R. Dee, 2003).

Gene Smith, *The Shattered Dream: Herbert Hoover and the Great Depression* (New York: William Morrow, 1970).

Robert Sobel, *The Great Bull Market: Wall Street in the 1920s* (New York: W. W. Norton, 1968).

8 To Fear or Not to Fear

Jonathan Alter, *The Defining Moment: FDR's Hundred Days and the Triumph of Hope* (New York: Simon & Schuster, 2006).

William J. Barber, *From New Era to New Deal: Herbert Hoover, the Economists, and American Economic Policy, 1921–1933* (New York: Cambridge University Press, 1985).

Adam Cohen, *Nothing to Fear: FDR's Inner Circle and the Hundred Days that Created Modern America* (New York: Penguin, 2009).

Paul Conkin, *The New Deal*, 3rd ed. (Arlington Heights, IL: Harlan Davidson, 2002).

Frank Freidel, *Franklin D. Roosevelt: Launching the New Deal* (Boston: Little, Brown, 1973).

Charles Hearn, *The American Dream in the Great Depression* (Westport, CT: Greenwood Press, 1977).

Susan Estabrook Kennedy, *The Banking Crisis of 1933* (Lexington: University Press of Kentucky, 1974).

Katie Loucheim, ed., *The Making of the New Deal: The Insiders Speak* (Cambridge: Harvard University Press, 1984).

Eliot A. Rosen, *Hoover, Roosevelt, and the Brains Trust: From Depression to New Deal* (New York: Columbia University Press, 1977).

Arthur M. Schlesinger, Jr., *The Crisis of the Old Order* (Boston: Houghton Mifflin, 1956).

Jordan Schwartz, *The Interregnum of Despair: Hoover, Congress, and the Depression* (Urbana: University of Illinois Press, 1970).

T. H. Watkins, *The Hungry Years: A Narrative History of the Great Depression in America* (New York: Henry Holt, 1999).

9 Voices from the Great Depression

Ann Banks, *First-Person America* (New York: W. W. Norton, 1991).

Timothy Egan, *The Worst Hard Time: The Untold Story of Those Who Survived the Great American Dust Bowl* (Boston: Houghton Mifflin, 2005).

James N. Gregory, *American Exodus: The Dust Bowl Migration and Okie Culture in California* (New York: Oxford University Press, 1989).

Donald H. Grubbs, *Cry from the Cotton: Southern Tenant Farmers' Union and the New Deal* (Chapel Hill: University of North Carolina Press, 1971).

Anthony Lee, *Painting on the Left: Diego Rivera, Radical Politics, and San Francisco's Public Murals* (Berkeley: University of California Press, 1999).

Robert S. McElvaine, *Down and Out in the Great Depression: Letters from the "Forgotten Man,"* rev. ed. (Chapel Hill: University of North Carolina Press, 2007).

Amity Shlaes, *The Forgotten Man: A New History of the Great Depression* (New York: Harper Perennial, 2008).

William Stott, *Documentary Expression and Thirties America* (Chicago and London: University of Chicago Press, 1986).

Studs Terkel, *Hard Times: An Oral History of the Great Depression* (New York: Pantheon, 1970).

10 The New Deal: Critics and Limitations

Bernard Bellush, *The Failure of the NRA* (New York: W. W. Norton, 1975).

Irving Bernstein, *Turbulent Years: A History of the American Worker, 1933–1941* (Boston: Houghton Mifflin, 1970).

Alan Brinkley, *The End of Reform: New Deal Liberalism in Recession and War* (New York: Vintage Books, 1995).

Alan Brinkley, *Voices of Protest: Huey Long, Father Coughlin, and The Great Depression* (New York: Vintage, 1983).

Lizabeth Cohen, *Making A New Deal: Industrial Workers in Chicago, 1919–1939* (New York: Cambridge University Press, 1990).

Albert Fried, *FDR and His Enemies* (New York: Palgrave Macmillan, 2001).

Alonzo Hamby, *For the Survival of Democracy: Franklin Roosevelt and the World Crisis of the 1930s* (New York: Free Press, 2004).

Janet C. Irons, *Testing the New Deal: The General Textile Strike of 1934 in the American South* (Urbana: University of Illinois Press, 2000).

Mark H. Leff, *The Limits of Symbolic Reform: The New Deal and Taxation* (New York: Cambridge University Press, 1984).

William E. Leuchtenberg, *The Supreme Court Reborn: The Constitutional Revolution in the Age of Roosevelt* (New York: Oxford University Press, 1995).

James T. Patterson, *Congressional Conservatism and the New Deal: The Growth of the Conservative Coalition in Congress* (Lexington: University Press of Kentucky, 1967).

Clyde P. Weed, *The Nemesis of Reform: The Republican Party during the New Deal* (New York: Columbia University Press, 1994).

T. Harry Williams, *Huey Long* (New York: Knopf, 1989).

11 People of Color in the Age of Roosevelt

Suzanne Forrest, *The Preservation of the Village: New Mexico's Hispanics and the New Deal* (Albuquerque: University of New Mexico Press, 1989).

Mario T. Garcia, *Mexican-American Leadership, Ideology, and Identity, 1930–1960* (New Haven: Yale University Press, 1990).

James Goodman, *Stories of Scottsboro* (New York: Vintage, 1994).

Abraham Hoffman, *Unwanted Mexican Americans in the Great Depression: Repatriation Pressures, 1929–1939* (Tucson: University of Arizona Press, 1974).

Lawrence C. Kelly, *The Assault on Assimilation: John Collier and the Origins of Indian Policy Reform* (Minnetonka, MN: Olympic Marketing Corp., 1983).

Kenneth Philp, *John Collier's Crusade for Indian Reform, 1920–54* (Tucson: University of Arizona Press, 1977).

George J. Sanchez, *Becoming Mexican American: Ethnicity, Culture and Identity in Chicano Los Angeles, 1900–1945* (New York and Oxford: Oxford University Press, 1993).

Harvard Sitkoff, *A New Deal for Blacks* (New York: Oxford University Press, 1978).

Patricia Sullivan, *Days of Hope: Race and Democracy in the New Deal Era* (Chapel Hill: University of North Carolina Press, 1996).

Graham D. Taylor, *The New Deal and American Indian Tribalism: The Administration of the Indian Reorganization Act, 1934–45* (Lincoln: University of Nebraska Press, 1980).

Raymond Wolters, *Negroes and the Great Depression* (Westport, CT: Greenwood Press, 1970).

Judy Yung, *Unbound Feet: A Social History of Chinese Women in San Francisco* (Berkeley: University of California Press, 1995).

12 Women in the New Deal Era

Blanche Wiesen Cook, *Eleanor Roosevelt*, Volume 2: *The Defining Years, 1933–1938* (New York: Viking, 1999).

Melvyn Dubofsky and Stephen Burnwood, eds., *Women and Minorities during the Great Depression* (New York: Garland, 1990).

Laura Hapke, *Daughters of the Great Depression: Women, Work, and Fiction in the American 1930s* (Athens: University of Georgia Press, 1997).

Alice Kessler-Harris, *In Pursuit of Equity: Women, Men, and the Quest for Economic Citizenship in 20th-Century America* (New York: Oxford University Press, 2001).

Suzanne Mettler, *Dividing Citizens: Gender and Federalism in New Deal Public Policy* (Ithaca, NY: Cornell University Press, 1998).

Lois Scharf, *To Work and to Wed: Female Employment, Feminism, and the Great Depression* (Westport, CT: Greenwood, 1980).

Bernard Sternsher, *Women of Valor: The Struggle Against the Great Depression as Told in Their Own Life Stories* (Darby, PA: Diane Publishing Company, 1990).

Susan Householder Van Horn, *Women, Work, and Fertility, 1900–1986* (New York: New York University Press, 1988).

Susan Ware, *Beyond Suffrage: Women in the New Deal Era* (Cambridge: Harvard University Press, 1981).

Susan Ware, *Holding the Line: American Women in the 1930s* (Boston: Twayne, 1982).

13 Raising the Walls in Turbulent Times

Warren Cohen, *Empire Without Tears: America's Foreign Relations, 1921–1933* (Philadelphia: Temple University Press, 1987).

Frank Costigliola, *Awkward Dominion: American Political, Economic, and Cultural Relations with Europe, 1919–1933* (Ithaca, NY: Cornell University Press, 1984).

Robert Dallek, *Franklin D. Roosevelt and American Foreign Policy, 1932–1945*, 2nd ed. (New York: Oxford University Press, 1995).

Lewis Ethan Ellis, *Republican Foreign Policy, 1921–1933* (Piscataway, NJ: Rutgers University Press, 1968).

Paul Fussell, *The Great War and Modern Memory* (New York: Oxford University Press, 1975).

Irwin F. Gellman, *Good Neighbor Diplomacy* (Baltimore: Johns Hopkins University Press, 1979).

Thomas Knock, *To End All Wars: Woodrow Wilson and the Quest for a New World Order* (Princeton: Princeton University Press, 1995).

Eric Roorda, *The Dictator Next Door: The Good Neighbor Policy and the Trujillo Regime in the Dominican Republic, 1930–1945* (Durham, NC: Duke University Press, 1998).

David F. Schmitz, *Thank God They're on Our Side: The United States and Right-Wing Dictatorships, 1921–1965* (Chapel Hill: University of North Carolina Press, 1999).

Ronald H. Spector, *Eagle Against the Sun: The American War with Japan* (New York: Vintage, 1985).

William C. Widenor, *Henry Cabot Lodge and the Search for an American Foreign Policy* (Berkeley: University of California Press, 1980).

14 The Great Debate: America Encounters World War II

James MacGregor Burns, *Roosevelt: The Soldier of Freedom* (New York: Harcourt, Brace, Jovanovitch, 1970).

Steven Casey, *Cautious Crusade: Franklin D. Roosevelt, American Public Opinion, and the War Against Nazi Germany* (New York: Oxford University Press, 2003).

Wayne S. Cole, *America First: The Battle Against Intervention, 1940–1941* (Madison: University of Wisconsin Press, 1953).

Wayne S. Cole, *Roosevelt and the Isolationists, 1932–45* (Lincoln: University of Nebraska Press, 1983).

Robert A. Divine, *Reluctant Belligerent: American Entry Into World War II* (New York: John R. Wiley, 1979).

Justus Doenecke and John Edward Wilz, *From Isolation to War: 1931–1941*, 3rd ed. (Arlington Heights, IL: Harlan Davidson, 2003).

Waldo Heinrichs, *Threshold of War: Franklin D. Roosevelt and American Entry into World War II* (New York: Oxford University Press, 1990).

Richard M. Ketchum, *The Borrowed Years, 1938–1941: America on the Way to War* (New York: Anchor, 1991).

Jon Meacham, *Franklin and Winston: An Intimate Portrait of an Epic Relationship* (New York: Random House, 2003).

Ronald Takaki, *Double Victory: A Multicultural History of America in World War II* (Darby, PA: Diane Publishing Company, 2000).

Neil Wynn, *The Afro-American and the Second World War* (Teaneck, NJ: Holmes & Meier, 1976).

15 Popular Culture and the Great Debate

Mark Bernstein, *World War II on the Air: Edward R. Murrow and the Broadcasts that Riveted a Nation* (Naperville, IL: Sourcebooks, Inc., 2003).

Michael Birdwell, *Celluloid Soldiers: The Warner Bros. Campaign against Nazism* (New York: New York University Press, 1999).

David H. Culbert, *News for Every Man: Radio and Foreign Affairs in Thirties America* (Westport, CT: Greenwood Press, 1976).

Nicholas John Cull, *Selling War: The British Propaganda Campaign against American "Neutrality" in World War II* (New York: Oxford University Press, 1995).

Bernard F. Dick, *The Star-Spangled Screen: The American World War II Film* (Lexington: University Press of Kentucky, 1985).

Morris Dickstein, *Dancing in the Dark: A Cultural History of the Great Depression* (New York: W. W. Norton, 2009).

Thomas Doherty, *Projections of War: Hollywood, American Culture, and World War II* (New York: Columbia University Press, 1993).

Gerd Horten, *Radio Goes to War: The Cultural Politics of Propaganda during World War II* (Berkeley: University of California Press, 2001).

D. H. Hosley, *As Good as Any: Foreign Correspondence on American Radio, 1930–1940* (Westport, CT: Greenwood Press, 1984).

Clayton R. Koppes and Gregory D. Black, *Hollywood Goes to War: How Politics, Profits and Propaganda Shaped World War II Movies* (Berkeley: University of California Press, 1987).

David Welky, *The Moguls and the Dictators: Hollywood and the Coming of World War II* (Baltimore: Johns Hopkins University Press, 2008).

Index

Note: Page numbers in italics refer to figures

America Between the Wars, 1919–1941: A Documentary Reader, First Edition.
Edited by David Welky. Editorial material and organization © 2012 John Wiley & Sons, Inc.
Published 2012 by John Wiley & Sons, Inc.